PIMLICO

224

WILD OLIVES

William Graves is Robert Graves's son and Literary
Executor. He still lives in Deyá, but earns a living as
a geologist consulting to the oil industry.

He is married with two children.

WILD OLIVES

Life in Majorca with Robert Graves

WILLIAM GRAVES

PIMLICO

Published by Pimlico 2001

2 4 6 8 10 9 7 5 3 1

Copyright © William Graves 1995

William Graves has asserted his right under the Copyright, Designs
and Patents Act 1988 to be identified as the author of this work

First published in Great Britain by Hutchinson 1995
First Pimlico Edition 1996
Reissued by Pimlico 2001

Pimlico
Random House, 20 Vauxhall Bridge Road,
London SW1V 2SA

Random House Australia (Pty) Limited
20 Alfred Street, Milsons Point, Sydney,
New South Wales 2061, Australia

Random House New Zealand Limited
18 Poland Road, Glenfield, Auckland 10, New Zealand

Random House (Pty) Limited
Endulini, 5A Jubilee Road, Parktown 2193, South Africa

The Random House Group Limited Reg. No. 954009
www.randomhouse.co.uk

A CIP catalogue record for this book is available from the British Library

ISBN 0-7126-0116-3

Papers used by Random House are natural,
recyclable products made from wood grown in sustainable forests.
The manufacturing processes conform to the environmental
regulations of the country of origin

Printed and bound in Great Britain by
Bookmarque Ltd, Croydon, Surrey

In Memory of Henry MacDonald Prain, 'El Capitán'

No, here they never plant the sweet olive
As some do (bedding slips in a prepared trench),
But graft it on the club of Hercules
The savage, inexpugnable oleaster
Whose roots and bole bunching from limestone crannies
Sprout impudent shoots born only to be lopped
Spring after Spring.

From 'The Oleaster' by Robert Graves

INTRODUCTION
AND ACKNOWLEDGEMENTS

When my father, Robert Graves, poet and author, died in 1985, I was astonished to find that he had named me executor of his Will. We had been at loggerheads during the last five years before a slow but remorseless illness had taken him down into the darkness of final senility, so I regarded myself as the least likely of my siblings to have been chosen for the task. Indeed, I had never even considered it. At school I had taken up science, and went on to earn a living as a geologist as a reaction to Father's fame and to my English teachers' ill-founded expectations of me. My astonishment gave way to shock when I realized that, since he had specified no one else, I also became his de facto literary executor.

Sorting out the Will and setting up the arrangements for the royalties from Father's copyrights to be paid to my mother, brothers and sisters was fairly simple. Getting ready to be the literary executor of one of the great writers of the twentieth century was not. Fortunately, I had a reasonable amount of free time between jobs consulting to my oil company clients, and I set about rereading Father's books, essays, short stories, and even his poems. I acquired first editions of his books, and of those to which he had contributed; I also bought any books written about him. I gradually built up a working library. Soon, with the help of his literary agent, I was confidently deciding what should and should not be published.

I reread his best-selling autobiography, *Goodbye to All That*, which he published in 1929 when he was thirty-four, and I studied the biographies and books about his life and works. I read the published selections of his letters and then, with complete fascination, those he had written to me and which I had kept. In doing so I found myself trying to unravel our relationship, which had started so wonderfully and had ended so unsatisfactorily. He was forty-five when I was born, and fifty when he returned with his young family to resume his life in Deyá, a small mountain village in Majorca. As a child, Father's early ordeals on the Somme, described in *Goodbye to All That*, had meant to me as little as the tarnished medals in a brass tobacco tin at the back of the chest of drawers in my bedroom at Canellún, the house I grew up in. Now, as I read his war poems for the first time, those terrible days came sharply into focus. His years with Laura Riding, the American poet, had always seemed less remote to me. I knew little about her, other than that she had built Canellún, but signs of her former presence were everywhere in the house. Reading about her in Father's unpublished diaries, I began to feel that I knew her well. Indeed, Father's behaviour towards me was becoming clearer and my emotions less confused. I found myself quizzing the old men and women of the village on how they felt about him. They told me things about the Deyá of my childhood that I did not know or had forgotten, and I relived scenes long past.

I realized that among my memories were valuable clues, perhaps not even apparent to me, to the understanding of the later part of Father's remarkable life. Slowly the idea of this book evolved: partly as personal catharsis, and partly as a contribution to those interested in the environment in which Father moved and worked. Throughout the following chapters I have described what I remember about our family and the village during my childhood, my youth and early years of marriage. Where possible I have cross-checked facts, although certain memories are bound to have fractured in the kaleidoscope of time. The main narrative covers the years from 1946 to 1970.

Writing this story, and attempting to make it readable, has made me appreciate the brilliance of Father's craftsmanship. Indeed, he has helped me throughout with his grammar, *The Reader Over Your Shoulder*, a book he originally wrote for my half-sister Jenny, after she had asked him for tips on how to write. It has made me realize that my most important task, as his literary executor, is to ensure both his prose and his poetry is read and enjoyed by generations to come. Sadly, it has also made me realize that, although my roots really are in Deyá, that enchanted Deyá, which was also Father's, no longer exists.

Producing this manuscript was rather like moulding a sculpture out of clay. I began with a block, a chronological account of all I remembered, and then slowly beat and kneaded it into shape, scraping out chunks, moving bits around, and filling in where needed.

The earliest version was savaged by an editor friend, and I was pushed to the verge of despair. I rewrote it twice more before I finally found it a home.

Among those who have helped, encouraged and advised me, I wish to thank Beryl Graves, Sofia Graves, Philip Graves, Catherine Dalton, Frank Delaney, Deborah Baker, Joanna Goldsworthy, Stella Irwin, Dunstan Ward, my editor Tony Whittome, and above all, my father's assistant Kenneth Gay. My thanks also to the oil companies on whose oil rigs most of this was written; to Enrique Foster Gittes for the use of his father's 1940s painting of Deyá; to the Robert Graves Copyright Trust for allowing me to quote from his letters and poems; and, of course, a special thanks to my wife Elena who may now want to read the outcome of the five-year gestation she has endured.

Finally, my apologies to those I may have inadvertently hurt through my narrative. Mistakes, of course, are my own.

WG

In the text, abbreviations at the foot of quoted letters stand for the following names:

JR – James Reeves
CG – Cicely Gittes
RG – Robert Graves
WG – William Graves
SJ – Selwyn Jepson
RF – Ruth Fainlight
AL – Aemilia Laraçuen
KG – Kenneth Gay
BG – Beryl Graves

WILLIAM GRAVES - Grandparents, Uncles, Cousins, Siblings

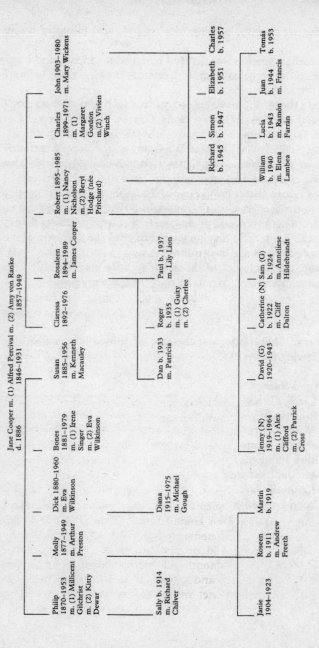

Jane Cooper m. (1) Alfred Percival m. (2) Amy von Ranke
d. 1886   1846–1931   1857–1949

Philip 1870–1953 m. (1) Millicent Gilchrist m. (2) Kitty Dewar

Molly 1877–1949 m. Arthur Preston

Dick 1880–1960 m. Eva Wilkinson

Bones 1881–1979 m. (1) Irene Singer m. (2) Eva Wilkinson

Susan 1885–1956 m. Kenneth Macauley

Clarissa 1892–1976

Rosaleen 1894–1989 m. James Cooper

Robert 1895–1985 m. (1) Nancy Nicholson m.(2) Beryl Hodge (née Pritchard)

Charles 1899–1971 m. (1) Margaret Gordon m.(2) Vivien Winch

John 1903–1980 m. Mary Wickens

Sally b. 1914 m. Richard Chilver

Diana 1915–1975 m. Michael Gough

Janie 1904–1923

Roseen b. 1911 m. Andrew Freeth

Martin b. 1919

Dan b. 1933 m. Patricia

Roger b. 1935 m. (1) Guity m. (2) Cherlee

Paul b. 1937 m. Lily Lion

Jenny (N) 1919–1964 m. (1) Alex Clifford m. (2) Patrick Cross

David (G) 1920–1943

Catherine (N) b. 1922 m. Cliff Dalton

Sam (G) b. 1924 m. Anneliese Hildebrandt

Richard b. 1945

Simon b. 1947

Elizabeth b. 1951

Charles b. 1957

William b. 1940 m. Elena Lambea

Lucia b. 1943 m. Ramon Farrán

Juan b. 1944 m. Francis

Tomás b. 1953

CHAPTER I

1

Our small aeroplane approached the massive grey mountains that broke out of the blue sea below.

'Look! there! there!' Father roared excitedly beside me, jabbing his big, slightly ink-stained forefinger with its ragged flat nail at the window and narrowly missing my nose. 'Look, William, see those white rocks? There's the beach. We'll go for a swim tomorrow!' He turned around in his seat to make sure Mother had seen. 'Look, Beryl, there it is; that's Deyá.'

'Deyá, Deyá!' I shouted back, to make myself heard over the drone of the engines. I could only see a coastline, but for weeks Father had been telling me of this wonderful place we were now going to. I was almost six years old.

His large rugged features, broken nose, blue eyes, heavy lips, the shock of unruly curly dark hair, were alive with anticipation. 'There, Beryl, over there on the fifth corner of the road, that's Canellún.'

Just as I turned back to look ahead, the mountain rose to meet us and, suddenly, we were passing low over the craggy peaks, above a flock of perplexed sheep which looked up at us and scurried away. Then, just as suddenly, the mountain dropped away from us and we were on the other side, losing height over brown fields and toy houses. As we dropped lower I could make out a forest of spiky windmills with boxlike bases, almost like the ones we had made at school in Galmpton with my teacher, Miss Horsham, for Victory Day. The pilot turned around and motioned us to fasten our safety belts. Father did up mine, Mother did up my three-year-old sister Lucia's and held my eighteen-month-old brother Juan tightly in her lap. Then with a bump and a bounce we landed on the earth strip of the small Son Bonet airfield. It was the sixteenth of May 1946.

1

The flight mechanic opened the door, lowered the steps and lifted Lucia and me to the ground. It was warm in the bright noon sun and there was a crowd of people watching and waving to us. To them we were a sign that things were slowly returning to normal. The Second World War was over and our air-taxi was the first civilian flight from Europe to land in Majorca since July 1936, the year the Spanish Civil War had begun. Mother followed us down the steps carrying Juan. As Father emerged from the aircraft, an old man broke away from the crowd and hurried towards us. He wore an oversized jacket and a black beret. His ears were large, his nose and cheeks hung loosely on his face. His mouth was curved in a smile, his small eyes glistened with tears. He and Father embraced, both of them slapping each other's backs. At fifty Father was over six feet tall, broad-shouldered and athletic; he engulfed the smaller man. I looked at this foreigner with interest. I was not used to seeing grown-ups crying. Both were speaking Spanish and I picked out only our names. Father turned to Mother. 'Beryl, this is our good friend Jöan Gelat.'

Mother was small and slim with dark hair, intelligent blue eyes, high cheekbones, a good mouth and a clear complexion. She spoke no Spanish. She shyly stretched out her hand. Gelat pulled himself together, blew his nose, took her hand and kissed it. I decided he was very strange. We were ushered into a building where policemen in funny black patent-leather hats looked at our passports, opened the bags and made Father fill in forms. Eventually we carried our luggage outside to Gelat's large American station wagon.

From the airstrip we drove towards the mountain range, along narrow winding roads, through orchards of almond trees between which had been sown the now tall green wheat. The roadside ditches were ablaze with colour: bright red poppies, yellow daisies, large blue heads of garlic, slender pink gladioli and spectacular blooms of asphodel. As we entered a shadow-filled pass between high cliffs, Gelat changed gears and we ground up a steep hill until we emerged into a calm light-grey landscape of terraces with dry-stone walls and gnarled, unregimented, ancient olive trees, occasionally highlighted by splashes of golden-yellow broom. Above us, dark wooded peaks were silhouetted against an azure sky.

The car floor was hot, and the open window pane rattled in its recess by my face, which was sometimes in the shade and sometimes in the sun. I had reached the age at which children cease being infants and become boys. When I first went to school in England, my hair had been cut and it was now getting dark. I no longer suffered from the indignity of the fair curly hair which I had as a baby. I felt very independent. This was an adventure I wanted to savour. But I must have dozed, because when I next looked up we were twisting through woods of evergreen Mediterranean oak with tantalizing glimpses of the sea. As we came down a hill and around a wide bend, Father asked Gelat to stop. Father jumped out, pulled me through the open window and we both admired the breathtaking view. In front of us was the Deyá coastline, with the Soller promontory in the far distance reflected in a mirror-calm sea. Here and there the bluish-grey glassy surface was streaked with dark blue ripples formed by a lazy breeze. Somewhere between sea and sky, the horizon was lost in the haze. From the water's edge and its border of bright green pine trees, terraces dotted with greenish-grey olive trees and the occasional deeper green of carob, almond or fig trees, rose step-like until they reached the oak forests at the foot of the towering cliff-face of the Teix. Father squatted down next to me and pointed to a house about halfway up the terraces, between sea and mountainside.

'There, William, there is Canellún,' he said quietly.

As we drove on, Father pointed out the Deyá church perched on the top of a steep hill, the Puig, against the backdrop of the reddish cliffs of the Teix. Stone houses with green-slatted shutters hugged the flanks of the hill and spread down to the valley below, the Clot. The main road cut through the saddle between the Puig and the mountainside. Here, lined with houses, it became the Deyá main street up which we now drove. Even though it was siesta-time, the villagers stood on the pavement or leaned over the café railings to witness the return of the *senyor de Canellún*.

We did not stop: Father was in a hurry to get home. He raised his chin absently at the villagers, a gesture I was to know so well, and we drove out the other side of the village, around a few more corners, through the open green wooden gates, up the gravel drive to Canellún. Gelat stopped at the top, behind the large stone house. All the green shutters were open and an old lady was standing in a doorway. She rushed up to Father and kissed him on both cheeks. She was Gelat's wife, Madora. I wriggled away when she tried to kiss me.

'William, you go and explore. See if you can find the front door,' Father said, and began to unload the car.

2

Canellún is set in a two-acre garden, sandwiched between the main road and the old footpath to Soller. U-shaped in plan, it has two storeys, a cellar and an attic, and is built of local limestone. Because of the slope of the land, the mountainside at the back of the house is level with the ground floor, and, at the front of the house, it is level with the cellar. At the side of the house is the *depósito*, a large covered-over water reservoir with a tiled surface. It forms a sizable terrace and is surrounded by a low wall to sit on. The main drive is fifty metres long, and, from the garden gate, leads past the *depósito* to the back of the house and the kitchen door. It is easier to get to the house by the drive than by the stairway to the *entrada* door, reached by a narrow path which branches off at the garden gate. The one-acre Canellún garden extends from a small torrent at the Deyá end, past the front of the house, to an old gravel pit. The torrent bed is dry and runs only after a heavy rain. On the other side of this torrent, set in another large garden, is a smaller one-storey house, Can Torrent, also part of the property.

I did as Father had told me and ran around the house and found the flight of cobbled steps leading to the front door. I pushed open the screen door – the massive pine-wood two-leaved main door behind it was open – and found myself in the *entrada* or hall. The cool shiny yellow floor-tiles reflected the spiral legs of an old mahogany table, the prints on the whitewashed walls and the heavy wooden ceiling beams. The silence was broken only by the intermittent buzzing of a horsefly half-heartedly trying to get through the screen door. To the right of the *entrada* was the dining room and, through it, the kitchen. To the left of the *entrada* – judging by the pens and bottles of ink on the table – was Father's workroom. Next to it, in what I was to know as the pressroom, stood a large black printing press. I went over, fascinated, and touched its metal frame, handles and levers. I returned to the *entrada*, took the stairs to the floor above, and wandered along the corridor, opening doors to all the rooms and peering into each one. There were five bedrooms, all spotlessly clean, the beds made up, and, at the end of the corridor, a bathroom and a lavatory. I ran back downstairs into the sun, circled once around the hot *depósito*, pretending to be an aeroplane, and then went to explore the shady patio which the U-shape of the house forms at its rear. There I found two doors, one of wood leading to Father's workroom, and another one, with slats, painted green like the shutters, behind which was a French window that led back into the *entrada*.

I wandered along the neatly laid out gravel paths amongst fruit trees, which I later learned to recognize as apricot, peach, cherry, plum, loquat, crab apple, almond, lemon and orange. There were also several older huge knobbly carob trees, as well as the ubiquitous, gnarled, millennial olive trees. I sat on each of the stone benches I came to by the side of the path. I went past pergolas covered with grape vines, and mimosas and oleanders, also a royal palm and a tall monkey puzzle tree. Herbaceous borders all around were planted with geraniums and roses against a backdrop of grey cineraria. The vegetable garden, at the gravel-pit end of the lower terrace, held potatoes, tomatoes and tall, pale metallic-green broad beans. An irrigation ditch for the vegetable garden ran next to the massive wall that bordered the main road and was fed by water from the *depósito*. The valve to open the water was in a sump which formed a small pond. As I knelt to inspect it, a frog plopped into the water. I heard footsteps on the gravel path and looked up. Father was carrying my white sun-cap and put it on my head.

'Come,' he said lowering his hand for me to take. I held on to his enormous forefinger and he took me down some steps I had missed earlier, through a tunnel, and into a shady walled area at the base of a cliff-face of the old gravel pit.

'This is the grotto,' he announced. At one end was a raised platform with a table made of an old millstone and, beside it, another stone bench. At the other end of this secret garden was a pergola covered with a grape vine and in the middle stood two walnut trees. It was too much for me to take in all at once.

3

That evening we went down to the *Fàbrica*, Gelat's house in the village, where we had been invited for supper. We walked along the main road, which followed the hillside's contours through the terraced olive groves, Mother wheeling Juan in his pushchair, Lucia riding on Father's shoulders and I running ahead. The road's metalled surface was narrow and slightly arched. There were wide grassy ditches on either side, and the occasional stone-walled drainage culvert running underneath for rainwater run-off, into which I climbed and hid. As we rounded the first corner we saw in front of us the Puig, rising majestically from within the surrounding valley, and crowned only by the stone church with its squat bell-tower on top. The hill was silhouetted against the towering cliff-face of the Teix, which the setting sun was bathing in golden-red hues. We came into the village, leaving the Puig behind us, with houses on our right and a lemon orchard, its trees drooping with bright yellow fruit and sweet-smelling white blossom, on our left. Two old men sat on a bench of stone slabs by the roadside. I noticed that each had covered the stone with a sheet of newspaper so as not to get his trousers dusty.

'*¡Don Roberto! ¿Como está?* How are you? And your voyage? Good?'

'How are you, *l'amo*? And you, *mestre Jöan*?' said Father, shaking their hands. We went on, past the grey stone houses and a tangerine orchard on our right and then down the main street to the *Fàbrica*, its bright purple bougainvillaea beckoning us from afar, Father striding ahead, but stopping to talk to everyone he passed.

As we approached the *Fàbrica* I could hear a babble of voices, which died in sudden expectation as we climbed the stone steps and went across the open verandah to the main entrance. It was so quiet it was hard to believe that anyone was at home. Then, as we walked through the door, pandemonium broke loose.

'*¡Don Roberto! ¿Como está?*'

'. . . How many years has it been?'

'. . . How was your trip?'

'. . . Meet my wife!'

'. . . How did you find the house?'

Father fielded the questions, embraced the men, kissed the women and introduced Mother. A wizened old lady came up to kiss me.

'What is your name, little one?' she asked. I stared back, not understanding a word. 'Look what a handsome and serious boy!'

she continued, showing me off to a prickly-faced old man. I fled behind Mother's skirt. I hated to have people make a fuss over me.

There was great coming and going, but soon the throng left and we sat down at a large table, Gelat's family – his wife, his son and daughter, their respective wife and husband, and the grandchildren – and us. I was grateful to be put next to Juanito who was only a couple of years older than I. Gelat wanted Father to have a real Majorcan meal to celebrate his return, and gave us *sopas mallorquinas* and *porcella* – not the most appropriate meal for a tired young English boy. *Sopas* are made of thinly sliced, crisp, oven-dried brown peasant bread, soaked in a vegetable broth and covered with cauliflower, cabbage, broad beans and whatever else is in season; a little unrefined olive oil is then poured over the top. There were plates heaped with pickled capers and samphire, sliced fresh peppers and bright red radishes to be eaten with the dish. *Porcella*, suckling pig, is baked slowly in a large outdoor charcoal bread-oven, and served a sizzling golden brown. Soon I got down from the table and played with one of Juanito's toys that I had taken a fancy to. It was a motorcycle made from two pieces of pressed tin with the outline of the machine and the rider painted on each side; a clockwork mechanism drove two small wheels beneath the rider's feet. I had never seen a toy like it in England. Clutching it, I fell asleep in the corner.

Back at Canellún Father washed me down with a wet flannel and put me to bed.

'This used to be my bedroom, you know,' he said, slipping on my pyjamas. 'It's a very special room.' It was at the front of the house, just above the *entrada*, with a wide built-in-cupboard, a large oak chest of drawers, a table and chair. Next to my bed with its crisp blue cotton bedspread were a bedside table and a bedside light with a wooden conical base. On the whitewashed walls hung a mirror, a large yellowish watercolour of an English farmyard with a black and white cow, and an oil painting of a pink house with a cabbage patch in front of it – there was a tree in this painting that later sometimes frightened me because one of the branches looked like a man hanging by his neck. My window looked out on to the vegetable garden and a clump of tangerine trees. I leant out with Father. Beyond the garden, the main road was hidden by a high wall covered in yellow Banksian roses, but over it we could see our olive groves on the other side, now under wheat. On our right shimmered the sea; in front, across the valley, the dark shadow of the hill we had driven down on the way to Deyá; on our left, part of the Teix. Above, in the evening sky, was the brightest star I had ever seen.

'What's that, Father?' They were always Mother and Father, never Mummy and Daddy.

'Venus, the Evening Star, darling,' he said as he closed my shutters. 'Now to bed!'

4

Next morning I woke up to the smells and noises of my new home. Mother had left my bedroom door open during the night so that I could call out if I were thirsty. There was the soon-familiar faint smell of whitewash and linseed oil – Gelat had had the house whitewashed just before we arrived – and the starchy smell of my cotton bedspread. The house itself was quiet except for the noise of water trickling into the lavatory cistern at the end of the passage. Father was already up, and I heard the crash of the bucket and then the squeak of the pulley as he drew water out of the rainwater well in the kitchen; I heard the fluttering of sparrows in the zinc gutters under the eaves of the roof, the distant braying of a donkey, the rumble and clatter of a mule and cart going by on the main road and the constant tinkle of sheep bells. But it took me many months before I could identify all those sounds.

I wandered downstairs in my pyjamas and found Father making a bonfire outside the kitchen door at the top of the gravel drive. He had piles of paper with which he was feeding it.

'Why are you making a fire, Father?' I asked.

'I am burning papers that once belonged to a lady called Laura,' he replied.

'Why?'

'Because she told me to.'

I helped him poke the ashes. 'And where is she now?'

'In America,' he replied. 'Come, let's see if there are any ripe *nisperos* on that tree.'

After lunch we went for our first walk to the Cala. We had come along the main road, down a cart track and had reached Son

Bujosa, the big *finca* with two giant palm trees standing watch over it by the front of the gate.

'That's a Majorcan bull mastiff,' Father said as a large ferocious black dog barked at us from the orange grove. 'I used to have one called Solomon who walked with me to the beach every day. I had to keep him on a lead because he once ran away and sucked a sheep's ear.'

I could not picture the vicious-looking dog we had just passed sucking a sheep's ear. 'Where is he now?' I asked.

'For many years, Solomon lived with a butcher in Palma who gave him nice pieces of meat, and then he died of old age.'

We continued down the cart track past a large sheep hut. The sheep were outside, dozing in the shade of the olive trees. As we went by they got up, their bells waking their companions, so that the whole flock took fright and moved away with a noisy jangle. At the end of the track we reached the Mirador and left Juan's pushchair by an olive tree. Father smiled at Mother's look of uncertainty.

'No one will touch it, darling, you could leave your purse hanging from this branch and it would be here when we came back.' We continued down a narrow path with steps, through a pine wood bordered by a large expanse of bare grey limestone. We emerged from the wood and stopped at a small salient overlooking the Cala.

The Cala is a narrow cove opening to the north-west with limestone promontories on both sides. To our left, the vertical cliffs of the pine-forested Punta de Deyá stretched out for almost a kilometre. To our right the cliffs, less abrupt but just as spectacular, were unevenly covered with shrubs of myrtle, cistus, hypericum, lentisc, rosemary, euphorbia and large tufts of *carritx* grass, and ended in a brilliant white rock stack, a sentinel guarding the entrance to the cove. Below us, a terraced slope sown with already-ripening wheat reached down to the boulder-covered beach. At the near end of the beach was a huddle of fishermen's huts and slipways. By them, a torrent bed still carried the winter flow from springs up in the Deyá valley. Along the beach, a couple of metres from the shoreline, an enormous smooth boulder stuck out of the sea. However, my young eyes were riveted to the centre of the scene: the turquoise water so calm and clear that, even though we were still fifty metres above, I could see every shimmering rock and stone beneath it.

We made our way down the cobbled steps, past neatly laid out vineyards on our night, through the wheat-covered terraces and reached the torrent at the bottom. We turned right and followed the stream along its last few metres down the gully, went past a narrow humped bridge, which crossed to the main group of fishermen's boathouses and slipways built into the rock, and reached the deserted beach itself.

Father left us as we changed into our 'bathing dresses', and hurried along the sandy shore to the massive rocks at the far end. There, using the climbing skills he had learned as a young man on the cliffs of Harlech Castle in North Wales from his teacher George Mallory, he quickly made his way around a rugged overhung ledge, his body leaning backwards, his outstretched fingers feeling for holds above, his bare feet searching for support and, reaching a small natural platform, he rather less impressively belly-flopped in. Father invariably climbed around to that platform to dive into the Cala and I never saw anyone else who could manage it.

While Juan toddled along beside us, Mother, Lucia and I collected, among the pebbles at the water's edge, many-coloured glass 'beads', the polished remnants of broken bottles thrown into the torrent up in the village and washed down by the swirling water over the years. Although Father loved his daily swim, he disliked the inactivity of sitting in the sun. Coming out of the sea, he showed me how to make sand-balls, dampening the sand with seawater, and turning them in his massive hands; and how to play 'ducks and drakes', skimming the smooth flat pieces of broken brown roof tiles over the surface of the water. Tiring of our games, he climbed up the side of the cove to pick a handful of rock-samphire and brought it back for us to taste. To this day, I associate its salty, slightly astringent flavour with the Cala in summer.

5

'Come on, time to be going,' said Father. The sun was sinking behind the Punta de Deyá and the shadow was making its way towards us at the far end of the beach. We gathered our things and started up the path by the torrent-bed. I ran on ahead.

'This way, William,' Father shouted in his best parade-ground voice. I had missed the turning, and come to a wide metalled track. I ran back and followed them up the steps.

'Where does that road go to?' I asked.

'Up to Deyá through our land,' he replied. But we never took it: we always went the Son Bujosa way.

It was a slow climb. Juan was still unsure on his feet and had a perpetual scab on his nose from falling over on his face. Lucia, although a little older, had a tendency to wilt when necessary. Father often was forced to carry them both. He allowed us three stops for drinks of water out of his green felt-covered water flask. This set the pattern for future climbs: the first drink, sometimes with a sugared almond, was in the shade of a large lentisc bush; the second, by a white rock next to the vineyards; the third, on the stone bench at the Mirador where we had left Juan's pushchair. The Mirador is an ugly stone cube which a former owner of Son Bujosa had been building when he died of a heart attack. Since he left no plans, his heir, perplexed, had converted it into a one-room studio and put benches and a balustrade around the flat roof. It was empty. We climbed up the stone steps to the roof and peered down through iron railings at the peaceful Cala below, now entirely in shadow, and watched the fishing boats slowly motor out to lay their nets.

6

We were too young to go to the beach every day, and the next afternoon Father took us to see more of the village. We walked into Deyá but, instead of following the main road down towards the *Fàbrica*, we took the winding cart track up to the Puig. We cut out the first hairpin bend by climbing some stone steps. At the top of the steps was the Estanco, a general store, also licensed to sell stamps and State-monopoly tobacco and cigarettes. Father went in to say hello, and the lady behind the counter gave us each a sweet. The smell of onions and potatoes, of lemons and oranges, of sacks of rice and sugar, of dried sardines in round wooden boxes – tail-to-tail in the middle, the heads with their glazed eyes on the rim – of rope-soled *espardenyas* and palm-leaf plaited baskets, and of vats of wine, all mixed distinctively with the smell of Ideales, the cheap strong black cigarettes smoked by the villagers, and the slightly rancid smell of olive oil, which the Estanco also dealt in as wholesalers. On the shelves stood tins of sardines and condensed milk, bottles of wine and brandy, jars of boiled sweets, short white paraffin-wax candles for use at home and long yellow beeswax candles for use in church processions.

We left the soporific odours of the Estanco and continued up the cart track on our way to the Puig. To our right, separated by a high wall, were the olive groves which covered that side of the hill. To our left was a row of houses, the Estanco being the first. At about thirty-metre intervals the Stations of the Cross were depicted on painted tiles in gothic sandstone frames set in the stone wall. Each Station carried the name of the large farm or institution which had paid for it. Since we were approaching the church, these were the later Stations and in them Jesus – with brown shoulder-length hair, a beard, and wearing red robes – was already shown stumbling beneath the weight of the Cross and being whipped by Roman centurions. Father sent me on up the hill to see what the next picture would be. Here, Jesus was being stripped of his robe by two centurions, and some ominous over-sized nails with large round heads were lying on the ground next to the Cross. In the following Station, Jesus, dressed only in a loincloth, was being gorily nailed to the Cross, blood dripping from his hands and feet. By the time we reached the top of the hill He was hanging on the Cross with the two thieves as companions. He did not look unhappy.

'Up here,' Father said as he climbed some steps leading towards the back of the church. He had a large iron key in his hand which he fitted into the grey weather-beaten door of a house, slightly recessed from the main body of the church. 'This is the Posada.' The floors were paved in stone, the walls uneven and the ceilings high. Through a door in the side of the house, I went into the garden and at the back of it I found some disappointingly empty stables. The house was under-furnished – just tables and a few chairs, some plates and prints on the walls – but it had a friendly feeling to it. I climbed the high narrow stairs and looked in all the rooms but found little of interest to me, only a couple of damp-smelling beds which I jumped on. Soon I was running out of the door and following the path by the side of the church.

The main portal of the church was shut but a heavy wooden door in the wall opposite it was ajar. I squeezed through and found myself in a small enclosure with dark cypress trees and walkways of cement, all puzzlingly inscribed with crosses and writing. There were wilted flowers in bottles, and small puddles of candle grease. I wondered what this strange place was. The door creaked and I expected to see Father, but it turned out to be a priest wearing a long black cassock. He looked surprised when he saw me, but smiled, and began talking to me in Spanish. I fled back to the Posada.

'Father, what is that place at the end with the tall trees?' I asked.

'So that's were you were,' he said. 'Come on. Let's all go to the cemetery. It has the best view in Deyá.'

'There's a priest,' I said.

'Good. That will be Don Guillem. I had better meet him.'

The next afternoon Father took us to Ca'n Madó. We walked through the village and, on the narrow curve after the cafés, we stopped a moment to talk to the women at the public washing-house, the *rentaderos*. Three women, dressed in shades of faded grey, were bent over the stone troughs. Each had a pile of clothes and a wooden box with dark brown, sticky home-made soap. I recognized Gelat's daughter-in-law, Aina, who spread the soap on her husband's shirt, scrubbed it with a bristle brush, dipped it in running water, pulled it out and squeezed the soap out on the slanting stone. I ran on. We followed the road under the cool plane trees – the Clot lay below us on our right, the Puig rising behind it – past the turning into Es Molí, and walked up the short drive to Ca'n Madó and on to Father's terraces. Gelat had planted them with early tomatoes, peppers and runner beans to complement the crop of broad beans and potatoes in Canellún's garden.

While the others picked vegetables, I wandered towards the old water mill to look at Gelat's *turbina*, which produced the village electricity. Outside, on a grassy bank by the stream from the reservoir overflow, lay the paddles and the old millstones for grinding flour which it had housed before the new generator was installed. At that moment Gelat arrived in his station wagon. The old man motioned me to follow him into the building. The large green-painted machine, with its drive wheel and wide leather strap, took up a whole room and smelled of burned oil. On one of the walls was a large black panel with switches, breakers and dials. I watched, fascinated, as Gelat opened the sluice gates. The wheels slowly gathered speed, the drive-strap flapping noisily as it turned the alternator. The needles on the dials crept up. Suddenly, with a flip of his wrist and the air of a magician, Gelat slammed the main switch on. The light bulb on the ceiling above us flickered and then burned brightly. Gelat beamed, and bunching his fingers, kissed them. He then threw the switch again, closed the sluice gates, and plunged us back into silence and gloom.

Together we walked out into the warm sunlight, across the stream, and up to Father who had almost filled his basket with vegetables.

'He is an inquisitive one,' said Gelat of me. 'Maybe one day he will be an engineer.'

In spite of his strange behaviour at the airport, I was beginning to like the old man. He was my first real contact with the village.

CHAPTER II

1

One afternoon, at the beginning of September, storm clouds gathered over the Teix, blocking out the bright sunlight and darkening the mountains. Mother, Lucia and I knelt on the sofa under the dining-room window and watched. Presently a bolt of lightning lit up the landscape. We tensed for the second it took the sharp clap of thunder to reach us. The window panes in front of our noses shook and the echo rumbled around the valley, leaving an uneasy silence in its wake. Then we heard the 'splat-splat' of the first raindrops hitting the *depósito* terrace. More thunder and lightning followed and soon the rain was a solid curtain of water. It gathered in puddles and, joined by rivulets stained reddish-brown by the earth from the terraces above Canellún, it made its way down our drive and ended in the torrent, which soon became a frothing mass of water.

The summer days had been mostly tranquil and sunny under bright blue skies, the nights warm and balmy, the sea calm. At times, northern winds had lowered the temperature, cleared the air, highlighted the horizon and whipped up waves so that they stood out, brilliant white, against an indigo sea. At others, clouds clung motionless to the sides of the Teix. Father called these 'boiratic' days, a word he made up from *boira*, the Majorcan for mist, and he claimed they gave him a headache. We had a bad sirocco which blew hot, dry and blustery up from the Sahara desert. Like tongues of fire it burned the leaves and buffeted the ripe apricots from the trees. Father fastened the shutters to prevent them from slamming, and shut the windows and doors to keep out the dust which hung in a reddish haze over the mountains. The sirocco lasted a nerve-racking three days, relieved, finally, by a few drops of muddy rain. Our thunderstorm, however, was different. It came from the north-west and marked the end of our first summer in Deyá.

2

The Deyá we came to in 1946 was a village of five hundred Catholic souls, a small agricultural community living mostly off the olive crop, with a little help from the carob and the almond crops. The land between the trees was rotated with wheat or broad beans, or left fallow for sheep to graze on. Where the terraces were irrigated, potatoes, tomatoes and lettuces grew alongside lemon and orange trees. Small vineyards provided wine for local consumption. Down at the Cala the half-dozen fishermen caught more than enough for the village needs. There were several charcoal burners in the mountains, two carpenters, three master builders, two butchers, three grocers. There was an hotel and an inn, two cafés, and a glove-sewing cottage industry. Deyá had not changed significantly for centuries.

In an agricultural community where summer rainfall is low and there are no wells, owning the right to a few hours of water from one of the springs is a vital asset. There are two large springs in Deyá and several smaller ones. The smaller ones tend to dry up in summer. Of the large two, by far the greatest flow comes from the one at Es Molí which drove Gelat's electricity turbine; the other was above Es Recó. When we arrived water was mostly distributed along tiled open *siquia* water channels, and stored for use at the other end in an *aljub*, a large open tank, which could be the size of a swimming pool or larger. The contents of the *aljub* were then used to water the terraces as and when needed. Discussions over water rights could easily draw blood. The rights to the springs are recorded in quarter-hours in the Town Hall, and the system dates back to the time of the Arabs.

When the Arabs and Berbers who had held Majorca for five centuries were defeated and ousted in 1293 by King Jaime the First of Aragón, some of them, living in small mountain villages such as Deyá, stayed on. Over generations their descendants were absorbed into the new settlers' families but vestiges of their Islamic traditions persisted.

When we arrived the villagers tended to live below their means so as not to give their neighbours reason to be jealous. Only close relatives were admitted to the hearth of their houses. They would never admit to things going well.

'Well, *l'amo* Tomeu, we finally got the rain we needed!'

'So long as it does not overdo it, *mestre* Joan, and knock down that swollen terrace-wall of mine!'

As with most mountain peoples, they were interbred, and disliked newcomers, even if these came just from the village in the next valley.

Old stone houses, like our Posada, had metre-thick walls, small unmatched windows, and low-angled, lichen-covered roofs of Roman tiles. Inside, the walls were spotlessly whitewashed, the stone-paved floors gleamed. Often each room was set at a different level, following the contours of the hillside. The *entrada* always had numerous chairs set against the walls, a table in the centre, and the inevitable aspidistras in flowerpots strategically placed on stands in the corners. This was neutral territory and was used for entertaining more distant relatives, or neighbours when they came visiting on weddings, funerals or feast days. The front door was always ajar and, if visitors wanted to attract the attention of those within, they put their heads around the door.

'Hail, Mary the Purest!' they shouted.

'Conceived without sin!' would come the reply.

Hidden from view, at the back of the house or sometimes to one side of the *entrada*, was the *foganya* or hearth. Its *campana*, the bell-shaped continuation of the chimney flue, which was open to the sky, extended low into the room, and stone benches, draped with sheepskins, were built around the open fireplace. It was around this mesmerizing flame that life revolved in winter: cooking, eating and even sleeping. The cistern, in the house or in the patio behind, collected the rainwater from the roof and provided the drinking water. Villagers claimed that every cistern tasted different. Through the back door of the house, in the patio, was a pink hydrangea, being tended for the village feast of Sant Joan, and kept jealously out of sight.

Deyá split naturally into its three main neighbourhoods: the Puig on the hill below the church; the Clot in the valley below; the Porxo in between, more or less level with the main road. Women of each neighbourhood shopped at the same store, washed their clothes at the same *rentaderos*, and, in early winter, picked olives as a group. In their spare moments they huddled together, shelling almonds, stitching crochet squares or darning socks. In summer they sat outdoors in the shade, in winter in the *entrada* of one of the houses around a brazier, warming their feet. They kept an eye on all that went on. Deyá births were exhaustively discussed, as were courtships, marriages, illnesses, deaths, but above all, anything remotely smelling of scandal. Certainly the new family at Canellún came in for close scrutiny.

The men from the various neighbourhoods socialized more than the women. On weekdays after work or on Sundays they met at the cafés for an *anís* and a cigarette over a card game of *Truc*. Although an onlooker might think from the shouts in that smoke-laden atmosphere that a fight was brewing, in general they helped each other out. The tall ladder, the extra-long watering hose, the wheelbarrow brought back from France, the allotted hour-of-water from the spring: all were at everyone's disposal if needed. However, favours must be returned. So long as everyone complied with the system there were no problems. If not, things still remained friendly on the surface, but at night chickens might be let out of their coop, a harness cut, or spring water diverted. Everyone knew everyone's business; the women doing their laundry at the public *rentaderos* took care of that.

'Did you hear my husband's sheep got out on to the main road last night?'

'Really? Are you sure they weren't let out? Think about it . . . .'

3

Soon after the storm, in late September 1946, Lucia, Juan and I started at our village schools. There were three: the boys', the girls' and the infants'. The boys' school was next to the Town Hall in the Porxo, the small square at the foot of the road that wound up to the Puig. In one corner by the school stood a neo-gothic wellhead over a cistern which stored the rainwater off both buildings.

My schoolmaster, Don Gaspar Sabater, a thin, verbose man with a squint, had taken up teaching while he was becoming established as a journalist. Don Gaspar taught us in Spanish, as was compulsory under Franco's laws, but my friends spoke *Mallorquín*, a dialect of Catalan, which is as different from Spanish as is, for example, Italian. I was soon chatting away to them in it.

We sat at wooden desks chewing our pencils, and looked up at Don Gaspar sitting above us at his table on a raised platform.

Behind him was the blackboard, a large map of Spain, a crucifix and the mandatory photograph of Generalissimo Franco, here in a business suit, looking rather fat, prosperous and pleased with himself. We learned the rivers and mountains of Spain parrot-fashion, and recited them in the same sing-song as our multiplication tables, the Visigoth kings or the story of Adam and Eve. We spent hours at calligraphy, laboriously copying endless lines of 'l's and 'i's. I became Don Gaspar's star pupil and years later, whenever we met, he would commend me on that lovely handwriting – unfortunately, it deteriorated from then on.

Although we followed the Spanish national curriculum, reading, writing and basic sums were all that was considered necessary for village schooling. Don Gaspar was not a bad teacher, although he understandably seemed more interested in his new motorcycle than the Visigoth kings.

'Which is the best motorbike in the world?' he would ask.

'A Lube!' we dutifully chanted back. The Lube was the only motorcycle made in Spain at the time. Don Gaspar's usually gleamed on its stand outside the school, but if he had just returned from his journalistic duties in Palma and the bike was the slightest bit dusty, one of the punishments for talking in class was to polish it. This was infinitely preferable to having to stand, or even kneel, with arms outstretched in a corner of the classroom.

The infants' school, to which Lucia and Juan went, was run by the nuns. There they were taught to pray and to read. Mother got a daily report from Juan: 'Mother! Tolito bit Margarita, Gasparín bit Antonia like this, Tolito pinched me like this, and Marquitos made *caca* in his trousers.'

Father collected us after school and took us home for lunch, but as the following summer approached, he arranged for Catalina, the ten-year-old daughter from the Estanco, to walk Lucia and Juan back home. I tagged along behind pretending I was not part of the group. In those days, before DDT and insecticides, there was a wealth of butterflies – fritillaries, whites, tortoiseshells, brimstones, swallow-tails, blues – on the wild flowers in the ditches by the roadside. It often took us twice as long as expected to get home, especially in May and June, when we trapped them under our straw hats.

19

4

Although difficult to reach, Deyá's praises had been sung for as long as travellers had toured the island. The village's most celebrated foreign resident had been the Austrian Archduke Ludwig Salvator, a cousin of the Hapsburg Emperor, who, in the 1870s, had bought a large farm within the Deyá parish boundaries and several farms in the neighbouring village of Valldemosa. The *Arxiduc*, as he was known, was a keen amateur natural historian and anthropologist and published many books, monographs and papers. Over the years, he attracted numerous men of science and letters to his table. Most were entranced by the beauty of Deyá. The story goes that one of them felt that the only possible addition, to attain absolute perfection, would be to be serenaded by canaries, and he duly had several dozen pairs let loose; they soon succumbed to the weather and predators. In 1892 the *Arxiduc* was paid a royal visit by his aunt, the Empress Elisabeth (Sissi), in her 1,800-tonne Imperial yacht, *Miramar*, which she berthed in the nearby Puerto Soller. In 1906 King Edward VII and Queen Alexandra arrived at his residence for a visit but the *Arxiduc*, who had not been advised, happened to be in Palma. They had to admire his museum instead.

The *Arxiduc*'s secretary was Deyá-born, Antonio Vives, who later married an Italian countess. Don Gaspar, our teacher, was married to the secretary's grand-niece, Juanita. They lived with her father, Dr Vives, who had recently retired from his village practice after having a stroke. At school Don Gaspar loved telling us stories about the *Arxiduc*, to which he tried to impart certain moral overtones. He told us of the time the *Arxiduc* gave one of his labourers his old *espardenyas* saying, 'Here, there's a couple more weeks' wear in these.' The labourer, a Deyá man, preferring to remain barefoot rather than wear those smelly old things, threw them under a lentisc bush. The *Arxiduc* came across them again the next day, shrugged, took off the new ones he was wearing, and put back on the old ones.

Don Gaspar told us of the black Majorcan sow the *Arxiduc* had kept for over ten years, just to see how long her tusks would grow. To everyone's amazement they grew like a wild boar's, in the shape of a corkscrew. Don Gaspar told us of the fortune the

Arxiduc spent on building a road along the coast, when it was obvious to the villagers that it would be washed away by the sea; and of the effort and money he put into planning and building paths leading to lookout points, just so that he could admire the view. Perhaps because he felt it reflected badly on Antonio Vives's illustrious master, Don Gaspar did not tell us that the name '*Porxo*' is all that remains of a seventeenth-century covered walkway which once stood on the site of our school and the Town Hall. The *Arxiduc* had indeed paid for these new buildings, but he had carried off the walkway's lovely sandstone arches to his farm.

Archduke Ludwig Salvator died in Brandeis, near Prague, at the beginning of the First World War; but by then he had put Deyá on the map. In the early Twenties an hotel opened and year-round foreign residents became a familiar sight. The village was also the summer home of several wealthy families from Palma and Barcelona. There was enough demand for a *telegrafista* to be appointed, and the white-bearded retired sea captain who took this job set up a wood-and-brass morse telegraph in his front room, opposite the café. He died in 1948, shortly after we arrived, and was replaced by a new appointee from Palma.

By 1929, when Father and Laura Riding first came to Deyá, many writers and painters had already visited the village and there was a significant number of English and German residents. Almost all of them left when the Civil War broke out on 18 July 1936.

5

Slowly, I became aware of the work on the terraces: sowing, reaping and threshing of wheat; trimming the vines and picking the grapes; pruning the olive trees and gathering the green olives from their branches for pickling, and the ripened black ones fallen to the ground for making oil. Lying in bed when I awoke, I could distinguish the harsh, sharp beat of almond harvesting from the poised, slow beat of that of the carob bean. Both crops were knocked down from their branches with long bamboo canes. I knew the guttural stop and start commands farmers shouted at their mules when ploughing the baked earth between the olive trees. I could tell the sound of stone being chipped by *margers* who built and repaired the dry-stone walls which held up the terraces. Those terraces had been a feature of Deyá, and the villages of the mountain range, since the Moors had introduced the technique in the eighth century. New terracing went on all the time, an art passed down from father to son.

I also began to understand about village names. Family surnames, paternal and maternal, were used only on official documents. Gelat's surnames were Marroig Más. His nickname came from the house he lived in. Village houses acquired the name or nickname of their first occupant; thus Ca'n Roig was the house of the redhead, and Ca Madò Coloma was the house of Mistress Coloma. Ca'n Gelat was named after a man who owned a cow; the milk was made into ice-cream (*gelat*). When the house changed occupants, these acquired its name, becoming 'of' Ca'n Gelat. The head of the family would be called 'Gelat' for short. I was *Guillem de Canellún*; Father, however, was not 'Canellún', but was given the title *Es Senyor de Canellún*. Perhaps my first inkling that Father was not perfect came when I realized that our house was misnamed. 'Canellún' supposedly meant the 'far house' – *al.luny* being 'far' in Majorcan – but it actually means 'the house belonging to far away', which is nonsense. The larger properties were called '*Son*' as in Son Bujosa and the villagers often referred to our house, more correctly, as *Son Al.luny*. 'Can Torrent' was also misnamed. It supposedly meant 'the house by the torrent' but 'Ca'n Torrent' would mean 'the house belonging to Torrent'. Hence my spelling of Canellún and Can Torrent.

In October we had stopped going down to the beach, and by November the weather turned cold and damp. The worst month of winter was February, when snow occasionally powdered the mountain tops and the sun did not climb out from behind the Teix until mid-morning. Canellún was not an easy house to heat. The fireplaces did not draw properly and the dining room, where we were allowed to play, the nursery being too cold, was always smoky. I hated going upstairs along the cold passage to the lavatory and, if it was not raining, preferred to go out through the kitchen to relieve myself behind an olive tree. The damp in the house was pervasive. I shivered in bed until it warmed and Mother wore a coat indoors unless she was sitting by the fireplace. Father, however, never seemed to notice. He took the chill off his workroom with a brazier and he sat at his writing table wrapped in a blanket. When he felt stiff, he went outside and chopped wood for exercise.

The long dark evenings were so boring that even the arrival of Maria the Washerwoman was an event. She washed the clothes in the Puig *rentaderos* and then ironed them using a huge iron filled with glowing coal. Twice a week she brought the laundry back on a large wicker tray and laid each piece out neatly on the *entrada* bench.

I followed the seasons, not so much by the weather or the crops in the valley, as by the fruit in our garden. The first fruit of spring were juicy yellow *nisperos*, or loquats; Father taught me to squeeze them into my mouth and then spit out the stones. Next came cherries. We had three cherry trees, one in the Canellún garden and two by Can Torrent. The secret was to pick them before they were pecked by birds. After the cherries came apricots and, during the week they were ripening, I could usually be found up the tree by Father's workroom searching for the least green fruit. Once they were fully ripe, I helped Father pick a crateful to bottle; later I was indignant when I realized he had left none on the tree for me. By the time the apricots finished at the end of June, plums were ready. The red Victoria variety on the tree by Can Torrent was disappointing, but the yellow ones near the irrigation sump were firm, sweet and often were covered with drops of resinous sugar where their skin was broken. I had stains down the front of all my shirts. July and August were lean months in terms of fruit in the garden, but autumn was heralded by *acerolas* and bunches of grapes which ripened at the beginning of September. The *acerola* is a sweet yellowish-red crab apple, of which I could hold three or four in my young hands. We had a vine arbour by the side of the *depósito*, and another over the grotto. The grapes had been sprayed with copper sulphate against mildew, so Father taught me to wash the bunches with the water in the irrigation sump before I ate them. September was also the month for figs, of which some forty varieties grow in Deyá, from the large green smooth ones to small bluish-black wrinkled ones. I loved eating them with almonds, and I cracked the pitted brown shells with a stone on the side of terrace walls. In October came pomegranates, which opened with a tearing sound and spilled their bright red juicy seeds all over me; and then there were persimmons, which looked like oversized tomatoes with sweet, soft, slippery orange-coloured flesh. Winter was the season for oranges and tangerines. Tangerines ripened just before Christmas. They were so easy to pull off the branch and to peel that my progress around the garden could be traced by the bright pieces of rind I had left along the edges of the paths. Oranges ripened soon after. The Navel variety on the trees by the Can Torrent gate were by far the best. The top of the fruit was puckered like a human navel and it had no pips. I adored them and even today I can find no fruit to compare to the majestic Deyá-grown, tree-ripened Navel oranges. I remember feeling sorry for Adam, shown in my school-book being expelled from his garden in Eden, and wondering whether his oranges were as good as ours.

6

When he met us at the airstrip in 1946, Gelat was still a very important person in the village. Before the Civil War, however, he had been the most powerful. His given name was Joan and his lineage was Marroig Más. Jöan Marroig Más had started out tenant farming and then ran a small bar with which he made enough money to buy up the village's only industry, a loss-making *Fàbrica*. This consisted of a large warehouse on the main street with a steam engine which, at different times, drove a soap-making machine, a flour mill and an olive press. The pips and residue left over after pressing the olives served as fuel for the steam engine boiler. Soap, too, was a by-product of the olive-pressing process. Gelat got rid of the flourmill and the soap-making machine, and in their place installed an electricity generator to supply the grid which he had laid out in the village. His venture into providing electricity was so successful that he exchanged the steam engine for a more powerful single-cylinder diesel, and then removed the oil press. After the First World War he had bought a car in France to taxi people to Soller and Palma, and when this could no longer cope with the demand he started a bus service to Palma. He was, however, always short of capital.

In 1929 Father and Laura Riding arrived in Deyá. Gelat judged, by the money they spent in the café, the telegrams they sent, and the number of taxis they took, that they must be rich. Indeed, Father had just published his best-selling *Goodbye to All That*. Gelat, with the peasant's inborn charm, broke with tradition and opened his home to them. He agreed to stop his morning bus to Palma in front of their house to pick up their mail. Soon the *Senyors* were stopping by the *Fàbrica* every afternoon for a chat and quick game of cards with him and his family. Gelat became their friend and factotum.

In 1932 Don Bernardo Colom, who owned the *finca* of Son Canals, sold the *senyors* a plot of land on which to build a house. Don Bernardo had made his fortune in Cuba – it was common for villagers to emigrate for a few years – and was married to a Cuban. He was rich by village standards and Gelat's pretty young daughter and Don Bernardo's son were courting. The plot was a kilometre past the village on the road to Soller, the next town up the coast, in a spot that got plenty of sun in winter. Naturally, Gelat acted as middleman. He arranged that *mestre* Pep Salas was to build the house according to the *senyora* Laura's plans; and he went to the site every day to oversee the masons' progress, and make sure the builder was not cheating.

Subsequently, again with Gelat as middleman, Don Bernardo sold the *senyors* three more tracts of land. On the first, next to Canellún, a friend of theirs built Can Torrent, which later became part of the property. Of the other two, the larger, some eight acres of terraced olive groves, was separated from Canellún by the main road; the smaller, some three acres of pine woods, was down by the Cala. Father and Laura originally bought these to prevent them being acquired by a German speculator. Although Father paid for all the properties other than Can Torrent, everything belonged to Laura. Where legally possible, the deeds were in her name; where not, they were in Gelat's.

Laura now planned to build a university on the plot above the beach. To reach it she drove a costly five-metre wide, stone-metalled road from the main thoroughfare, through our upper terraces, through the neighbouring land, to the valley bottom and down to the beach. The work was overseen by Gelat. Initially, to pay for these projects, Laura had hoped to divide the upper land into building plots, and, perhaps, also build an hotel. However, just as the road was completed, a freak rain storm produced such a flood that the torrent rose over its banks, broached the road and washed away large parts of it into the Cala. The road could not be repaired at once, nor were any plots sold, but Gelat kept his inevitable cut. To cover the debts, Canellún had to be mortgaged, and it was to settle the mortgage that Father wrote his next best seller, *I, Claudius*. Afterwards, Father felt the road was unlucky: he did not like us going that way to the beach.

Gelat was commissioned by a bank to dispose of one of the large *fincas* in Deyá, Es Molí, whose owner had fallen on hard times. Gelat split the property into its various houses and small tracts of land and sold these to villagers who were working in France or in Cuba and who had ready cash. For himself Gelat kept Ca'n Madó, an old flour mill, together with its water rights to the substantial spring which drove it. He removed the mill's machinery and in its place installed a Swedish-made turbine – he persuaded the *senyors* to pay for it – driven by the same head of water to power his Deyá grid, instead of the now worn-out diesel generator at the *Fàbrica*. In exchange for the turbine, he made the Ca'n Madó orchard and vegetable garden over to Laura, although the deeds, of course, remained in Gelat's name. His *turbina* unfortunately used up far more water than he anticipated; and, led by Dr Vives, the other villagers who shared water rights complained. It all ended in litigation.

Gelat started his *turbina* up at dusk. When he did, light bulbs that had been left on the night before, glimmered and then burned brightly. At the time, and for the few years after we arrived, the output was perfectly sufficient for the village needs. Around midnight, he shut it down. To warn his users to prepare their candles and switch out the lights, he dimmed them three times. A couple of minutes later the electricity would go off.

With the turbine providing electricity for his grid, Gelat sold the old diesel, and built a café in the part of the *Fàbrica* where the oil press had once stood. The Salón Deportivo 'Concordia' had a large floor area, and Gelat added in a snooker table, a dance floor and an elegant stage for dance bands and travelling acts. Father and Laura abandoned Margalida at Jaume the Butcher's café, which they used to frequent, and Gelat gave them their own table at the Salón. They went there most evenings to play cards, listen to the news on the wireless which Father had paid for and, when Gelat had a band, to join in the dance.

One house which had been part of the Es Molí property was the semi-ruinous Posada on the Puig. It abutted on the church and the Es Molí owners had once used it to stable their donkeys during Mass and then, having taken holy communion, return to it for a breakfast of pastries and hot chocolate. Gelat convinced Laura they should buy the Posada from him although, since the house was now rented by the church, it took considerable negotiation with the priest, and money had to be passed to the bishopric before they got hold of the key.

In the Deyá municipal elections of May 1936 Gelat stood for Mayor on the Socialist Party list, and won. However, his term was short-lived. Two months later, after the Civil War began, Gelat was removed from office and then arrested and, in view of his Socialist politics, accused of having built the Cala road to help a Republican landing. He spent six months in the Palma prison.

7

When, in 1936, General Franco led the Nationalist uprising, the Majorca military command at once sided with him. This put all villagers who had voted Socialist in a difficult position. Fortunately, few could be accused, as Gelat was, of being overtly Communist or Socialist. The people of Deyá were by nature apolitical. During the Republic they had been prepared to pay lip service to any party candidate standing for election, whether on the Right or the Left – provided they were not asked to sign anything. Nevertheless, there were a number of disagreeable incidents in Deyá during the three years of the Civil War.

Perhaps the most unsettling event occurred within four days of the uprising, when five open cars drove into Deyá after midnight, carrying eighteen armed Falangist youths, looking for a Socialist councillor from the inland town of Inca, who was in hiding. They had been wrongly informed, and stopped at Dr Vives's house. When nobody opened up, they fired at his door. Those bullet marks are still visible almost sixty years later. Dr Vives himself was a Nationalist, and had feared the youths were Communists sent by Gelat, with whom he was in litigation over the water rights. The Doctor escaped through the back door, hoping to be hidden in Don Bernardo's *finca*, he also being a Nationalist. It was after midnight, the turbine was shut off, and Dr Vives could not see where he was going. First he lost his *espardenyas* and then, hearing a shuffling of footsteps, he climbed a carob tree and hid. The shuffling continued intermittently throughout the night, and it was only at dawn that he realized the noise was coming from a tethered mule, not any armed guards. Meanwhile the Falangists got Gelat out of bed to turn on the electricity, found the Inca councillor at the Hotel Costa d'Or in the nearby hamlet of Lluc Alcari, and took him back to Palma – where he was shot.

The sea bombardment took place about a year later, a less personal but no less dramatic affair. It happened early one evening in late spring after work, when most of the men were in the café. Suddenly a loud bang was heard, as if there were rock-blasting nearby. Everyone rushed out into the street, and heard the next shell whistle over and explode on the terraces above. The head of the Deyá Falangists was being shaved by Blau the Barber, in his little shop by the Porxo, and he ran out wiping the soap off his face.

'¡No pasarán!' he shouted. 'They won't get through! ¡A las armas! Take up your arms!' Then another shell exploded nearby, and he quickly changed his tune. '¡Al refugio! To the shelter!'

The vaulted passage behind Ca'n Vallés, a manorial house built by the Arxiduc's secretary close to the Town Hall, had been deemed to be the village bomb-shelter. Xesc Parrageta, his leg withering after having once been one of the strongest men in the village, came out on his crutches carrying a stool, and sat in the middle of the Porxo square hoping to be hit. In the cemetery young Francisco Mosso, who was in the militia, held the garrison's binoculars and looked out to sea. He too was lame: some time before he had smashed his leg against Gelat's taxi when cycling home from hunting rabbits in the woods. What he saw was a Republican cruiser lying some three miles offshore. Two more shells came whistling over, one on each side of the Puig, barely missing the church. The old ladies, who regularly attended vespers, later said it had been protected by Sant Joan, Deyá's Patron Saint.

Quite what the cruiser was aiming at, Francisco could never decide, and concluded that it must have got either its orders or its position wrong. Most of the shells hit the terraces above the village and two did so without exploding. When the next morning the Captain of the Puerto Soller Submarine Base drove up to Deyá, Francisco showed him where the unexploded shells lay. One of them had fallen near the Canellún Grotto. There the Captain told Francisco, who was pretty muscular in spite of his gammy leg, to put the dud shell into their lorry. To this day he still remembers how he refused to obey, until the Captain laughingly pointed out that the shell had lost its igniter in flight.

Paseillos – short walks – given by the Falangists at Ca Madò Pilla, in Valldemosa just outside the Deyá parish bounds, were a constant reminder to the villagers of the war's seriousness. The Falangists drove their victims up from Palma at night, and took them down the path to a beautiful lookout point built by the *Arxiduc*. From the top of a 200-metre drop on to the rocky shore below, they pushed their hapless victims to their deaths. Deyá fishermen, on the way to set their nets, averted their gaze from the mangled bodies being pecked at by black vultures. After a *paseillo*, the monks from the Valldemosa hermitage climbed down the cliffs early the next morning – supposedly collecting samphire or capers for pickling – to administer the last rites. There was nothing they could do or say or they themselves would have been executed. Even so, they managed to rescue and hide one of the victims, little more than a boy, who had survived by falling into a pine tree.

Perhaps the worst consequence of the Civil War on Deyá was the way it polarized the inhabitants and brought out long-standing jealousies, hatred and petty vendettas, which had more to do with inheritances, mistresses and water rights than with politics. Those who had voted for the Socialists in the 1936 elections were in an especially delicate position. March the Fisherman, who was one of Mayor Gelat's Socialist councillors, had a family of four. The house next to the Town Hall became the Falange headquarters, and there were youths on guard at all times. When the March boys passed by on their way back from school, they were 'captured' by older village boys who had been given Falangist uniforms to wear. They were called Reds, and sometimes kept locked up for hours. March was wise enough never to complain: the *paseillo* was a real possibility if he did.

Magdalena the Butcher's elder brother, Pere Ferrer, had been an ardent Socialist. After the shoot-up at the Doctor's, he took to the mountains. Every evening his younger brother left food and newspapers for him to collect in a hiding-place near March's house, at the Viña Vieja. Unfortunately, March's dog barked when it heard Pere come down from the hills at night for his things. March's children loved their dog, but March knew that if the Falangist hotheads got Pere, he would be taken on the *paseillo*.

A dog's life is not worth a man's . . . . So he took the poor animal out in his boat, tied a heavy stone around its neck, and threw it overboard.

For a time Pere lived close to the village in a good dry cave, beneath a gigantic oak tree, near the ruins of a lookout tower; however, one day a Deyá Falangist sympathizer, out mushroom picking, found his newspapers in the cave, and denounced him. Pere was warned in time and moved on. By the time his next hiding-place was discovered about a year later, the political situation was somewhat more settled, so he came down from the mountain and gave himself up to the *Guardia Civil*. He was taken to Palma and exiled to the small island of Cabrera for four years. There he managed to survive on the meagre rations, which he supplemented by catching crabs and prising limpets off the rocks. Pere Ferrer returned to Deyá after the war, but died a broken man a couple of years later.

The village's only loss at the hands of the Falangists was Pere Parrageta, Xesc's brother. He owned an orchard which, in spite of the curfew, he used to water on Monday and Thursday evenings, when the rights to the spring were his. One evening after dark, on his way back from watering, he was stopped by a group of young Falangists from Palma, who, mistaking him for Magdalena's brother, drove him away. By the time the local Falangists had telegraphed Palma, it was too late.

When we arrived, there were still villagers who would readily report anyone with Republican tendencies to the authorities, so none of the events of the Civil War were ever discussed in public. However, virtually everyone in the village had been intensely emotionally affected by these events, so that they formed an integral if unspoken part of the Deyá psyche. Over the years, I gleaned snippets of what had happened, but it was not until after Franco's death in 1975 that I was told the full stories by March the Fisherman, Francisco Mosso, and others who had lived through it.

8

In 1939 after Franco's victory, the new regime demanded that village mayors should have a clean, non-Republican record. This caused little problem in Deyá, since the village elders made sure – over their game of dominoes in the café – that the right names were submitted to the authorities. However, they could do little about the increased power wielded by the Catholic Church. Don Guillem, the new Priest, expected everyone to attend Mass on Sundays in their Sunday best: suits for the men, long sleeves, stockings and veils for the women – even on the hottest summer day. He made sure the traditional mourning periods were strictly adhered to: three years for a parent or spouse, two years for a brother or sister, one year for an uncle or aunt. Because of these rules, almost everyone wore black or grey. Even my school-friends had a black ribbon sewn to their coat collar for the death of a close relative.

Spain suffered a severe drought just after the Civil War, and the harvests were bad. This, together with the lack of foreign aid, meant that the flour, sugar, coffee, rice and lentils sold at the Estanco were rationed and of poor quality. The flour was mixed with maize, the sugar a dirty grey, the coffee blended with chicory. The rice and lentils both contained small stones, and women would sit in their spare moments outside the front door in the shade, swirling handfuls of either around in plates, and picking out the grit.

Nevertheless, villagers rarely went hungry. *Pa amb oli*, fresh bread smeared with olive oil and tomato, and *sopas mallorquinas*, dry bread soaked in vegetable broth, formed the heart of the local diet. The grocery shops stocked most of what they needed, and practically everyone owned a few terraces of olive trees and grew wheat on them. Most also owned a piece of land with water rights on which to grow tomatoes, peppers and potatoes. Fishwives brought the morning catch up from the Cala, and blew their conch at their stops in the Porxo, the Puig, and the Clot; but when they could, men climbed down the rocky cliffs with their fishing tackle, and returned with fish of their own. The two butchers, both called Magdalena, each killed a sheep every Monday, and most villagers ate meat once or twice a week; again, most kept a few hens to kill for a special occasion, and a pig which they slaughtered before Christmas. Small game abounded in the mountains, and it was not uncommon to see the spotted ginnet cats, weasels and rabbits close to the village. Rabbits and partridges were the main quarry for hunters like Francisco Mosso and, in the season, shots reverberated across the valley.

Unlike Son Canals, which Don Bernardo owned and ran, most of the large *fincas* belonged to wealthy families from Palma or Soller. These engaged tenant farmers, *amos*, from Deyá to look after their property. No salary was paid: the *amo* gave the landlord 'half' the produce, and kept – a larger and better – 'half' for himself. The landlord came to the *finca* only for short visits, when the *amo* would prepare him a good meal and then go over the accounts; except in summer, when the landlord and his family might stay for the month of August to get away from the Palma heat.

Olives were Deyá's main crop. They ripen in December and the large *fincas* engaged a dozen or more *gallufas*, women olive-pickers from the other side of the island, to help bring in the harvest. Every so often a *gallufa* married one of the Deyá boys and stayed on. All twenty-eight olive presses in the village and *fincas* were working during and immediately after the War. The oil was supposed to be sold exclusively to a government monopoly, but this was hard to control.

The extra oil the villagers kept back they exchanged for essentials. This was usually done by the women, who would take a monthly trip in Gelat's bus carrying a five-litre tin of contraband oil in a large wicker basket of dirty clothes. They invariably worried when the bus stopped in Valldemosa, and the *guardias* climbed in and cursorily looked over the passengers. Of course, Gelat's son Jöan, who drove the bus, was paying the *guardias* off, but one could never know when there might be a new one who did not abide by the agreement. In Palma they took the oil to one of a number of small grocery shops, sold it for a decent price and then bought a little black-market coffee, sugar, flour, condensed milk, or soap. They carried their booty back in the bus to Deyá, hidden under the same dirty clothes.

It was only natural, under the rationing imposed, that smuggling should flourish, and Deyá's age-old vocation took on a new lease of life. The shipments, delivered from Tangier in deep-sea trawlers, now included, not only the usual cartons of cigarettes, but also rice, flour, coffee and sugar. The boxes of cigarette cartons and the 50-kilo sacks were offloaded at one of the many small jetties along the coast and quickly hidden in nearby caves. Later, the contraband was moved on dark nights by young men, wearing special harnesses to ease their heavy loads, all the way up and over the 1000-metre-high Teix to villages on the other side of the mountain range.

Half a dozen *guardias* with their families were stationed in Deyá to maintain the peace and to prevent smuggling. Their headquarters, a room with a desk and a photograph of Franco – in uniform – was next door to Dr Vives's house. The *guardias* came mostly from rural parts of mainland Spain and did not speak Majorcan. They were grudgingly accepted by the villagers since their wages, small as they were, proved a useful injection into the local economy. However, none of the *guardias* ever fully integrated, even though some of them married village girls.

9

Excluding Gelat, perhaps Castor the Postman was the villager whom Father's return, after the War, had affected most. The weight of his mail sack had more than doubled with the letters the *senyor de Canellún* received. Castor came from the mainland and had been appointed to Deyá by the Postal Service long before the war. During the Civil War he was anonymously accused of failing to deliver a letter, lost his job and was sent to prison. It was a blatantly trumped-up charge, but he had unforgivably voted for the Socialists in the 1936 elections. However, since Castor was married to a local girl, he had been reinstated by the time we arrived.

Castor's day began at six in the morning, when he emptied the postbox by the Estanco, postmarked the stamps, and took the letters in the mail sack to Gelat's bus, which left for Palma at half-past seven. At half-past three every afternoon, Castor collected the mail sack from the bus when it returned. By the time Castor had carried the sack to his house on the Puig, sorted the letters, and put them in his postman's issue leather bag, it was five o'clock. Castor himself decided on the village limits within which he was required by law to deliver the post. Canellún, he decreed, was definitively outside, so he left our letters at Ca'n Pep Mosso, which was both a grocery shop and a small café with verandah at the back. Father found it more pleasant and convenient than Gelat's Salón, which was now little frequented.

Father sat at a table on the far end of the café verandah with a coffee in front of him, and waited for Castor to arrive. There was usually someone to talk to but, if not, he always carried a clip-board with some work, a pen and a bottle of ink in his large basket. When Castor appeared through the café door Father grabbed his pile of mail, rushed back to his table, put on his glasses, tore open each letter and, after avidly reading the contents, threw it into the basket. He then hurried home, basket slung over his shoulder. Later that evening he would return to the village carrying a pile of letters in answer to those he had received, and post them in the box by the Estanco.

As with Castor, most villagers were affected, directly or indirectly, by our arrival. Some were called in for jobs at Canellún. Miquel the Carpenter came shortly after we arrived, to take measurements for nesting boxes in the chicken run Mother was to have built. Miquel was illiterate and he carried a rod with him on which he carved the appropriate measures. He built the village coffins by mentally comparing the length and breadth of bodies to that of his wife, and then had her lie on his bench while he cut the box to fit.

After he had made the nesting boxes he walked over once again to Canellún.

'Hail, Mary the Purest,' he shouted.

'One moment please,' said Mother, skipping the response, and going to fetch Father.

'Ah, Miquel, a small brandy, a cigarette?' Father always offered brandy.

'If you insist, Don Roberto.' He was pleased to see Father again and complimented him on the state of the house. Father did not invite him to sit down. Father liked standing when he came out of his study. Eventually Miquel got around to the point of his call.

'After all these years you have been away, your shutters need tightening and a new coat of green paint. That way they will last you a lifetime. Whenever you are ready I can come to collect them.' It was not that he needed the extra work. It was just that he had made the shutters and wanted them to look their best. Like many of the villagers, Miquel thought foreigners somewhat simple when it came to looking after their houses and land.

Pep Salas the Builder had also been called in for an estimate on the chicken run. He had built both Canellún and Can Torrent and always listened gravely to the way Father wanted something done.

'*Sí, Don Roberto,*' he said and then proceeded to do it the 'right' way. He had been taught to do things correctly and nothing would budge him. He was also an amateur dowser and it was he, when building the chicken run, who convinced Father that he should dig for water in the Can Torrent garden. The well was dry, and wire netting covered the abandoned hole for years afterwards.

Often, as we were being made ready for school, Joana the Fishwife would walk regally towards the house, a large wicker basket balanced on her head.

'*¡Senyora, o senyora!*' she would screech. She was a very thin old lady, her face a network of wrinkles, and she wore a dark grey cotton dress of a nondescript pattern and cut, which had passed countless times through the *rentaderos*. When Mother actually wanted to buy from her, she came out with a plate. Joana lowered her basket, lifted the damp sack which covered it to display a mass of flapping fish, and stood questioningly with a pair of ancient roman-scales in her left hand. Mother then pointed to her choice. It was usually red mullet: she was not yet ready for squid, prawns, or the various multicoloured and silvery fish whose Majorcan names we had still to learn. Joana weighed the mullet, and slid them on to the plate.

'*¿Cuanto?*' asked Mother, one of the first words she learned, and held out some dirty one-peseta notes.

There were four general stores, and all sold much the same things. We used both the Estanco and Ca'n Pep Mosso. There were two main bakers, although the Clot shop also made and sold its own bread. We bought ours from Gabriel the Baker, who had a sign in English over his shop on the Puig which announced *KAKES & PASTRYS*. Magdalena the Butcher, whose shop was on the main road, had her husband Jaume slaughter the weekly sheep. They fought all the time. Jaume was deaf but had an eye for young girls. Before the war his first wife, Margalida, had run a café in the front part of the premises which Father, Laura and their friends had frequented. When they moved to the Salón, Gelat's new café, Margalida was hurt and stopped talking to them. They began buying their meat from Magdalena Ferrer whose shop was on the Porxo, and we continued doing so after the war. The village gossip was that our Magdalena had had an affair with a married *guardia*; this became public knowledge, and she had never been able to marry afterwards. She now lived with her bachelor brother who did her slaughtering. Father had accounts at all the shops we patronised in much the way the owners of the *fincas* did. Every three or so months he would settle up. Father would never check the bill. He would pay, roll the bill into a ball, and hand it back; not that he was not interested – it was a question of trust.

We had clothes made or mended by one of the several seamstresses in the village. Both Mother and Father wore their oldest clothes in the house and in the village. A jersey with a darned elbow, or trousers with a patch on the knee, were quite acceptable to them and, I suppose in comparison with the villagers' blacks and greys, they always looked well dressed to me. If, however, they were going down to Palma, they smartened up. Mother liked to wear soft pastel colours, her Jaeger suits being favourites. Father wore a suit and tie and one of the colourful waistcoats he had bought before the war, made of peasant cotton cloth or silk, and on which he sported antique silver buttons. He always wore his green pork-pie hat.

When they went to Palma, they took Gelat's taxi. His son Joan drove. Joan would open the Canellún front gates and back up the drive to the kitchen door. He had inherited none of his father's panache. He always carried an adjustable spanner in one greasy hand and a cotton rag in the other. Petrol was hard to come by, so the old pre-war American station wagon was powered, as were most cars and lorries, by a *gasogeno*. The gas which replaced the petrol mixture was produced by the incomplete burning of almond shells in a monstrous cylindrical pressure-chamber, bolted to the back of the vehicle. *Gasogenos* had to be lit several hours before a trip, generally in the middle of the night, and were notoriously unreliable. One day, with Father and Mother already in the car, Jöan was waiting behind the steering wheel for the pressure to build up. I stood on the *depósito* wall, ready to wave them goodbye. Then, muttering under his breath, Jöan pulled out his spanner and cotton rag from under the driver's seat and got out of the car to check the flame. There was a deafening explosion. Jöan staggered back, suffering nothing worse than burned eyelashes and a singed ego. I smiled at his colourful swear words. After their return Mother reported that he had blown the car horn on every single bend all the way to Palma.

10

Mother came of a very English background. She was born on 22 February 1915. Her father, Sir Harry Pritchard, was a solicitor, senior partner in a law firm specializing in drafting Parliamentary Bills, and one-time President of the Law Society. Her mother, Amy, came from a family of doctors and scientists and was a church-goer. Beryl and her twin brother Hardinge were the youngest of five and they lived in Hampstead. She had gone to day school in Harley Street, taken piano lessons, and kept an alligator as a pet. All the brothers and sisters went to Oxford. Hardinge read Law and was a member of the Moral Rearmament Group. Beryl read Philosophy, Politics and Economics (PPE) at St Anne's and joined the Oxford University Labour Club. Her tutor said she had 'an excellent PPE brain'.

Mother must have been very much in love with Father, twenty years her senior, and have trusted him implicitly, to come on this adventure to a Spain ruled by Generalissimo Franco, against whom many of her contemporaries had volunteered to fight. She did not care for the sun or the food and she was bitten by mosquitos; we three children were a handful. However, when she arrived she immediately pushed herself to learn Spanish by reading *Don Quijote de la Mancha*. She sat in her workroom above the kitchen, with the *Quijote* on a book-stand and a dictionary by her side, taking notes. Within a year she was proficient. However, both she and Father spoke Spanish with strong English accents and neither ever learned to speak Majorcan[1] which Lucia, Juan and I were now fluent in.

In the village, Mother and Father's circle of friends and acquaintances was small. Father still stopped in at the *Fàbrica* to see Gelat most days on his way to the post, but Mother was not Laura, and the friendship became more distant. This at least put the villagers more at ease, since they had not really approved of Gelat's closeness to him. In their minds a *senyor* was a *senyor* and a worker was a worker; just as oil floats on water, each has his place and should not mix. My parents' easiest relationship was

---

[1] Indeed, most of the non-English words we used around the house were Spanish and not Majorcan. For example *depósito* is a Spanish word and I have kept it in the text because it was part of our everyday usage.

probably with my schoolmaster Gaspar Sabater and his wife Juanita, who were *senyors*. Father used Gaspar's library in his research for *The Isles of Unwisdom*, a book about the only woman admiral in Spanish history. And Mother got on well with Juanita. Dr Vives had given his daughter a comparatively good education, and she was one of the few Majorcan women in Deyá to whom Mother could take her questions about children or servants or the best buys in Palma shops. Juanita brought her two boys along to Canellún to play with Lucia and Juan. Although Gelat's and the Doctor's families were again on speaking terms after the water-rights litigation, Mother and Father's friendship with the Sabaters must have irritated Gelat.

Apart from us, very few foreigners had ventured back to Majorca after the war. Those who were on the island had mostly stayed throughout the Civil War and later the Second World War. The only British subjects in the village were Jessie Broadwood, an old English lady who had stayed on because of her numerous cats; and the Pring-Mills who, although they came to Deyá about the time we did, had spent the war in neighbouring Valldemosa. Major and Mrs Pring-Mill's son Robert later became my sister Lucia's tutor of Catalan at Oxford. Although neighbourly, they had little in common with Mother and Father other than their nationality. Indeed, Mother regarded both Mrs Broadwood and the Pring-Mills almost as right-wing extremists. My parents made their real friends in Palma.

When Mother and Father went to Palma in the taxi, their first stop would be breakfast with Cyril and Lisa Morrison, one of the few recently arrived foreign couples in Majorca, on their yacht *Rosalind* anchored at the Club Nautico. 'Squirrel' – the nearest I could pronounce his name – was an ex-Indian Cavalry officer who had taught himself to sail, and was one of the first in the yacht charter business in Palma. After breakfast, Mother and Father would shop in the open-air central food market for certain meat, fruit and vegetables they could not get in Deyá, and in one of the better grocer's shops for butter, ham and tinned food. At eleven they would join William Cook, an American painter and long-time friend of Gertrude Stein, for coffee at his usual table in the Bar Fígaro. There they would leave their baskets behind the counter so as to spend the second half of the morning at the bank, the post office or doing more general shopping. Father could never resist visiting one or two antique shops. At half-past one, when the shops shut, Mother and Father would meet again at the Bar Fígaro to pick up the baskets. Sometimes, during the course of the morning, they visited the Gittes family or, exceptionally, they would stay over and have lunch with them.

The Gittes were their best friends on the island. Archie was an American painter, Cicely an English concert pianist; they had four children. At the outbreak of the Civil War they were living in Genova, on the outskirts of Palma. When food became scarce, they thought they might fare better in a village further from town, and they moved up to Deyá. To begin with things were fine. Archie painted Deyá landscapes. He and Cicely took Father's dog Solomon – usually chained up in front of the *Fàbrica* since his master had left – for walks. The children went to the school. The Gittes's troubles started when Archie was suspected of being a spy by the *Guardia Civil*. These would not allow him out with his easel, for fear that he would send maps to the Republicans. Then the Second World War started and Cicely's small allowance, on which they had been living, failed to arrive. Finally, painting indoors all day, Archie developed tuberculosis. They were helped out by Antonia who cleaned house for them. Not only would she not let them pay her wages but she lent them a little money and initiated Cicely into the practice of olive oil contraband. Shortly before we arrived in Deyá the Gittes had returned to Palma to give their children better schooling. Archie and Cicely now lived in the old quarter behind the Cathedral. Among their friends they found excellent teachers who had been purged for their Republican ideas, and who provided magnificent private tuition for their bright children.

11

Mother was not a natural cook: she cooked out of necessity, not out of pleasure, and it took her some time to come to terms with the unfamiliar ingredients. With time she greatly improved, but I do not remember any dish she made that I much cared for as a child. Her mutton stews were watery; she overcooked the aubergines, marrows and runner beans; she even managed to make the wonderful fresh fish tasteless. Father was a considerably more experienced cook, but he rarely spared the time. His contribution was the salads which he enjoyed preparing, with tomatoes, peppers, cucumbers, lettuces, and sometimes unexpected ingredients such as *acerolas*, grapes or melon. For pudding we mostly had fresh fruit, although sometimes in winter – as a change from oranges – Mother gave us stewed apricots or plums from Father's bottles in the cellar. These lay next to his jars of bitter-orange marmalade, blackberry jam, *acerola* jelly, and tomato chutney – some of it still of pre-war vintage. Bottling fruit and making jam, jelly and chutney, together with gardening and washing-up, were Father's therapies whenever he got stuck in his writing.

We soon adopted some of the local customs, and Father arranged with Gelat to have a pig fattened, killed, and made into sausages for us. For six months he carried the Canellún leftovers for our pig in his basket on his way to the post. It was a black Majorcan pig with the peculiar meaty tassels typical of its breed hanging under its snout. It started as a piglet and grew into a sizable sow. A *matanza*, a pig killing, was an important event in a villager's calendar, and we had ours in December as was customary. So as not to upset Mother and us, Father made sure we arrived at the *Fàbrica*, where the event was taking place, when the pig was already dead. Later, in other *matanzas*, I saw how the butchers stuck a large knife into the throat to bleed the beast, and heard its distressing death squeal. Our animal had already been cut up. The meat lay on a scrubbed table next to a hand-turned mincing machine; the bones were being boiled in a cauldron over an open fire; the intestines had been washed clean. I then watched, fascinated, as men with bloodied hands ground the meat, and pinafored old women prepared it and filled the guts to make sausages. There were two basic fillings. One was the red *sobrasada* paste, seasoned with sweet red pepper and other spices, and used to fill short, fat, or long, U-shaped sausages, or even large round ones which had to be bound with string to prevent them from splitting. The other was the black *butifarrón* paste, mixed with the pig's blood and seasoned with black pepper, pine kernels and aniseed, then stuffed into the lengths of intestine which were knotted to make chains of small sausages. I loved the delicate, sweetish, peppery red *sobrasada* spread on brown peasant bread. The *butifarrones*, which are usually sliced lengthways and fried, I found too strong for my young palate.

It was a sunny day and, when the work was over, we had lunch around the now clean wooden table outdoors. *Matanzas* carry overtones of pagan sacrifice, of which Father was very much aware, and they are always followed by a celebratory lunch. To Mother, it was more of a social obligation. I just loved eating out. Madora, Gelat's wife, had prepared *sopas de matanzas* – much the same as ordinary *sopas* but served with pork meat – in a large low earthenware pot over the open wood fire. The grown-ups had wine, we children sweet fizzy lemonade; and afterwards Father and Gelat made short speeches. We then crated the *sobrasadas* and *butifarrones* and loaded them into a donkey cart. At his invitation, I climbed in next to Gelat, and we drove up the Puig road to the Posada. Father walked beside us. At the Posada I helped Father carry the sausages up a narrow staircase to the dusty loft, where we hung them on nails driven into the roof beams and left them to cure during the colder winter months.

After frequent '*mañanas*' and the usual delay, Mother's chicken run was finally built in the Can Torrent garden. Mother bought a cock and ten Minorcan hens which were soon laying lovely, large, delicious brown eggs. A soft-boiled egg, timed by the kitchen sand-glass, became my favourite treat. Mother allowed some eggs to hatch and purchased – as she had been advised to do – a bantam hen which looked after the chicks better than the Minorcans did. Mother had a wonderful way with all animals. In the mornings I helped her feed the hens, scattering maize around the run, while she filled the earthenware drinking bowl. It was easy to tell when one of them had laid an egg by the excited cackling they made. On hot afternoons the hens sat in the shade of the overhanging olive tree, uttering long-drawn-out, soporific, clucking sounds. The cock started crowing well before dawn, and if I was awake, I listened to him, and to the echoing quality of the replies he received from his counterparts on the farms. It made me feel good knowing that all was well in the valley.

CHAPTER III

1

One Thursday at the end of July 1947, Gelat's grandson Juanito and I were playing in the garden. The church bell struck the midday Angelus – three sets of three rapid chimes. It sounded throughout the valley and the men working the terraces tidied away their tools and went home for lunch. Juanito got on his bicycle. At Canellún we did not eat until one o'clock, so I offered to ride with him part of the way. For I had a small red bicycle which Gelat had unexpectedly wheeled up the Canellún drive one day and given me. It was not even my birthday. I had soon learned to ride it on our walks to Ca'n Madó.

Juanito went ahead. On the first corner in the road I was pedalling furiously to catch up with him, my head bent low under my straw hat, when something made me suddenly look up. For a split second my sight was filled with a tall chrome-plated radiator grille, a black mudguard, a gleaming headlamp. It was one of the taxis that drove through Deyá every Monday and Thursday full of tourists. It was rounding the bend on the wrong side, freewheeling to build up pressure in its *gasogeno*. I do not remember the impact. Nor do I remember the pain as I lay screaming by the chicken-wire fence at the edge of the road, clutching my injured leg. The car had knocked me off my bicycle and, as I fell, a large part of my right foot was torn away by the pedal.

My screams soon brought Mother and Father, who later confessed they thought a pig had been run over. Father wrapped my foot with the tea towel he was carrying, in which he had been drying a lettuce for one of his salads, commandeered the taxi and rushed me down to Soller and Dr Rovira, who gave me first aid and sent me on to the hospital in Palma. It was a bad wound, and I spent about a week in hospital, mostly under sedation, until the doctors felt my foot was sufficiently healed to send me home. However, since I had to be taken back to the out-patient

42

department every day to have my bandages changed, I could not return to Deyá. Archie and Cicely Gittes kindly solved Mother and Father's predicament by taking me in.

Father carried me through an archway into a shady patio lined with aspidistras and up wide stone steps to the Gittes's flat. I was put to bed in a cool room from where I could see the patio, and get my first glimpse of Mother and Father when they arrived on their almost daily visit in Gelat's taxi to take me to the hospital. Cicely was a cheerful, chubby blonde lady who wore her hair in a bun and had a peculiar way of enunciating her words. She spoiled me and, much to the disgust of her four boys, gave me rather more than my share of the scarce food. I lost weight in spite of all her pampering. The clumsy doctors who dressed my wound hurt me terribly, and I whimpered through the hot nights with the pain.

At first my foot seemed to be healing, but then it got worse. After about two weeks it was obvious to Cicely that things had gone seriously wrong. Back in hospital, the doctors shrugged their shoulders and said my foot would have to come off. Mother and Father desperately telephoned and telegraphed everyone they knew or heard of who might be able to help. They were about to rush me back to England for a second opinion when, miraculously, they were told of a surgeon in Barcelona who had worked in the British Army under the famous Dr Trueta, and had learned his new method of grafting skin over war wounds. One month after the accident, the day before the Palma doctors were planning an amputation, Father bundled me in a blanket and carried me from my hospital bed on to the Barcelona boat; the next morning he delivered me to the Clínica Adriano.

Dr Gabarró examined my foot and, X-ray in hand, began cursing the doctors in Palma: there was still gravel from the road in the wound.

'It's a miracle you did not get gangrene,' he growled. Unlike the Palma doctors, he was gentle and kind, and quickly built up my confidence, so that I no longer trembled with apprehension when he came to see me. A couple of days later he was ready.

'Guillem,' he said in Catalan, which was much like the Majorcan I spoke, 'I am going to operate on you tomorrow; would you like to watch? It won't hurt. I'll give you an injection.'

'No, thank you, Doctor,' I replied, feeling squeamish.

It was the first skin graft ever to be performed in Spain, and Dr Gabarró had a large audience in the teaching theatre. He removed a patch of skin from my thigh and grafted it on the foot. When I awoke from the anaesthetic, I had plaster on both my foot and my thigh. The operation was successful and, a couple of days later, the nurses hooked up a device with a handle by which I could pull a bar against my toes to start developing some strength in them.

The month I spent in the Clínica Adriano was perhaps the only time in my life I could count on Father's undivided attention. At home he was either working, or off for a quick swim or on some errand or other. He never really sat back and relaxed when we were around. At meal-times the three of us squabbled for his notice. There were certainly few opportunities for me to be alone with him. Even to stand at the bathroom door and watch him shave was a treat. He used the end-bits of ordinary soap which he kept in a wooden bowl, a balding shaving brush and a Rolls Razor. He grimaced into the small round mirror framed in the white painted cupboard high above the washbasin and pulled his nose up to shave his upper lip. He was not very thorough, and his face was always prickly. Fortunately, however, one of his evening chores was to bathe us before Mother put us to bed, and I gladly suffered his somewhat harsh – and haphazard – flannelling until I was about eight years old. For after the bath he sat me on his knee, dried me in a large bath-towel, and sang me songs or told me made-up stories.

Having his full attention in hospital was like a continuous bath night. My favourite song was a nonsense rhyme about three monkeys washed up by the tide, which he sang to the haunting tune of 'The Duke of Grantham'. Others in his repertoire were 'The Campdown Race Track', 'Casey Jones', and 'Goodnight, Ladies'. We had a long ongoing story about Deyá in Roman times, how young village boys were given a sling when they were my age, and had to hit a target before they were allowed their breakfast of *pa amb oli*. In that way they became very good sling shots, and Roman Emperors came to Deyá to see if young Toni and young Xesc were as good as their Balearic Slinger fathers. The best slingers would then be taken by the Emperor to Rome to fight in the legions. It was my own private historical novel. If Father were smoking, he kept me amused by blowing smoke rings so that the second ring went through the first. He told me silly nursery rhymes which were different to the ones Mother had read me:

> Jack Sprat would eat no fat,
> His wife would eat no fat;
> They threw the beastly stuff away
> And gave it to the cat.

It was during this month that his pale blue laughing eyes, his wonderful smile, his prickly face, and his constant presence formed such a strong bond that, even when he behaved so appallingly towards me in later years, I never ceased loving him.

While I was in the Barcelona hospital, Mother came over for a haemorrhoids operation. Since long before we arrived in Deyá, she had been in pain most of the time. She was often in bed, and must have felt miserable and homesick – away from her friends in an unfamiliar country. She had become highly strung and shouted at Father, at me and especially at mischievous Juan. Since Mother was brought up in an age and a social background in which emotional confrontations were to be avoided at all costs, her outbursts must have added to her misery. In spite of her illness and her bad temper, she still embodied, for me, routine and stability. Father was wonderful, but when I fell down or needed reassurance, I went to Mother. One of my greatest pleasures was being read to by her. She had a beautifully modulated reading voice that made the back of my neck tingle. It mattered little whether the book was *Robinson Crusoe* – my children's edition with coloured pictures – or *The Barretts of Wimpole Street* or *The Phoenix and the Carpet*. They were all thrilling when she read them.

Mother was put in the bed next to mine at the hospital. When the nurses had wheeled her back into the room, after her operation, Father went for a walk.

'Mother's asleep. If I'm not back when she wakes up, ring the bell for the nurse.' It did not occur to him to warn me of how she might feel, waking up after the anaesthetic; perhaps he did not know. I was alone and even now, while the experience of my foot is buried deeply in some recess of my mind, I vividly recollect that awful moment when Mother began to stir.

'I must go to feed the hens! Quick! I must go to feed the hens!' she muttered.

'But, Mother,' I said, 'they are in Deyá.'

'Yes, yes. It's time to feed them.'

I could not get any sense out of her. I was terrified. I burst into tears and rang for the nurse.

The change in Mother's temper after the operation was dramatic, and she never again raised her voice at any of us. Indeed, I cannot remember Mother and Father ever having a fight. Since Father was not one to hold back a sharp word, and it takes two to quarrel, this is a mark of Mother's reserve. She also began to take on more responsibilities, deciding where to meet friends in Palma, or where to buy a wireless set, or when to see a doctor about having my adenoids out.

Three weeks after my operation I was back in Deyá. As soon as the plaster was removed I went back to school. Though I had lost the tendons in my foot to all but my big toe, I soon stopped limping and began to run with my friends. However, the scar tissue remained thin and tender, and I always had to be careful not to hit it; I could never play quite as roughly as the others. Nor, when I was older, was I ever able to use hard sports wear such as football boots or scuba flippers, which could easily rub and open a sore. My 'bad' foot never grew to quite the length of my 'good' one, and I still have shoes made to measure. I have never knowingly had a complex about the scar – but it is perhaps a subconscious fear of hurting my foot that has always made me abhor physical violence.

2

Mother had been doing Father's typing but, when she was ill, things got behind. *King Jesus* had just been published and was selling well, and by June 1947 Father could afford to bring his friend Karl back to Deyá to take care of the secretarial work. Karl Goldschmidt, a graphic artist, had been in Deyá before the war, when he had been 'adopted' by Laura Riding. He was small, lean, and very fit. He had been born in Germany in 1912, of Jewish parents, and at first spoke little English, but both Laura and Father spoke German. In the beginning, Karl helped them with the printing press and then, as his English improved, began to do their typing. At the outbreak of the Civil War, all three left Majorca together on a Royal Navy destroyer. Father persuaded the ship's Captain not to transfer Karl to a German ship – and back to Hitler's Germany – thereby almost certainly saving his life. Karl never forgot this. In England Karl obtained leave to stay and work and, when the Second World War broke out, he served first in the Pioneer Corps and later in the Royal Navy. In the Pioneers he had been made to change his name – as a protection in case of capture – and he became known as Kenneth Gay. When the war was over, he was granted full British citizenship and he retained this name; but we always called him Karl. After the break with Laura, and whenever his wartime commitments allowed him, Karl had continued working with Father. He was staying with us in Galmpton when he met his future wife, Rene, who was also a friend of my parents. Mother and Karl had always got on well. Indeed, they had met when he, Robert and Laura were in England in 1938 – and Mother knew how close the friendship between all three had been.

The village was rife with rumour when the word got around that Don Carlos *es secretari* was coming back. Carlitos – only Gelat called him that to his face – although young, had been much respected for his immaculate turn-out and his punctiliousness. As with any new gossip, the women at the *rentaderos* discussed his impending return at length. It was with some trepidation that they looked forward to seeing him again. How would he fit in with the new *senyora* and her children? They remembered Don Carlos as being as protective of Laura as Don Roberto had been.

'The *senyor* and Carlitos were like a large bull mastiff and a small fox terrier around a bitch in heat. And his temper . . .! Don't you remember how he set upon the Son Beltrán boy for horsing around and "accidentally on purpose" bumping into *senyora* Laura . . . ?'

Indeed, it was hard for the villagers to imagine Father and Karl together again, but without Laura. They had now got used to the new family at Canellún and hoped that things would still be all right.

Karl arrived with Rene just before my accident, and they moved into Can Torrent, where he had been living at the outbreak of the Civil War. He proved a great help to Mother. He spoke Spanish fluently, and knew the village and its characters. He was clever with his hands, and always willing to repair a blown fuse, or to unplug a drain. He took it upon himself to ensure that Gelat's water supply reached Canellún. Later, Karl acquired a wireless set and tuned in every evening to the BBC. Although we had our own set in Canellún, neither Father nor Mother were methodical listeners, so when there was important news such as an election result, or the winner of the Oxford and Cambridge Boat Race, he would come across to tell us. Karl soon learned to read between the lines of the heavily censored *Baleares* newspaper for items of interest to us all. He also kept us up to date on local news and gossip.

However, Karl was not always easy to get along with. Mother's chicken run was just outside the Can Torrent kitchen and for some time he put up with the cackle, the crowing and the smell of her precious hens. But when Rene became pregnant soon after they arrived, our crowing cock was dispatched, to let her sleep. Fortunately, I still heard his friends across the valley crowing among themselves. The hens followed shortly afterwards. Furthermore, Karl reduced my fruit-picking territory. I lost access to the particularly good cherry tree opposite his front door and the Navel orange trees by his front gate. There were no written rules, but after he had chased me away a couple of times, I became circumspect about approaching them unless I knew he was in Palma or Soller.

Then there was the matter of the water supply. The water tank in the Can Torrent attic was, for some reason, fed by the tank in Canellún's attic, and the system was plagued by airlocks. A large cast-iron wheel with a handle outside our kitchen door pumped the *depósito* water up. Karl turned the wheel what he considered a proportionate number of times for the water he used in Can Torrent. But airlocks spoiled his reckoning. In exasperation, he would pace up and down in front of Father.

'For Christ's sake, Robert,' he moaned in his marked German accent, 'I did two hundred turns this morning, and the tank is empty again. You can't have pumped your share!'

Karl came over to Father's workroom before nine o'clock every morning with what he had typed the day before and to pick up that day's work. As well as typing, he checked references, read proofs, and helped Father with letters to publishers and literary agents. When Mother had been doing Father's typing she had never criticized his work, although she only praised what she really liked. Karl, however, though he never commented on Father's poetry, often acted as editor for his prose. From behind the closed workroom door we could all hear his tense raised voice: 'Robert, this isn't good enough!' or 'For Christ's sake, Robert, you can't say this.' Karl seemed to have learned the technique from Laura and, knowing just how good Father's writing could be, insisted on it being perfect – however many drafts he was required to type.

3

Laura had furnished Canellún exquisitely, if somewhat unconventionally. Most of the tables and chairs were Spanish early-nineteenth-century hardwood. She and Robert had found them in Palma antique shops, when old furniture was both cheap and plentiful. Only the sofa and the single divan beds were brand-new. The set of dining-room chairs – five wide leather-covered straight-backs and a narrow one with armrests for Laura to preside in – were a gift from Gelat. He had them specially made from the wood of a large mulberry tree, cut down fifteen years before on the waning moon, whose trunk, as was the custom, had then been kept under water in an *aljub* until the wood was needed. It had then been allowed to dry in the shade, covered with sacks, before being cut into planks for making the chairs. Laura had hung the walls of Canellún with painted plates from the Manises kilns, good prints, several paintings by John Aldridge and beautiful silk batiks by Len Lye. Bowls, vases and mirrors had also come from antique shops. A large still-life oil painting by Mezquida, a seventeenth-century Majorcan, dominated the dining room. Every item Laura had placed, museum-like, in just the right spot.

During the ten years Father had been away, Gelat had kept Canellún in immaculate condition. Strangely, Mother altered nothing when she arrived. The tables, chairs, the sofa and beds – all remained in exactly the position she found them. She did not even change the sofa covers or the curtains. Laura's clothes remained in a cupboard in the Nursery, her pre-war photo album stood on its shelf, her portable gramophone and records on the bookcase in the pressroom where we found them. Perhaps Mother instinctively realized that there was something shrine-like to Father about the way Canellún was left at the outbreak of the war. However, with children around, Mother could not succeed in keeping the house up to Laura's impeccable standards.

We always had at least one maid. They arrived before breakfast, and left after lunch. They did the housework, the washing-up, the laundry and ironing, and helped Mother with the cooking, although none of them could keep up with the disruption caused by three small children. Mother went through two or three maids before she hit on the Carrillo family. Papa and Mama Carrillo were immigrants from the province of Murcia, in the south of Spain, and were known in the village as the Murcianos. Maria, their eldest daughter, worked for us for three years, until she married a charcoal burner. When Maria left, her sister Francisca, who had often come to help, replaced her. Later, the Carrillo twins, Antonia and Salud, took over and stayed with us for many years. All were intelligent and hard workers and responded well to Mother's easy nature. None of them, especially the twins, stood for any nonsense from us children. I was always on a war-footing with them, because as soon as they washed the floor, I had an uncontrollable urge to cross the still-wet tiles, and I took care that they did not grab me by the ears.

Mother spent her day overseeing the maids, shopping, cooking, watering the garden and, when we were not in school, looking after us to make sure that we did not disturb Father. He spent all morning at his desk. At one o'clock, when lunch was ready, Mother would send one of us to call him. His workroom was reached through the pressroom. The Crown Albion hand-press, which he and Laura had brought over from England in 1929, and on which many beautiful Seizin Press books had been printed, was no longer there. It had been sold to a printer in Palma. The only signs left were the wooden blocks cemented into the floor tiles where it had once stood. Instead, the pressroom was now lined with bookshelves, and had become part of Father's library. The door to Father's workroom was always closed. It had a noisy spring, and made a creaking sound. To be allowed to open it gave me a wonderful feeling of trepidation. The workroom had a very special smell of books and ink. Father sat behind his desk, heavy reading-glasses on, pen poised in his hand, and a surprised look on his face as though wondering why he was being called. 'Coming!' he would say, completing the sentence he was working on.

We each had our place at the big oak dining-room table. Father sat with his back to the window, and I next to him. Mother sat opposite Father, and Lucia next to her. Juan sat at the head of the table in the narrow armchair, which had once been Laura's. Father would tell us in simple terms either about what he was working on – the Spanish woman admiral and the discovery of the Solomon Islands – or about life in England, or about witchcraft, or any other subject that interested him at the moment. Mother joined in but never contradicted him, unless he was telling us something too unconventional. Then she would say: 'Oh really, darling . . .!' and Father would look suddenly sheepish. When visitors were present – few in those early days – we were allowed lunch with the grown-ups, but not supper. We ate off East India Company china with English Georgian silver. Father was strict about table manners: 'Don't eat with your mouth open', 'Don't fidget', 'Don't rock your chair', 'Keep your elbows off the table'. Bad manners made him angry, and a second warning earned a sharp rap on the head with a silver teaspoon.

4

I was a fairly quiet child at home. I never read avidly but I did enjoy looking at the pictures in Hilaire Belloc's *Cautionary Tales*, in Edward Lear's *Book of Nonsense*, and in the ten volumes of Arthur Mee's *Children's Encyclopaedia*. We had a Philips wireless, and at a quarter to seven on weekday evenings I listened to 'Dick Barton, Special Agent' on the BBC. When Father was not working, I would beg Mother to put one of the 1930s dance records on the portable wind-up gramophone which Laura had bought before the war. The first two lines of 'Begin the Beguine' and 'You and the Night and the Music' are engraved in my brain for ever. Although occasionally Mother would play Snap or Happy Families with us around the dining-room table, she left us pretty much to our own devices, and intervened only when I teased Lucia, who was too young to be of any other interest to me.

The choice of toys in the Palma shops was meagre. For girls they sold dolls with rag bodies and cardboard heads whose faces became soggy and disintegrated when kissed. For boys they sold clockwork cars made of tin, and heavy cap-pistols. One toy I especially liked was a small metal speedboat with a copper water boiler. The boiler was heated with a tiny olive-oil lamp which forced steam out of its exhaust. This moved the boat quite fast through the water, making a most realistic noise. Most of my toys were brought over from England. My red 'Jettex' racing car was propelled by a solid fuel cylinder, and I had to tie a string to it so as to make it go in circles around the *depósito*. I had a Hornby train set, and I built stations for it with my set of tiny building bricks and water-soluble mortar.

Then there were always the cats to play with. Shortly after we arrived in Deyá, Mother heard a mewing sound from the terraces above the grotto and came back delightedly clutching a ferocious black kitten with a white medallion mark under its chin. Blackie soon became tame, suffered stoically the onslaught by us children, and grew into a sleek female resembling the cat goddess statues of Ancient Egypt. At about this time we were also given Linda. As a kitten Linda was thought to be a female, but he unexpectedly grew into a large nondescript tabby-and-white tom, whom not even Mother could like. One morning there was a great commotion in the cellar and howls were followed by horrendous screeches and flying fur. Mother could not make out which of the cats Linda was fighting until, after an extra loud screech, a wild civet cat flew past us up the mountain. Linda became a hero.

Whenever I could, I jumped on my bicycle, which had now been repaired, and went to see my village friends: Toni, Carlitos, Xesc, and Pepe. Together, we got up to all kinds of mischief. Mother would have been horrified if she had known how we trapped little birds with sticky gum on the edge of the spring they came to drink at, and wrung their tiny necks – my friends took the corpses home in their pockets for their mothers to cook; or how we caught frogs in the *aljubs*, put straws up their behinds, and blew them up; or how we tied tins to tails of cats unfortunate enough to get caught. We stole sweet myrtle-berries from a special tree on Son Bujosa land, and got chased away by the irate *amo*. We threw stones at each other and, my friends being better shots than I was, it was fortunate I was never hit[1].

On schooldays we were expected to line up in front of the school and await Don Gaspar's arrival, but he was often half an

---

[1] *Mallorquín* has the word *trenc* for a stone-inflicted head-wound, which must have been common when Balearic slings were still in use.

hour late for lessons. So we took turns to stand guard, while the others played hide and seek among the olive trees, behind stone walls, even in people's courtyards. *Madonas* of the houses bordering on the Porxo vied with each other for the most pristinely swept and watered, dust-less section of dirt road in front of their doors. They swore at us and chased us away with their brooms if we scuffed the surface.

Other than at Christmas, the only toys my village friends could hope for were those made by Xesc Parrageta. After he had unsuccessfully tried to get himself killed by the Republican shells in the bombardment during the Civil War, he had come to accept his infirmity. He sat, wizen-faced, in his courtyard on a low stool, crutches on the ground, a smelly half-full chamber pot at hand, moulding a charcoal-burning cooking stove from clay, which was his main line of business – there was not much of a market for his toys. His hand-carved spinning tops wobbled. One could not play even the simplest tune on his bamboo whistles, which he made with only three holes. Somewhat better were the slingshots, which he made from a forked oleaster branch and rubber from an old inner tube; but these were expensive. Clay marbles and *trac-tracs* were the cheapest and best value of his wares. I did not really enjoy playing marbles – usually on the ground in front of the school – because I did not have the skill needed to win. *Trac-tracs* I found more fun. Xesc Parrageta made them from half walnut shells cut down the middle, and a string tensed with a sliver of bamboo; we played them with our fingers like a rattle.

One of the great attractions for my friends, who did not come to Canellún any more than I went to their homes, was to rummage around our rubbish tip, where all the non-rotting refuse was thrown, to see whether they could find anything to play with. Among sardine tins, plate shards and worn-out shoes, were the remains of my discarded toys from England. These now took on a new lease of life. A broken Dinky car without wheels started a scramble to improvise something new for it to run on.

'Look, look, this red thing is almost good! It's a bus with two lots of windows as if it had two storeys,' cried Xesc, a small blond boy with almost Nordic features, whose father was a charcoal burner.

'That's silly,' said Pepe, son of one of the *guardias*. 'It would bump into the tops of bridges and people would be killed.'

'No, Xesc is right,' I said. 'That is the way they are.' However, I usually kept quiet about things difficult to explain, just as I kept from telling Mother about blowing up frogs. I knew instinctively that my home and my village life should be compartmentalized, and that only I had access to both.

5

When we first arrived, Mother and Father had tried to give parties for us children and our village friends. On Guy Fawkes Night – Father called him 'San Guido' so as to make him more acceptable to Don Guillem the Priest – we burned the Guy on a bonfire on the drive at Canellún, and let off fireworks. On our second Christmas Eve in Deyá we threw a party at the Posada. Father decorated the *entrada* with paper chains and dressed a pine as a Christmas tree. We ate sandwiches and drank lemonade. We played Blind Man's Buff, Pin-the-Tail on to a cardboard donkey, Musical Chairs using Laura's gramophone, and even fished for sweets in a large bin full of sawdust. I can still picture my new friend Toni March, Jöan March the Fisherman's son, splendidly clean in a brown-flecked homespun wool sweater knitted by his mother, and grey short trousers – his black hair wetted and combed with an immaculately straight parting – as he burrowed in the sawdust with the rest of us, and his look of joy when he found a sweet. However, the game which excited everyone the most was Find-the-Coin, for which Father had hidden a 5-peseta piece. At first there was a lot of pushing and shoving and running and shouting in the various ground-floor rooms, to find it. After five minutes, children began to crawl under tables, and lift up the raffia carpet. It was Xesc Burota, the charcoal burner's son, who finally spotted the coin above the doorway, hidden among the gilded laurel leaves of the red-and-yellow Spanish royal coat-of-arms, which Father had saved in 1932 from a rubbish dump, when the Republic had been proclaimed. Even the appearance of Father Christmas, who gave everyone a small parcel containing pencils, erasers and notebooks, did not mollify the unfortunates who had set their hearts on the 5-peseta coin. In the end, the party proved too much of a success. The following year, the parents of every child in the village – some forty in all, from infants to teenagers – wanted their offspring invited. It had to be stopped.

From then on we celebrated Christmas at home. We decorated our pine in the Canellún *entrada*, lit candles on it and sang carols – 'Adeste Fideles' in Latin – around it, waiting for Father to come downstairs dressed as Father Christmas with a sackful of presents. We hung out our stockings, and woke on Christmas morning to find them stuffed with coloured pencils, sweets, marbles, perhaps a Dinky Toy car or a balsawood glider – and always a few cold tangerines from our garden to make up the bulk. For Christmas lunch, at which Karl and Rene joined us together with old Mrs Broadwood, we had turkey with bread sauce and chestnut stuffing on Father's special bone-china plates – mostly chipped – which were used only on that occasion every year. The first year Mother had almost called off the meal when the turkey was led up the Canellún drive on a rope. Mother made the mince pies, and Rene the Christmas pudding. Father hid a Victorian silver threepenny coin in it and the finder was supposed to be blessed with good luck for the following year. We had hardly finished the meal when Karl and Rene were washing up at the marble sink while Father dried: Father liked to get things back to normal as quickly as possible so he could return to his desk.

Both Mother and Father had been brought up in church-going families, but neither was religious, although somehow their traditions and superstitions seemed to make up for it. We all made New Year's resolutions: mine was always not to tease Lucia, which I kept only until I next saw her. On Shrove Tuesday we cooked pancakes on which we squeezed fresh lemon juice and then sprinkled sugar. On Good Friday Mother baked hot cross buns. On Easter Sunday Father hid Easter eggs in the garden, and we had an egg-and-spoon race. We celebrated our birthdays and not our saint's days as my village friends did.

Father held it unlucky if, on New Year's Day, the first person to cross the threshold of the house was not a 'dark stranger'. Antonio Murciano, the father of our maids, who had one of the darkest complexions in the village, knocked on the door just after midnight – knowing he would leave with a bottle of brandy and a box of cigars.

Giving a blade was supposed to cut friendship and if we were given a knife as a present we had to pay the giver ten centimos. When we found we had left anything behind as we started on a trip to Palma, and had to return to get it, we sat in a chair, and counted to ten before running back to the car. Bad luck was brought on by spilling salt, but could be counteracted by throwing a little over one's left shoulder. Breaking a mirror brought seven years' bad luck, regardless.

I never questioned our customs and superstitions. They were part of being English. However, I made sure that Toni or Xesc never knew of them. I could explain London's double-decker buses, but why Friday the Thirteenth should be unlucky at Canellún – unless Father broke a plate – when Tuesday the Thirteenth was unlucky in the village, was beyond my grasp.

Christmas is the most important feast in the village calendar. At Midnight Mass, one of my friends, a seven- or eight-year-old boy, stood in the pulpit dressed in a velvet tabard and holding a sword aloft, and sang in a high treble voice the half-tone cadences of the medieval *sibila* chant. Christmas trees were unknown. Instead, in the *entrada* of every house, children built a *Belén*, a model of Bethlehem made out of cork, local moss and silver-paper ciga-rette wrappers, and peopled it with clay figurines of shepherds, sheep and poultry. The central feature was always the manger with Joseph, Mary and baby Jesus; above hung the star which had guided the Three Kings on their camels to it. Lunch on Christ-mas Day consisted of stuffed squid, followed by suckling pig, and that by fruit, *turrones* and marzipans both made of almonds and sugar.

On the eve of January the fifth, my friends left a shoe on their windowsill for one of the Kings to fill; and woke the following morning on the Feast of the Three Kings to find their presents next to the shoe. To those who had been naughty, the Kings left black joke-charcoal made of sugar. Presents, like toy cars or cap-pistols, had been ill-afforded and, after they were un-wrapped, my friends' parents put them out of reach so they were not broken. The real difference between my friends and myself was not that I had many more toys than they did, but that I could play with them even if they got broken.

On the sixteenth of January, the eve of Saint Anthony's feast, a bonfire was lit on the Porxo. Neighbours brought out *sobrasadas* and *butifarrones* to cook and share around the embers; the village bards made up verses about events of the past year, which they sang in a high nasal tone to the drone and beat of the *ximbomba*. This ancient drum-like instrument is played by sliding a wet hand up and down a cane, which is attached to the middle of a pig's bladder stretched over the mouth of an earthenware pot. The next day, on Saint Anthony's feast, Don Guillem blessed the village animals. *Amos* brought their mules and donkeys, hunters their dogs, *madonas* their cats, and children their puppies.

On the Wednesday before Easter, women spent all day filling baking-tins with small round *empanadas*, which they took to the baker to put in his wood-fired oven. The pastry of these pies, either sweet or savoury, is made of flour, lard and water, and the filling was chopped lamb or peas. On Easter Sunday the neighbourhood women visited each other to try *empanadas* and swap recipes.

Church processions formed an essential part of village life. Lucia and Juan loved to join them and were often taken by the Carrillo girls. I only ever went once. This was on our second Good Friday in Deyá, the Easter after my accident. I bought a long yellow beeswax candle at the Estanco and went up to the church with my friend Toni March. The rattle of the giant wooden clapper in the belfry was summoning the faithful. For during the three days while Jesus was buried, no outward sign of joy was permitted, not even the chime of the church bell. In Palma, as in the rest of Spain, cinemas closed and radio stations played classical music only. Toni and I entered the church through a side door used by the men and sat in one of the front pews. Women came in through the main door at the back, and sat in the rear. Don Guillem was saying Mass, and a statue of Christ was lying on a catafalque, ready to be carried out. Flickering candles were reflected in the neo-classical gilded altar panels, which contrasted with the stark lines of the nave's stone and whitewashed walls – much as the gold braid of Don Guillem's robes and trappings contrasted with his congregation's dress. The smell of frankincense from the altar mixed with the smell of wood-smoke in the clothes of the men sitting around me.

Presently the procession began to form. At its head were three older boys dressed as acolytes in white cloaks, carrying lanterns on wooden poles. Don Guillem took his place under a scarlet canopy borne by four village youths. Behind him were the town councillors, the Mayor at their head, holding his rod of office – a rod which Father had originally given Gelat when he had held the appointment before the War. Six Penitents – the church only owned six outfits – with their long pointed hoods and staring eye-holes, came next. One of them supported a large cross which he would drag along the entire way.

As the procession moved off, the men of the congregation formed two files behind the Penitents. I got into line with Toni and we lit our candles. Behind us came the statue of Christ on its catafalque, carried on the shoulders of four men in acolyte vestments. Women and children brought up the rear. The route followed the road down one side of the Puig, past the nuns' convent, through the Porxo, up again by the Estanco, and back to the church. The dusty road surface had been watered, and covered with green myrtle shoots. At each of the thirteen Stations of the Cross we stopped and sang 'Lord, Lord, forgive us our sins'. As we shuffled down the way I could see bonfires, which had been lit in the forecourts of most of the big *fincas* in the surrounding hills, and long plumes of smoke and sparks rising from them as brushwood was added. By the time we reached the Porxo, the eighth Station, I had had enough of asking forgiveness. I left Toni and the procession and went up to his father's bonfire on a terrace above the village.

As I approached, I heard the thrilling crackle of fire; soon I could smell it. Tending a bonfire counted as being at the procession, and was a useful compromise for men like Joan March the Fisherman, who went to church only for funerals. He ruffled my hair affectionately, and asked me where Toni was. I pointed towards the procession, which we could see winding its way up the Puig, picked out by the flickering light of the candles. Don Guillem's voice, leading the congregation's chant, carried clearly on the cold night air. As with the quasi-sacrificial pig *matanzas* and the Saint Anthony bonfires, the Holy Week fires were a tradition handed down from time immemorial, and more akin to Father's White Goddess than to the figure lying on the swaying catafalque, still making its way up the hill. Indeed, like the fires and the *matanzas*, most of the local traditions had their origin in old pagan rites.

In 1944, still in England, Father had been studying the bardic mysteries of Wales and Ancient Ireland when he suddenly realized that he had discovered a simple prose-key with which to unlock the poetic myths of Egypt, Greece, Syria and Palestine. This discovery and its consequences grew into a literary work, *The White Goddess*, which he described as a 'handbook of poetic mythology'. He did not claim that his thesis was rigorously scientific, but he was convinced that he had found the matriarchal religion of the ancient bards, which later had been supplanted by the patriarchal religions of first Greece, and then Rome. Although I did not really understand Father's White Goddess, the mysteries of the winter solstice and the rebirth of the new god-king, I was clearly more attuned to Father's ideas than to Don Guillem's.

Don Gaspar's school was run by the State but, curiously for a country that was officially Roman Catholic, we did not even have morning prayers. The lesson on *Religión* in our single school-book came immediately after *Higiene*, and we recited the Commandment 'I will not commit adultery' in the same uncomprehending parrot-like fashion as 'I will wash my hands before all meals.' Often, I went to Mass on Sundays to be with my friends. I attended their First Communions so that I could go to their fast-breaking parties where we had cupfuls of thick hot chocolate and plates of *ensaïmadas*. These are Majorcan buns made of a flaky pastry of flour and lard – *saïm* – coiled into a spiral, and liberally sprinkled with icing sugar. When we were about nine years old, we were also poured a glass of cheap champagne to toast with, and allowed to smoke a smuggled cigarette. It was great fun and, even though Mother did not approve of this minor debauchery, she never stopped me from going to First Communions.

As a *Protestante* I would be due for a long stint in the *Purgatorio*, but this did not appear to worry Toni or Xesc. However, they could not suspect – I myself only found out later – that not only had we never been christened, but that Lucia, Juan and I had been born out of wedlock. As such, we must surely have fallen into the category of heretic, and could expect to roast for Eternity in the flames of Hell. Nevertheless, even had Don Guillem known, I doubt whether it would have stopped him blessing our house when he did his rounds every Easter.

'Father! Father! The Priest is coming!' I shouted excitedly as he came up the drive, a white surplice over his cassock, a stole around his neck and a black bonnet on his head. He was accompanied by his two acolytes, Toni Marranchó, whose mother worked for Karl and Rene, and Miquel of the Bakery, both wearing white surplices. These boys were about my age, but went to the Palma seminary, so did not go to school with us. Toni was holding a scarlet silk parasol over Don Guillem; Miquel carried the silver utensils.

'Then open the patio door!' snapped Father. Somehow it did not seem right to let them enter through the kitchen door. I let them in, and we stood in the *entrada*. Don Guillem read a short prayer in Latin, swung smoking incense in the baroque silver censer, and sprinkled holy water on the walls and floor with a silver aspergillum. Miquel then held out the silver collection plate, expectantly, for Father's customary generous donation.

St John the Baptist's day, the Deyá fiesta, falls on the twenty-fourth of June. Father claimed it derived from a pagan festival on the summer solstice. In 1948 the celebrations followed their usual pattern. A stall had been erected in the Porxo in front of the school, and sold peanuts, sweets and firecrackers. The Soller band played pasodobles up and down the streets. All the events were heralded by letting off noisy rockets, which left dogs whimpering under tables. Members of a Palma repertory company put on a *comedia*, and a folk-dance troupe from the inland village of Selva performed and invited the villagers to join in. Our young men and women were furious at Don Guillem for not permitting ballroom dancing – which was allowed in other villages – and grumbled behind his back. However, there was no question but that the priest had the final authority on village morals.

The foot race events were strongly contested over some fifty metres uphill, on the main road from the *Fàbrica* to the Fonda, the inn close to the Doctor's house. Prizes – a packet of cigarettes, a bottle of brandy, a live chicken – were tied to a tall bamboo shoot, to be snatched by the first across the line. The *cintas* were our favourite event. Silk ribbons, embroidered by the schoolgirls, with a ring stitched on to one end, and rolled over a cylindrical wooden core, were strung on a wire high above the road. We boys were given a peg which we had to thread through the ring while riding our bicycles. If our aim were true, the *cinta* pulled away with a thrilling jerk, and a long coloured streamer flapped behind us.

Money was another difference between my friends and myself. I was not conscious of being well off by comparison with them since, usually, we did not need money. However, they knew.

'*Guillem*,' said one of the elder boys, perhaps Juanito, 'why don't you take some notes from your father's basket? He'll never notice, he has plenty. Then we can buy lots of firecrackers, go to the *comedia*, and let them off.' Not to lose face, and having little sense of money, I found two 100-peseta notes in Father's basket – in those days this was over a week's wages – and put them in my pocket. In the jostling to see the Soller band go by, I lost both. My friends and I searched among the fiesta litter on the streets, but to no avail. The boys were very disappointed but we squeezed in to see the *comedia* anyway, and then I joined my family and went home with them. I was already fast asleep when Father turned on my bedroom light.

'Did you take these from my basket, William?' He was holding up the missing notes which Maria the Washerwoman had found in the street and rightly assumed to have been Father's.

I woke up at once. 'Yes, I'm sorry,' I replied, not only feeling extremely vulnerable, but wetting myself with fright.

'If ever you need anything, just ask me. Don't ever, ever, do a thing like that again!' Father never again referred to the incident, but it was the very first time he had spoken to me that harshly, and I miserably knew that I had done something terrible. I did not fall asleep again until I heard the cocks crowing across the valley.

CHAPTER IV

1

In 1948 we made the first of our yearly summer trips to England. Karl and Rene looked after Canellún, fed the cats and took care of the mail. In London, we stayed with my cousin Sally Chilver in St John's Wood, and went by bus almost every day to Mother's parents in nearby Hampstead. They had a large garden with a tennis court on Heath Drive, and we picked gooseberries and raspberries in the vegetable patch. Grandpa was an elderly gentleman, who had a large yellowish snuff-stained moustache, and wore pince-nez glasses, and grey spats over his shoes. By that time, Sir Harry was over eighty, but he still went to work at the law firm. He made us 'rabbits' by tying knots in his handkerchief and told us stories which always ended with the 'rabbit' jumping away. Grandma I remember as a grey-haired old lady who shuffled around the house whistling through her teeth. We had tea from a silver teapot, and were given white and brown bread sandwiches with fish paste and watercress, followed by fruitcake with icing. Our English was not that good, and it is much to Mother and Father's credit that when they spoke to us in English, we did not answer them in Spanish. Nevertheless, Grandpa found it very amusing that three-year-old Juan called the silver sugar-tongs the 'sugar snatchers'.

One morning we were taken to the zoo by my paternal grandmother, Amy Graves, whom I had never met before, and never met again. She was in her late eighties, and Father was very fond of her. I remember her vaguely, outside the zoo gates on Primrose Hill, as a sombre lady dressed from head to foot in black, with a black veil and carrying a black stick. She seemed older than anyone I had ever seen before. She put her cotton-gloved hand into her black leather purse and gave me a shiny silver sixpenny piece as a present.

We also saw Catherine and Sam, my half-sister and brother, Father's children from his marriage to Nancy Nicholson. Nancy was an artist and later became a textile designer. She had always been a headstrong feminist. When she and Father married, she refused to change her name to 'Graves' and insisted, to everyone's confusion, that girls in the family be called 'Nicholson', and boys 'Graves'. Indeed, she was the first married woman in England to have her passport in her maiden name. My eldest half-sister Jenny Nicholson was born in 1919 and David Graves, Catherine Nicholson and Sam Graves followed at two-yearly intervals. Tragically, my brother David was killed in Burma during the War, when I was three, and I do not remember him.

Jenny had gone to live in Italy. She had been a war correspondent in the WAAFS and had later married Alex Clifford, also a journalist, who had covered the North Africa campaign. Both had visited us in Deyá shortly after our arrival. That year, on our way to England, we went via Italy, and stayed with them for a fortnight at Portofino, where they had a small but lovely *castelletto*, which overlooked a coastline not unlike Deyá's. Jenny was wonderful to be around. She drove a large soft-top American DeSoto, and swore at drivers who dared dispute her right to occupy the middle of the winding Italian roads. She liked organizing parties, boat-rides, picnics and visits to the funfair. She always seemed to be doing something interesting and of my three half-brothers and sisters, she was the one I always felt closest to.

Catherine, plump and matronly, very bright but exasperatingly vague, had married Cliff Dalton, a brilliant physicist from New Zealand who had been an Oxford Rhodes Scholar. In 1948 Cliff was Head of the Fast-Breeder Reactor Division at Harwell, a highly sensitive post to hold now the Cold War was starting. Their eldest child, James, was Lucia's age and four more followed. Perhaps it was because she had her own family that I regarded Catherine more as an aunt than as a sister. Later, in 1950, when Cliff was appointed to the Chair of Mechanical Engineering at Auckland University, he, Catherine and their family went to live in New Zealand and I saw little of them for some years.

Sam had come down from Cambridge and now worked in an advertising firm. When Father left with Laura for Deyá in 1929, he was an infant, so he never had the opportunity to be as close to his father as to his mother Nancy. Sam came to visit us in Deyá just after I had my accident. The timing was unfortunate. Father kept having to go to Palma to take care of me, so again they could not spend much time together. Sam was never one for kicking his heels, and one afternoon he decided to climb the Teix, and was lost, overnight, on the craggy top; eventually he found a path leading down to a *finca* on the other side, above the Palma-Soller road. Unfortunately, one of the family on the *finca* had recently been murdered by a stranger, and the appearance of this young dishevelled foreigner was unsettling, so it was some time before they stood their guard-dog down and opened the door to him. Sam was deaf from measles contracted in Egypt as a toddler, and this, together with a marked speech impediment, made him diffi-cult to understand. When Sam managed to explain himself, they sent a messenger to Deyá, and Karl came in Gelat's taxi to take him back home. I enjoyed being with Sam. Although I also had difficulty understanding him, his eyes were full of fun; he liked horsing around and invented games for me to play. Sometimes he almost seemed to be my own age.

On the summer visit of 1949, we rented a basement flat near Victoria Station. My grandparents had just celebrated their golden wedding and had been given one of the early television sets by my uncles and aunts. I was enthralled watching 'Muffin the Mule'. Feeling, however, that I needed a bit more culture, Father engaged a young Oxford undergraduate, Martin Seym-our-Smith, to show me the sights of London. Neither he nor the sights impressed me much, and I remember little of the experi-ence. On the other hand, my visit to the Tower of London with Uncle Hardinge, Mother's twin, remains indelibly engraved on my memory. After our tour, when I was fascinated by the ravens and the Beefeaters and bored by the Crown Jewels, my uncle put me on a bus back home, and asked the conductor to let me off at Victoria. The journey home seemed endless and it finally dawned on me, passing row upon row of semi-detached houses, that we were driving out of London. Worried, I ran down the stairs to check with the conductor: on top and out of sight, he had forgot-ten me. He made me stay on the bus until it turned round at Crystal Palace and made its way back into London. A new con-ductor let me off at the right stop. I was exhilarated by my 'adventure'. I walked nonchalantly into the flat to find Mother,

Father and Martin in a panic, having phoned the police and the hospitals. It had not occurred to me that they would be worried.

On our visits to London, as well as seeing family and friends, Father also kept in touch with his literary agent, Mr Watt, and with his various publishers. To give Mother some peace, Father took me along with him to Faber & Faber, where he went to discuss *The White Goddess*, which was about to be published. T.S. Eliot was the editor. We were ushered into his large bright office with windows down to the floor on one side, a desk at one end and a conference table at the other. I drew pictures and played with my Dinky Toy car on the gleaming table surface while they talked. Then Mr Eliot came over to where I sat, carrying a saucer of water and a couple of cards.

'Now, William, let's play Photo-finish,' he said. 'Which horses would you like? Pick two.' I chose two brown ones and he wrote a 'W' opposite them.

'Now, Robert?' Father picked another two. We each of us put a shilling on the table. Mr Eliot then put the card he held in the water and the winning horse was revealed. It was mine.

We went to London for four consecutive summers. There I met boys of my age, but I never felt at home. In spite of the wonderful toys, chocolates and cakes, I felt a prisoner in the small flats where we stayed. Even visits to the zoo, the cinema, or to see my grandparents' television, could not make up for my yearning for Deyá. I longed for the heat of the sun, the cool of the sea, the sound of sheep bells. Above all I longed to be able to jump on my bike, without having to ask Mother, and ride down to the village to see my friends. It was a relief when, in 1952, Mother and Father decided that they could no longer justify the effort and expense of the yearly trip. Father's mother had died. In 1950 Sam had married Anneliese, a German nurse. Catherine and her family lived in New Zealand. Whereas in Deyá, in spite of Franco's dictatorship, more and more friends and visitors wanted to come and spend their summer holidays with us.

2

Father had financed Laura Riding's literary and other projects with an almost religious fervour during their years together. He wrote books she despised, but which he knew would sell; and she accepted the proceeds as her right. As she wrote in 1934 to a friend, '. . . the fact that I have the houses is then the fact that I have the houses.' Indeed, Canellún and Can Torrent were in Laura's name; the remaining properties were in Gelat's. After Laura had left Father, she 'returned' the properties to him, and sent a letter to Gelat, who held her power of attorney, requesting him to make over all the deeds to Father.

In May 1947 we drove in Gelat's station wagon to Sineu, a small town in the centre of the island. It was a beautiful ride. The wild gladioli were in full pink bloom, the deep red poppies grew spectacularly in the almond groves. While we wandered around the streets of Sineu with Mother, under the enquiring eyes of the locals, Father and Gelat went to see the town Notary Public. There Gelat officially 'sold' Canellún, Can Torrent and the Posada to Father on behalf of Laura, all for a nominal sum. Then we all went to a restaurant in a large wine cellar with big vats placed around the walls, and had a meal of suckling-pig and crème caramel pudding. The waiter filled earthenware jugs with wine from the vats, and Father toasted Gelat.

However, the houses situation was not really that simple. Since Laura had registered the houses Canellún and Can Torrent in her name, the law had changed, and the Ministry of the Army would permit foreigners living on the islands and on the coastline of Spain to own no more than two thousand square metres outside a village's limits. The Army refused to authorize the transfer of the deeds of Canellún and Can Torrent – La Posada was in the village – and the exchange became invalid. That same year, on the day after Boxing Day, Father and Gelat returned to the Sineu Notary Public, and put the houses back in Gelat's name. Since the land across the road and the land near the Cala were still in Gelat's name, as was the orchard at Ca'n Madó, another village house and Es Pinets, a piece of land on the far side of the valley, Gelat now officially owned all Father's properties. For most of these Father had paid premium prices. However, he was not seriously concerned. It was a fairly common situation, and several villagers including Pep Salas the Builder had properties belonging to foreigners in their name. And did he not have Gelat's word that things would soon be sorted out?

Towards the end of 1948, Jöan Gelat fell seriously ill and Father visited him every day at the *Fàbrica* on his way to collect the mail. Gelat had never fully recovered from his imprisonment. One morning in the spring of 1949, Don Gaspar arrived even later for lessons than usual. We had lined up and were ready to file into the school, but he did not hand over the key to the oldest boy to unlock the door, as he usually did.

'Boys,' he told us lugubriously, 'this is the end of an era. Don Jöan Marroig Más has just died. You are one of the first to know. The church bells will soon begin to toll. As a sign of respect we will not have classes this morning.'

Giving us a half-day off was indeed a measure of Gelat's importance in the village. For, in spite of Franco's victory, he still owned the bus service and both the electricity and the water grids; his Salón Deportivo, with its billiard table, table-football and stage, was the busiest bar in Deyá.

I ran back home, and the bells began tolling just as I reached the Canellún gate. First the slow majestic ring of the main bell, then the higher somewhat cracked pitch of the treble bell, and again back to the main bell. I broke the news to Father, who immediately went to the *Fàbrica* to offer his condolences to Madora, Gelat's wife; he took me along. I had to trot beside him, to keep up with his lengthy stride. His *espardenyas*, downtrodden at the heels and tattered around the edges, threatened to come off his large feet at every hurried step. On the Puig, the church bells continued their sombre discourse. When we reached the *Fàbrica*, we were unexpectedly ushered in to view the corpse. Most of my friends had already seen several *muertos* in their short lives but Gelat's corpse was my unforgettable first. He lay snugly in the coffin Miquel the Carpenter had just brought in, wearing his grey Sunday suit and a fedora hat. A handkerchief had been tied around his chin, as if he suffered from toothache. My friends told me later with glee that it was to keep his mouth closed before rigor mortis set in. Father stood over him for a long time, then took pen and paper from his basket, carefully drafted a few lines, pinned them to the inside of the coffin lid, and we left. Was it a poem, a prayer, or a benediction? Memories of their days with Laura must have come flooding back. Whatever he wrote, it went with the coffin to Gelat's grave.

The funeral took place that evening. I wore my best flannel trousers and held Father's hand. Mother stayed behind to look after Lucia and Juan. Once again we walked down to the *Fàbrica*.

The village men, in their black Sunday best, stood huddled in groups, and talked in low voices about the results of the olive season which was just ending, and the litres of oil that had been pressed. Four men, carrying the coffin on their shoulders, came down the side steps by the large purple bougainvillaea and, without further ceremony, bore it slowly up the road. Above the quiet shuffle of feet, I could hear the church bell tolling again in the distance. We followed behind the coffin. Occasionally, a new black figure would replace another, helping to carry the coffin. Up the main road into the Porxo and up the Puig road, the procession wound its way towards the church. We entered through the main door at the back; the coffin was placed on a bier in the aisle close to the altar. During Don Guillem's service, I felt comforted by Father's tall silent figure at my side. After Mass, the congregation filed sluggishly past the tearful mourners, presided over by Gelat's son Jöan, and lined up in the order of the closeness of their relationship to the deceased, to offer their formal condolences.

Next morning as I bicycled past the *Fàbrica*, I saw that the women were whitewashing the room Gelat had died in, as is the unspoken custom, to ward off evil spirits.

In accordance with Spanish law, Gelat's estate was divided up with a third to his widow, Madora, and two-thirds to the children of whom there were three – Joan, who now became known as 'Gelat'; Anita, who had married Dr Vives's brother and lived in Rennes; and Magdalena, who had married Marcos, Don Bernardo's son. Since Father's properties were still in Old Gelat's name, they became legally part of his Estate. It was young Jöan who 'inherited' our houses and land; and many years went by before the legal situation was finally sorted out.

3

One November afternoon, when I was ten years old, I was sitting on the pavement opposite the *Salón* with Toni March. We were discussing the merits of the strongman who, according to the notice in the window, would be giving an exhibition that Saturday. Toni was old enough already to go out, on holidays and weekends, in the fishing boat with his father and brothers; but he hated missing any show.

'I think he'll twist iron bars, like the strongman who came last year,' I said.

'But we've seen that done already,' complained Toni. 'Perhaps he'll eat a floor tile or a glass bottle, or . . . or . . . swallow a sword!'

Just then Guillem of the Puig skidded to a stop in front of us on his bicycle. He looked at me with an enigmatic smile. 'You had better get back home. Gelat has just been delivering something for you at Canellún in his lorry.' Guillem was a couple of years older than I, but had become one of my best friends.

'What . . . what sort of thing?' I asked.

'You'll see!' he said.

So I jumped on my bike, and pedalled back to Canellún as fast as I could. The gate was open and I sped up the drive. My jaw dropped in astonishment. There, in the middle of the *depósito*, stood a beautiful, brand-new, shiny black Raleigh bicycle. It had four-speed Sturmey-Archer gears, a Brooks saddle, and a steering-lock with a key. Unlike with Spanish bikes, the tip of the front mudguard was chromed. Mother and Father had had it shipped out from England for me – as a surprise.

At about this time we bought Isabela the donkey. Her previous owner, a woodcutter, had died at a ripe age in that year's flu epidemic. Isabela was a grey, overfed and pampered animal; soon we discovered that she was also independent-minded, and had a vicious kick and bite. She was already several years old, but had never had a bit between her teeth, nor had she been between the shafts of a cart or a plough. Father repaired the stable at the Posada for her, and arranged with Castor the Postman, who was now also our part-time gardener, to look after her. We bought a second-hand yellow donkey-cart and, with great patience, managed to break her in. '*¡Arri!*' and a flick of the reins got her started; '*¡Ouuu!*' and a pull of the reins stopped her. I learned to keep my balance while standing in the cart when she trotted. Every afternoon, I harnessed her and drove her down to collect the ice-blocks from Gelat's bus, and to carry them back, wrapped in sacking, to the icebox in the cellar.

Our neighbour, Major Pring-Mill, lent Father a jockey's racing saddle. Isabela, however, was so fat that when the saddle was strapped on it slid over her neck; we had to have a crupper made to slip under her tail, and hold the saddle in place. I was the only member of the family of the right size to ride her so, for much of the day, Isabela was mine. I trotted or cantered along the dirt-tracks on my way down to the beach and, when I reached the Mirador, tied her up under a pine tree, first loosening the saddle straps, while I went on for my swim. I enjoyed riding her; though now and then, without any warning, she would stop dead, and I would sail straight over her head. As I picked myself off the track, she would amble over to whatever greenery had taken her fancy, lower her ears, turn her back legs towards me and dare me to come close. I might seethe with anger at her, but I knew that losing my temper would do no good. I had to let her have her nibble and wait for her to raise her ears again. That was her sign she was ready for me to get back in the saddle.

Mounted on Isabela, my friend Mikey Rosenstingl fancied himself a cowboy like Buffalo Bill. I had met Mikey when I was in the Barcelona clinic for the operation on my foot. His father, Arnaldo, and Father had met through the Gittes family and became good friends. Like thousands of other Jewish refugees, Arnaldo, originally a Hungarian doctor, had found refuge from the Nazis for himself, his wife and only son in Franco's Spain. However, he was not allowed to practise medicine; instead he had opened an antique shop in Barcelona. Mikey, then an intense eight-year-old with bulging black eyes, sallow skin and unruly hair, delighted in long Spanish words I did not understand.

'You have a propensity for usurping my pencil,' he would say; or: 'Let me manipulate the venetian blinds to prevent the solar rays from entering.' Every day he had taken a bus halfway across Barcelona to visit me in the clinic. Later Mikey and his parents came to Deyá, first staying as our guests at the Posada, then buying a house in the Clot.

'Regard me, Guillermo,' he said, perched on the donkey's back. He was wearing his favourite green-and-white check shirt, somewhat discoloured from frequent washing. 'In the spectacle of the Rodeo, it is a question of equilibrium. You retain the reins tightly over the neck with your left hand, and your right arm extended over the posterior; your knees must encompass the saddle like this.' At which point Isabela bent her neck for a mouthful of grass and Mikey fell off.

Mikey was the first friend I had in Deyá who bridged the gap between my village life and Canellún. He spoke both Spanish and

Catalan and integrated easily with my friends. Neither Toni nor Xesc could pronounce Rosenstingl so they called him 'Rosito'. After falling off Isabela he became known as Rosito Bill. Rosito was an affable boy and did not in the least mind his nicknames. With him, not only could I go to the village to see my friends, we could also go swimming, which the priest, on moral grounds, had forbidden the Deyá boys.

On our second summer trip to England we brought back a yellow RAF-surplus inflatable rubber dinghy. We left it in the boathouse which belonged to Toni's father. Rosito and I walked down to the beach on our own, so that we could play with the dinghy, and avoid having to share it with Lucia and Juan. Rosito wore a swimsuit with shoulder straps, which I joked he had picked up in his father's antique shop, and he insisted was new and merely 'followed the regulations in force on the Barcelona beaches'. Rosito was highly intelligent and was always trying out some new idea. I could usually see the logic, and I would go along with his plans. However, more often than not there was some factor he had not accounted for. He loved experimenting with the dinghy's sail.

'Look,' he said, 'if we set the canvas perpendicular to the structure, any zephyr that approaches will propel it.'

It was a flat calm day, no 'zephyrs' came and we had to paddle back to the beach. Toni, watching us from his father's boathouse, roared with laughter.

Rosito's parents could spare him little pocket money, and when they came to stay he always thought up ways to earn a few pesetas. The carobs ripened at the beginning of September, and Father offered us a peseta for every sack we filled with the long hard black-brown beans. When we had two full sacks we called Father, but instead of giving us the expected two pesetas, he lifted one of the sacks in his big hands, shook it down and filled it from the other, giving us just one peseta, and the empty sack to fill again.

Perhaps to develop my creative talents, Mother and Father gave me a set of 'Punch and Judy' glove puppets for Christmas. After teasing Lucia with them for a few days, I had put them back into their box and forgotten about them. Rosito now decided we should put on a show. Together we wrote the sketches, rehearsed them and, when we thought them good enough, went to the village to put up signs advertising it. We could not decide on an admittance fee so we wrote: 'PRICE: PAY WHATEVER YOU FEEL LIKE'. We were unprepared for the crowds that appeared, not just children but many of their mothers as well. In Deyá, a show was a show, and it was something to talk about the next day at the *rentaderos*. We had fitted the puppet theatre into the back door of the Canellún *entrada*, and the audience sat outside on the patio. The show went well; but we had mistimed it, and it was over in about half an hour. We passed the hat and our takings were much better than we had hoped for. Since there was still daylight, and many people had arrived late, Rosito and I decided to give a second performance. We added some of the material we had not felt up to before, but now it proved to be too long, and the show began to drag. My brother Juan was one of those children who, when they like a story, want to hear it over and over until it becomes an old friend. Juan had enjoyed the first performance and he thought that the second was all wrong. He uttered a yell of despair, picked up the first thing that came to hand and flung it at the puppets. It happened to be a knife. Nobody was hurt, but he went into one of his crying tantrums, and our audience left in an embarrassed silence.

Friends from England began coming to Deyá. In the spring of 1950 Isobel Hawking, a friend of Mother's from her Oxford days, came for a few months with her three children. Stephen was my own age, and we got on well. However, when I was in the village with my friends, I found it impossible to include him. He must have found me very rude. I refused to speak English to him in front of them, because I knew they would mimic me. Indeed, if ever I was with them, and I saw Father approaching, I would quickly go and meet him to be out of earshot. One morning Toni and Xesc and I were discussing the end of the thrush-netting season and when Stephen approached and asked me in English how cold the water was in the Cala that day I ignored him. Who could be so idiotic as to want to swim in March, anyway? Later, on our way back to Canellún, I explained to Stephen about the *tords*: how huge flocks of thrushes migrated from Siberia and ate the olives when they got here; how Deyá families inherited passes on the mountainsides where the *tord* catchers hid with their almost transparent nets stretched between two long bamboo

72

poles and waited patiently for hours for the birds to hit them and be trapped; how *tords* were cooked stuffed with *butifarrón* and wrapped in cabbage leaves and were considered a delicacy. I realized how little I knew of Stephen's English world and how little he knew of mine. Even his sense of fun seemed strange to me. At Canellún that Easter we were waiting for the rain to stop so that we could go outdoors to look for our Easter eggs, which Father had hidden in the garden, when suddenly Stephen quietly but firmly said: 'Stink bomb!' and threw one under the sofa. We all fled into the cold *entrada* to get away from the smell of rotten eggs. When Stephen grew up, a wasting disease relegated him to a wheelchair, but by then he had become a cosmologist of genius.

4

I thrived on village life. No thoughts crossed my mind about what I would do when I grew up. And why should they? Like his father, Toni would become a fisherman; Xesc, a charcoal burner; Guillem, the town crier; Pepe would join the *Guardia Civil*; I assumed my life would proceed similarly and that I would end up doing something at Canellún. Our visits to London were forgotten as soon as I got back. I had no desire to be anywhere but Deyá.

It was the Gittes family's departure to the United States in 1949, to give their children a formal education, that really brought home to Mother the limitations of our local schooling. Father must have caught her concern. One day we were walking to the village along the road together when the road menders were at work. They had great mounds of stones, which they broke up with special long-handled hammers and placed in the potholes before tarring them over.

'You know, William, money does not grow on trees,' he said. 'If you do not work harder at school, you may end up breaking stones like these men.'

Indeed, I learned little, and there were so many *fiestas* and holidays that, to Mother, I seemed to be at home most of the time. Don Gaspar, a Franco sympathizer and trusted by the government not to publish anything derogatory, had been made editor-in-chief of a Palma magazine. He was now often away from school, leaving us in the charge of Don Alfredo, a painter friend of his with a waxed moustache. We all had great fun launching paper aeroplanes at him. Unlike Don Gaspar, he had no control over us. His first line of defence was slapping our hands with a small square ruler. But this was never enough.

'Who did that? You, you and you, kneel down facing the wall with your arms out,' yelled Don Alfredo. After about two minutes, my outstretched arms began to get heavier and heavier, and my knees impossibly sore. It was a mindless torture, immediately forgotten when over.

Lucia loved her convent school. Like the other village girls in the month of May – the Virgin Mary's month – she built a shrine in her bedroom decorated with lots of flowers and every evening said her three Hail Mary's in Spanish followed by three in Majorcan. She even asked Father to teach her the Lord's Prayer in English. Juan was very credulous, and came home from the convent school terrified by stories about the *Purgatorio*, hellfire, and the Man-With-The-Sack, who, the nuns told him, would carry him off to Soller if he were naughty. He was forever playing with matches, and one day started a fire in the dining room that burnt up our wireless. Afterwards, he was more worried about the Man-With-The-Sack than what Mother or Father might say. His wild attention-seeking tantrums became more frequent. He was a sensitive, frustrated child who probably needed more love and affection than he received.

Mother and Father considered sending me to a prep school in England, but then decided to keep me in Deyá, prepare me for the Common Entrance exam, and have me go straight to a public school. Mother had school-books sent from England and followed their instructions to the letter. Now, in the afternoons, instead of my going to the village school, Mother gave me English reading, writing and arithmetic lessons. We got on quite well, but it was very time-consuming for her. Father taught me Latin, and had me translate *Fabulae Faciles*. He told me to use my Spanish. This did not work: I could not make head or tail of the stories – myths with which I was entirely unfamiliar. When I had finished my translation, I would knock on his study door, pull down the creaky handle and go in to the smell of books and ink. Wearing his reading glasses, he was rather forbidding. He would go rapidly over my work, explaining where I had gone wrong as if he could not understand why I was so stupid. My eyes would go from desk-top to bookcase to the batik on the wall, to his collection of African charms on the mantelpiece. I came to dread the ordeal, and the feeling that I was wasting his time.

In the summer of 1950, Bill [W.S.] Merwin, a twenty-two-year-old American poet, turned up in Deyá. He had been a tutor to the Braganza family in Portugal, and Father asked him to stay on and tutor me. I now went to Bill in the mornings, and to the village school in the afternoons. I rode my new bike up to the Posada where he and Dorothy, his red-haired wife, were living. Their marriage must already have been breaking up, for I remember my shock and incredulity when I overheard Karl telling Mother that Bill sometimes locked his wife in the kitchen, so that he could get on undisturbed with his writing. We worked in Bill's study. He tried to teach me English, history, geography and maths, although I still did Latin with Father. One day, we were reading an Elizabethan courting ballad about a fellow playing his whistle. I immediately understood the play on words and blushed crimson; but when Bill asked me what the ballad meant, I was so embarrassed that I pretended not to know. He then made me undo my fly buttons and take out my 'whistle': I detested him for that, and gave up every pretence of trying to learn his lessons.

5

Mother and Father were not yet married. When, in 1929, Father left Nancy and came to Deyá with Laura Riding, there had been – at least on Laura's part – no question of marriage. Ten years later, when Laura left him, Father began living with Mother and I was soon on the way. Both wanted to get wedded, particularly because they knew it would make their ageing parents happy. Mother, who had earlier been married to Alan Hodge, a historian, received her divorce papers relatively quickly. Nancy, however, standing by her feminist ideals, had remained Miss Nicholson; divorce papers could not therefore be issued in the legal form of *Graves v. Graves*. Solicitors, including my grandfather Sir Harry Pritchard, were perplexed by the problem but could see no way out. In the end, it was my always-resourceful half-sister Jenny who persuaded her mother to style herself 'Nicholson alias Graves' and thus solved the legal dilemma. Father's divorce papers arrived in November 1949.

Mother and Father were married in May 1950 by the British Consul in Palma. The wedding party took place aboard the Morrisons' yacht *Rosalind*. The small gathering included Karl and Rene, Joshua Podro – with whom Father was at that time writing *The Nazarene Gospel Restored* – and Father's pre-war friend and poet Norman Cameron, who had originally built Can Torrent. We children were sensibly told nothing of the event. It never bothered me when I discovered a few years later that I had been born out of wedlock. As Father assured his own mother, we had always been Graveses 'in heart if not officially'. Indeed, I was amused when I found out that my uncle John, who kept the family records, had drawn three branches on the family tree under 'Robert': the first was for Jenny, David, Catherine and Sam; the second for Lucia and Juan and myself; and the third for my youngest brother Tomás who was born later. Our branch he labelled 'b', for 'bastard issue'.

The new marriage's first trial arrived soon enough. In November 1950, Judith Bledsoe came to Deyá. She was a young art student from California on a European trip. She had strikingly dark Mediterranean looks. Father took to her at once and, as he was apt to do with new and interesting people, gave her his undivided attention. Judith was quite overwhelmed when Father asked her to illustrate his book *Adam's Rib*, in which he unravelled the mythological roots of Creation in the Book of Genesis. I liked Judith – she helped me saddle Isabela – but grown-ups were grown-ups, and I had no inkling of the undercurrents that were flowing.

The women at the *rentaderos* must have smelled a rat even before Father himself realized what was happening. They had an uncanny nose for scandal.

'Did you know, Maria, that the *senyor* of Canellún has gone down to the Cala for his swim with that piece of skirt in tow?'

'Yesterday, the *madona* of Ca'n Simò told me that the *senyor* has rented one of the houses in Lluc Alcari for the girl, and that the *senyor* and the boy took her bags down in the donkey-cart.'

'The *senyora* of Canellún must be a fool to allow that girl around. Remember the trouble the *senyora* Laura had with the *senyor* and the German girl before the war . . . . And that wasn't his only escapade. Men – once they start they never stop. Ha!'

Soon Father was writing poems to Judith. According to Father, the magic in a poem – that quality which makes the hair on the back of one's neck stand on end – depended on how close it came to describing the presence of the White Goddess, the cruel Goddess, whose prime attribute was wooing the sacred king and then sacrificing him for his twin brother. Since writing *The White Goddess*, Father's poems had mostly been concerned with the mythological aspects of Her presence. Father loved Mother. However, Mother was no White-Goddess figure. She was fully aware she could never share his obsession with poetry as Laura had; nor did she share his new faith. Father now saw Judith as his Goddess's representative.

> The Goddess has been plaguing me lately very cruelly
> and I have managed to satisfy her by two or three poems
> written in arterial blood;° she appeared in Deyá during
> the last full moon swinging a Cretan axe. [RG to JR[1],
> December 1950]

Karl was shocked when he realized that Father had fallen for the girl. Judith, feeling the tension mounting, left Deyá and continued on her tour. It took several insistent letters from Father to get her back to work on the drawings. Mother – either unaware of any threat or emotionally unprepared to see the situation Karl's way – continued being friendly with Judith and commiserated with her about a new boyfriend who was being difficult. Perhaps Mother was right and Judith was too young to be interested in a fifty-five-year-old man, however vigorous and famous he might be. Judith's boyfriend arrived in due course and, their differences sorted out, she promptly left with him for England. She never produced the drawings. A barrage of poems and letters from Father followed her, and his infatuation lasted for a year or so. Almost ten years went by before his next Muse came along.

---

[1] A list of the recipients – eg JR = James Reeves – of the letters quoted in the text may be found in the introduction. Most of the letters have been published in full by Paul O'Prey in *Between Moon and Moon*, Hutchinson, 1984. Letters to me are in the Library at St John's College, Oxford.

6

I was eleven years old when I met Po Vidal. It was the first summer when his family spent their holidays in Deyá. Mrs Vidal came from Swiss aristocratic stock and Mr Vidal, once the Palma swimming champion, ran a small cabinet-making business. Po was the second of their five children. They lived in Son Reboll, a small farmhouse above the picturesque hamlet of Lluc Alcari and about two kilometres past Canellún on the Soller road. Madame Vidal – as we called her – kept open house for her children's friends: we were always welcome to stay for a meal or even remain the night. Po was a year older than I. His nose was hooked, his teeth crooked, yet he had great charm. I found he was a friend I could trust to turn up whenever he said he would. Toni or Xesc might arrange to meet me at the Salón; but Toni might be told by his father to help stack the nets, or Xesc might have to take a message to his father up at his charcoal kilns in the oak forest. Po and I spoke in Spanish, this being the Vidals' home language. However, Madame Vidal, who was born in Jamaica, always spoke to me in English with a pleasant Caribbean lilt, and I was never embarrassed if my parents addressed me in English in front of Po.

The Vidals formed part of a colony of Spanish families who all owned summer houses in or near Lluc Alcari. They would arrive at the beginning of July and leave at the end of August. These families kept very much to themselves. Many had spent their summers here since the turn of the century. Laura had known several of them, including their pre-war doyen, Don Sebastián Junyer, a well known Catalan painter. Laura had liked Sebastián's impressionist paintings, but she had preferred the modernist work of his young nephew Jöan Junyer and had bought two of his canvases which now hung in the Posada.

However, unlike Laura, Mother was shy; while Father was forever immersed in his work. Neither made any effort to mix socially with the colony. Mother may have felt that the Spanish middle class remained supportive of Franco's dictatorship although this could hardly be imputed to Mme Vidal, who always criticized the rubber-stamp government, and pointedly read the *Journal de Génève*. Certainly, the group was offputtingly Catholic – they even had their own Mass said on Sundays in the Lluc Alcari chapel. Mother also objected to the apparent lack of intellectual bond between husbands and wives. Father, when questioned, glibly attributed his lack of Spanish friends to the fact that they hardly ever invited people into their homes, and that their mealtimes were some two hours behind ours.

The children of the Lluc Alcari colony formed a large group to which Po introduced me. Ages ranged from toddlers to eighteen-year-olds; there was generally someone's spinster aunt who came along to look after the younger ones and to chaperon the girls. In spite of her reservations with the parents, Mother must have been very relieved to see how quickly I was drawn into the group; and later Lucia and Juan. We went on walks, spent hours at the beach, acted in plays, picked mushrooms in the woods. Po's parents arranged boat trips with picnics in secluded coves up the coast, and I was invited along.

Po and I went everywhere together, he on his silver-painted bike, I on my Raleigh. We went almost daily down to the Cala to swim, except when the sea was too rough. Then we often bicycled over to a house near Valldemosa, some seven kilometres away, where friends of Po spent the summer. It was a heavy uphill slog almost all the way there, but this was more than compensated by the exhilaration of riding back, bent low over our handlebars, racing each other all the way down to Ca'n Madó. We smoked cigarettes we rolled with pine needles; when I stole a real one from Mother, and we broke it in half to share, I was sick. One afternoon Po, I and two other friends were in the Canellún grotto, playing with toy boats of carob tree bark in a lake we had made by diverting the water from the Son Bujosa *siquia*. When suddenly the water stopped coming, I went up the steps through the tunnel to see where the blockage was. I found the *amo* of Son Bujosa pulling off his belt, ready to strap me. I fled, vaulting over our high garden wall on to the main road, and met up with the others, who had heard what was happening, halfway down to the Cala.

Po often ate with us at Canellún and I ate with him at Son Reboll. One evening I had supper at his house and afterwards we met up with others of the group by the side of the road overlooking Lluc Alcari. Cars rarely passed at that time of day. Some of us sat on the stone wall, others on the tarmac itself, enjoying the cool of the evening. I had promised Mother I would cycle back immediately after supper, but the conversation was too much fun and

I forgot. At midnight we were still happily chatting away when a light wobbled into sight along the road. There was something strangely menacing about it, even at a distance. Silence fell as we watched it approach. It was Father riding a bicycle which he rarely used. He pointed the light at me.

'William!' he barked. 'Home!' It was the first time since the money incident that he had been truly angry at me. I had no reason to feel afraid of him since he never really hit me or punished me. Occasionally he knocked Lucia's head against mine when I was teasing her, and she was being particularly whiny; or he rapped me on the head with a silver teaspoon to mind my table manners. However, this time there seemed to be so much anger in him, I felt that at any moment he might be violent. I abandoned my friends, and pedalled home as hard as my rubbery legs would let me. It was past midnight and Gelat's electricity was off. I hurriedly lit a candle, jumped into bed, and had blown it out before I heard Father closing the garden gate.

CHAPTER V

1

Mother told me to wear my grey shirt, short flannel trousers, knee-length socks and sandals. I thought these made me look horribly English; I was relieved, at least, that Father was taking me. My new school turned out to be only a three-minute walk from our new flat. A brown painted sign over the entrance proudly proclaimed *Estudios Universitarios*. We walked up to the master sitting at the battered desk in the entrance hall.

'Have him wait over there,' he told Father, assuming that I spoke no Spanish, and pointed to a wooden bench.

I sat down. Father shrugged and, lifting his chin in that familiar gesture of his, which meant 'Good luck!', strode out into the street. I was alone.

Boys were milling all around. Looking at them, I knew I had been right, and promised myself to wear something different tomorrow. Even chaps younger than I wore long trousers fastened around the ankles like knickerbockers. Perhaps Mother could make me some? They were a noisy crowd but at least they talked Majorcan among themselves. I wondered what this place would be like. Mother and Father's aim was still to get me through the Common Entrance exam, and I had already begun lessons in the mornings with my new tutor, Martin Seymour-Smith. My afternoons here at *Estudios Universitarios* were supposed to expose me to some Spanish culture and, by mixing with other boys of my age, prepare me for the rough and tumble in England. I had been given a book with drawings of public schools: most resembled church buildings; none was like this run-down looking place. The bench I was sitting on was covered all over in boys' scratched initials; the tiles on the floor were chipped, dirty and had chewing-gum stuck to them. Still, *Estudios Universitarios* was larger and grander than Don Gaspar's school in Deyá. I would miss my old school friends, Toni and Guillem and the rest, although I should still see them every weekend.

I was awakened from my thoughts by a group of boys who had gathered around me. One of them, perhaps two years older than I, with a sharp nose, pointed chin, straight, unruly fair hair, and wearing glasses, came up to me.

'You, what's your name?' he asked in Spanish.

'Guillem Graves,' I answered in Majorcan with my strong Deyá accent. I pronounced 'Graves' phonetically as it would be in Spanish, *Gra* as in 'gravel' and *ves* as in 'vestry'.

'You speak Majorcan?' he asked, astonished. A foreigner speaking the local vernacular like a native was practically unheard of. Besides, my English schoolboy clothes could hardly have prepared him for this.

'Of course.' I used the word *idò*, which has many shades of meaning – depending on the tone of voice used – from 'Of course', to 'Well, I never', to 'You had it coming'. At once, the whole hall was in an uproar.

'Where did you learn Majorcan?'

'How did you learn it?'

'Do you also speak English?'

'What language do you think in?'

2

Mother had finally come to the conclusion that if Lucia, Juan and I were to get anywhere in life, we needed a more formal education. Father no doubt felt that the Deyá schools would have been perfectly adequate provided we worked, and that our brilliance would have soon shone through. However, he respected Mother's wishes and, in September 1951, we moved to Palma. We rented the first- and second-floor flats of a brand-new four-storey block in a street named after Guillermo Massot, a little known Majorcan composer, in a part of town that was in the throes of development. The flats were large, the *primero* slightly more so than the *segundo*. Both had spacious sunny balconies at the back, overlooking a *Guardia Civil* barracks, and an old ochre-stuccoed farmhouse, boxed in by new buildings, with turkeys still running loose in the yard – the gobble of turkeys still brings back images from those Palma days.

We lived in the flat on the *primero*. It had a sitting room, dining room, kitchen, bathroom, and four bedrooms. At the rear, the dining room and kitchen opened on to the balcony, to the side of which was an outhouse with a second bathroom and a laundry room. The flat, like the one upstairs, was cheaply built and poorly finished. The doors did not close properly, and the reddish imitation marble floor-tiles wobbled and cracked. A nail driven into the wall to hang a picture went all the way through into our neighbours' flat; when a door slammed, chips of plaster fell off. It was not to be a permanent move, so Mother bought beds, pine-wood chests of drawers and bedside tables at a discount ware-house, and a second-hand sofa in the flea market. However, the tone was raised by the dining-room furniture, which Father bought from his antique dealer friends; and by pictures borrowed from Canellún and the Posada. In winter we were more comfort-able than in Deyá. There was a wood stove in the sitting room, its flue passing through the ceiling to the flat upstairs. The bedrooms had electric fires. We even enjoyed the luxury of hot water, with an electric immersion heater in the bathroom. Francisca, the second of the Carrillo girls, had consented to live in and work for us. We soon had a telephone installed.

To get away from household noise, Father took over the front room of the *segundo* flat as his study; and Martin Seymour-Smith, my tutor, lived in the remaining rooms with his wife-to-be Janet and with Laelaps, their large *Ibizenco* hound. Martin was a small, wiry and intense young man, with a prominent jaw, a large nose and piercing eyes. He had been a family friend since he was a schoolboy: his own father, Frank Seymour-Smith, was a retired librarian, who traced many rare source books for Father. It was Martin who had shown me around London, the year I got lost on the Victoria bus. Now, having just come down from Oxford, he was trying his hand – after Bill Merwin's failure – at preparing me for Common Entrance. Janet, tall, blonde, good-looking and bright, seemed happy to play second fiddle to him.

At that time, Palma was a friendly town of some 150,000 people, small enough that one met people one knew on every other street corner. Trams waited at the stops for children who were late for school; and nobody complained when the driver halted to pick up the *sobrasada* sandwiches his wife brought him.

Shops and businesses were open six days a week but they closed when there was a wedding or a funeral to attend. Shopkeepers, and even taxi-drivers, let you pay 'next time' if they could not change a 100-peseta note. On Sunday afternoons, young men and women in their Sunday best ambled up and down the central tree-lined avenue of the Borne; the girls arm in arm, giggling; the boys eyeing them and nudging each other. Their elders, on the stone benches, kept watch. At ten o'clock, when the Barcelona ferry blew its foghorn, announcing its nightly departure, everyone hurried home to supper. The streets were safe, not because of the sinister state-police – called the *Grises* after their grey uniforms – who patrolled in twos, one on each pavement, but because, in any given neighbourhood, everyone knew everybody else and petty crime was frowned upon. At night, every street block was assigned a night watchman; already in bed, I often heard the sharp hand-clap, or the shout of '*¡Sereno!*', when someone had forgotten the keys to the street door of his block of flats.

The people of Palma already knew Don Roberto, the tall writer from Deyá, who strode around town with a large peasant basket over his shoulder. Many, especially the antique dealers, remembered him well from before the War. All were puzzled why such an illustrious man did not live in the centre of town, or at least in Terreno, the neighbourhood most English and Americans frequented. They did not realize that the flats in Calle Guillermo Massot were simply a temporary base for our schooling and that, on the day there was no school – be it a holiday, weekend or mid-week fiesta – Don Roberto was on the bus, or in Gelat's taxi, hurrying back with his family to his beloved Deyá.

Indeed, Guillermo Massot proved to be a sensible choice. The rent was low and, since there were no large cafés in the neighbourhood, it was quiet. Around the corner was a grocery and a pastry shop; a dry-cleaner's was opposite; and there was a tram stop at the end of our street. The Deyá bus parked four blocks away. It arrived at half-past eight in the morning and my job was to get the 'mailbag' on my bicycle, which I kept chained to the banisters at the bottom of our stairwell. Gelat's driver handed me the leather briefcase, which contained both the mail and the work that Karl had typed the previous day. I would open it to see if that week's *Eagle*, my comic from England, had arrived. Just before lunch, Father filled the mailbag with his return work and any instructions for Karl, and either he or I took it back to the bus, which left for Deyá at half-past two.

When we moved in, the flat was at the very edge of town. For the first couple of years, we could look across the empty building site opposite and see the southern slopes of the Serra de Tramontana. I sometimes went for walks into the countryside with Father, Martin and Laelaps. Father found it useful to talk to Martin about whatever he was working on. He liked to hear how his ideas sounded and were received, before they went through Karl's editorial filter. Although I never understood much, I listened to their conversation with interest – Father was wonderfully persuasive. Five minutes' walk took us to the Riera torrent, which carried much of the rain run-off south of the Sierra. Downstream, the Riera skirted the town walls, and emptied into the Palma bay. We always followed it upstream, past the Psychiatric Hospital and the Municipal Cemetery, into open almond groves. In the torrent-bed lay pools of water fringed with bulrushes and full of frogs. My image of those walks is of a sunny, windless February afternoon, with green grassy ground underfoot, the pale pink almond blossom strikingly set against a bright blue winter sky; Laelaps is eyeing the sheep grazing on the bank, and pulling vainly on his leash; while Father and Martin, oblivious of landscape, dog, and me, dissect the poetry of W.H. Auden.

The flats were close to the dogtrack and we could hear a constant yelping of greyhounds in the distance. Juan loved to be taken there by Mother and Martin, to place 1-peseta bets on the dogs of his choice. Races were mostly run after dark, under floodlights. Through his virtually indestructible English National Health glasses, Juan intently followed his dog among the pack as it chased after the 'hare', which was pulled by a wire on the inside of the circuit. He won often.

We could also hear the trotting of horse-drawn hearses on their way to the cemetery. Funerals were far more formal than in Deyá. Instead of the coffin being carried on the shoulders of village men to the church for the *cuerpo presente* mass, in Palma it was delivered in a black and gilded hearse, drawn by four black horses wearing black plumes in their harnesses.[1] After the service, it was

---

1 Occasionally it was a white hearse carrying the poignantly small coffin of a dead child.

loaded back into the hearse, and the funerary cortege walked slowly behind it, to the point where one of the city gates once stood. After a final *adios*, the drivers whipped their horses into a trot towards the cemetery.

The Palma bullring was a fifteen-minute walk away. Father greatly enjoyed bullfights and, before the war, he and Laura had watched the legendary Juan Belmonte, Domingo Ortega and 'Joselito'. He began going again with Martin and Janet: Antonio Ordoñez and Miguel Dominguín were now the great matadors. One day Father took me along. Mother did not approve; she never went herself or allowed Lucia or Juan to go. However, as usual she deferred to his decision. At that first bullfight, I felt sick and walked out. Later, as I learned the technicalities, I went to the *corrida* at every opportunity, and came to love it. I realized that at its worst, a bullfight is just gruesome slaughter; but at its best, each movement, each pass of *matador* and bull, enshrines the beauty of a Goya engraving – we had a marvellous edition of these at home. As a young *aficionado*, I cheered the spectacular passes with the cape, which ended with the bull perfectly positioned beside the *picador*; the measured lance-work of the *picador* on horseback, receiving the bull on the run; the split-second timing of an impeccably placed pair of *banderillas*; the subtlety of a *matador*'s passes with the *muleta*; and, above all, the clean mathematical thrust of the death-sword.

3

Our mornings began by getting Lucia and Juan ready for school. Both Mother and Francisca cajoled them to wash and get dressed, gave them their *pa amb oli* for breakfast, and handed them their clean striped cotton school pinafores. Father walked them to the nearby *Colegio Mallorca* which, as a secular school, accepted unchristened children. It was not a success. After fruitless enquiries to find another, Mother and Father came to accept that the only suitable girls' schools in Palma were run by nuns.

The following year Mother managed to get Lucia admitted by the Teresan Sisters at Pont D'Inca, near the airport. Lucia wore a dark blue sailor suit uniform and went by school bus. She enjoyed school, and came top of her class. She still loved the rituals of the Catholic Church and was disappointed that, unlike her friends, she could not be given First Communion dressed in white chiffon. Father said that he would not object to her becoming a Catholic, if she still wanted to, when she had turned fourteen, and understood what the religion was about.

Meanwhile, Mother sent Juan to *Ramiro de Maeztu*, a school named after a Spanish journalist shot by the Republicans during the Civil War. Juan was unhappy there, and consistently got low marks. A second move, to the Franciscan Brothers, brought little improvement. He had always been a difficult child, and continued throwing tantrums when he did not get his way. The most trivial of things would upset him: even being given a smaller potato than Lucia for lunch could provoke a rage which ended in his flinging his glasses across the room.

While Lucia and Juan were prepared for school, I breakfasted and collected the mailbag from the bus. Then I went upstairs for my lessons with Martin. He and I got on as well as could be expected. He taught me all subjects except Latin, which I did with Janet. She had just taken Greats at Oxford and turned out to be an infinitely better Latin teacher than Father had been. Indeed, Janet would probably have made a more satisfactory overall tutor than Martin. It was she whom Father had hired to help him with his book on the Greek myths. Martin came with her to write a book, and was engaged to tutor me as an afterthought. Arrangements like this were very much a feature of the Canellún way of life: if help were needed, then the first halfway suitable person who appeared would be co-opted for the job.

Although the room Martin taught me in was sunny, I felt claustrophobic, and my mind wandered easily. There was little traffic and sounds carried far in the Palma mornings. I could hear the clip of the hearses, the clang of the tram bells, the gobble of the turkeys, the din of the bugler practising in one of the Infantry barracks nearby. From the street in front of the flat, came the cries of the mattress menders, knife grinders and gipsy rag-and-bone men. Halfway through my first lesson, I heard the key in the front door as Father returned from taking Lucia and Juan to school; then the squeak of the glass-panelled door into his study; finally the sounds he made fiddling with his brazier – he refused to use an electric heater – scraping the ashes off the top and to the side, and allowing the *orujo*, the fine charcoal pellets made from olive pips, to give off more heat.

After lunch, I hurried along to *Estudios Universitarios* where I was taught geography, Spanish, history and maths. I soon noticed differences between my Spanish and English school-books. In Spanish geography, France was separated from England, not by the English Channel, but by the *Canal de la Mancha*. In Spanish history, Felipe II's 'Invincible Armada' was destroyed, not by Sir Francis Drake, but by storms. In Spanish maths, long division was set out, not with the divisor on the left, the dividend on the right and the quotient on top, but with the dividend on the left, the divisor on the right and the quotient beneath the divisor. At first I found this confusing but, as with the village and Canellún, I managed to keep each in separate compartments.

Once we were settled in our schools, Mother organized extra-curricular lessons for us. Two evenings a week I was taught the guitar by *Maestro* Bartolomé Calatayud. He was an old man, with wispy long white hair, a damp cigarette-end dangling from his lip, who beat time to music with his foot.

'Like this, Guillem: *¡uno dos, uno dos!*' Calatayud disliked flamenco and gave me classical and South American scores to learn. One of my first pieces was a Beethoven minuet. On Friday nights, I went to Po Vidal's house in Terreno, where about a dozen of us assembled with guitars, lutes, mandolins and *bandurrias* – a six-string Spanish mandolin-like instrument – under the *Maestro*'s baton. Po played the *bandurria*; so did Juan when he was old enough to join us.

As we improved, we gave occasional concerts in the villages outside Palma. One summer, we played in Deyá at the yearly fiesta given by the proprietress of Ca L'Abad – a large *finca* near Lluc Alcari which had once been a Carthusian abbot's home. This fiesta was a feudal affair. Candles lit the stage on the terrace in front of the building, and the lady of the houses sat in a *loggia*, flanked by friends and her father confessor, looking down on it. The audience – villagers and the summer residents of Lluc Alcari – sat in front of the stage; but instead of playing to them, we performed to the *loggia*. Juan, who was only eight, was a great success. Sadly, when the lady died, the Ca'n L'Abad fiesta was discontinued. On her deathbed, she willed the estate to her father confessor, Don Bruno, a canon in the Palma bishopric. Don Bruno was a *Valldomosin* and therefore had no interest in enter-

taining the *Deyanencs*: the inhabitants of Deyá and Valldemosa
have been sworn enemies since time immemorial.

Lucia took ballet lessons from a Lithuanian émigré called Aina.
There was a rival ballet school in Palma, with greater social cachet –
Errol Flynn's wife exercised there – but Aina was the better teacher.
From time to time I offered to pick Lucia up, so that I might catch
a glimpse of the girls in their leotards. Sometimes I found Po there:
his elder sister went to the same class. Once a year, Aina's pupils put
on a performance at one of Palma's theatres and Po and I had to sit
with our families – often we took a box – through an interminable
Peter and the Wolf or *The Nutcracker Suite*. Father's light-hearted
verse about Lucia and her friends sums it up:

> Fairies of the leaves and rain,
> One from England, two from Spain,
> You who flutter, as a rule,
> At Aina Jansons' Ballet School,
> Dancing at the *Lírico*:
> Pirouetting, swaying, leaping,
> Twirling, whirling, softly creeping,
> To a most exciting din
> Of French horns and violin!
>
> . . . ['To Magdalena Mulet, Margita Mora &
> Lucia Graves']

4

Mother had a second operation, after which she went from
strength to strength. Her marriage had survived the crisis over
Judith. While Father got on with his work, she coped with the flat,
Canellún, the servants, us children and our schooling. She also
saw to the complicated logistics of getting us to and from Deyá,
with basketfuls of clothes, food, books and toys. She had become
reasonably fluent in Spanish and even found time to translate two
books into English, *The Infant and the Globe* by Alarcón and *The
Cross and the Sword* by Galván – both of which Father then
polished, and published under his own name.

Palma was very much a place of work for Father: not only did
we have the luxury of hot water, we also had electric light – unlike

the increasingly dim and unreliable light from Gelat's turbine – which meant that here he could write well into the evening. Mother and Father had little contact with the English and American expatriates, who lived in Terreno and frequented Larry's Bar; they avoided the likes of Errol Flynn, who spent part of the year in the Palma Yacht Club in his black *Zaca*, and of his fellow-actor George Sanders, who lived in Genova. They discouraged social visits from friends, and found it less time-consuming to have their mid-morning coffee at the Bar Fígaro with the Morrisons, old William Cook, or some of their new friends such as the one-eyed American poet Robert Creeley. Bob Creeley, introduced to us by Martin, later wrote a successful novel called *The Island*, mostly about himself and Martin, in which the Martin character describes tutoring the great writer's eldest son as 'a cushy job, but at times tedious'.

With few visitors in Palma, I looked forward to Saturday evenings in Deyá. After supper in Canellún, Karl and Rene, and any other friends who might be around, came over for coffee and a brandy, and everyone played 'The Game'. I was allowed to stay up and join in. The Canellún dining room was fairly small, with room for three on the sofa and another in the Chippendale chair by the fire; the rest had to sit around the large mulberry table. 'The Game' was a version of charades and consisted of silently acting out a phrase – picked by the opposing team from *The Times* – within the three minutes it took the sand in our kitchen hourglass to run through. There were signs for 'sounds-like', 'rhymes-with', 'short-word', 'yes', and other signs for the number of syllables in a word, and the number of words in the phrase. I thought Karl was the best and most imaginative player in getting his phrase or sentence across. He would, however, get amusingly frustrated and wring his hands and roll his eyes when his team got stuck. Although never as quick as Karl, Father loved acting and, with his mastery of words, was more than competent. He was inordinately pleased when his team won.

Sundays were also a treat, because that was the day Father liked eating out, to give Mother a rest. Before we moved to Palma, we went to the Pension Miramar, two doors up the Puig road from the Estanco, where there was a pleasant patio. But the owners had moved to new premises behind the *Fàbrica* and catered for the growing summer trade only. Now we ate at the Fonda, perched above the main road. The dining-room walls were covered with dozens of paintings, which over the years had been left as gifts by the artists – or in lieu of payment. Although mutton and fried potatoes were always on the menu, I usually chose from the Majorcan dishes: *sopas mallorquinas* (the bread-soaked vegetable soup), *llampuga amb pebres* (a local fish on a bed of grilled red peppers), *tords amb col* (thrushes stuffed with fat bacon and *butifarrón* and wrapped in cabbage leaves) and, my favourite, *llom amb esclatasangs* (pork cutlets with pan-stirred, fleshy *Lactarius deliciosus*, the mushrooms which grew in the woods in November).

5

Deyá and Canellún were still home. On weekends, I tried to catch up with everything that had happened during the week. One Saturday morning in the spring of 1952, I changed out of my Palma clothes, saddled Isabela, and went down to the Cala to see Toni. There was a buzz of excitement around the jetty.

' *¡Huep!* Toni. What's up?'

'Our new boat, *Sa Polsimada*. Come on, Guillem, we're going to try her out!' I climbed aboard the *llaud*. Although a little larger, she looked much the same as the other fishing boats on the slipways. Some seven metres long, *Sa Polsimada*, the 'Sea Spray', had a vertical bow and stern, a broad beam and a strongly sloping deck, so that waves breaking over her would run off over the low gunwale, and the rest drained through small openings at deck level. Hatch covers along the centre of the deck gave access to the engine, and an extra large hold. Toni's father took the tiller, while his elder brother Jöan unhooked the rope from the prow, pushed her off, jumped in, lifted the hatch, and started her up. We reversed into the middle of the Cala, then motored sedately out of the cove until we turned the Deyá promontory. Joan now opened the throttle and we cut through the water like a speedboat. I suddenly realized what made her so special. She was not designed for her ostensible use: to take day-trippers up the coast. *Sa Polsimada* was built for smuggling.

Jöan March was a heavy man, not very tall, but built like a rock and with a mariner's rolling gait. His leathery face was tanned from countless hours at the tiller, and his brown skull showed through his short cropped hair. Beside him on the deck was his pipe and ancient sealskin tobacco pouch which he always carried. In spite of having been a Communist during the Republic, and on the town council when Old Gelat was Mayor, he had done well for himself. Until the end of the Civil War, he crewed for an old fisherman who lived in Lluc Alcari. He then bought himself his first boat, the *Estrella* – on which he had taken me fishing with Toni – and was soon helping the smugglers offload their shipments. This paid well, but he needed something bigger and faster for the job. By the time he bought *Sa Polsimada* he was being addressed as *Patrón*, a sure sign of affluence and importance.

In the early Fifties, smuggling was at its zenith. Food-rationing had ended, and the standard of living in Spain rose rapidly, creating a need for luxury items. However, those available in the shops were highly taxed, and the smugglers, sensitive to supply and demand, now brought in cigarette-lighters, cameras, film, radios, nylon stockings, contraceptives – even medical X-ray equipment – with their shipments of tobacco. Majorca became a de facto free port and Customs checked everyone leaving the island for the mainland. The highly lucrative trade was financed by businessmen who had *secretos* built along the coasts of Majorca, either by enlarging suitably hidden caves, or by excavating them into the steep cliffs. They also provided wireless sets to communicate with the delivery ships, mostly surplus Royal Navy torpedo-boats – with English skippers – from Tangiers. These rendezvoused with the local fishing boats, at night, offshore and out of earshot of any patrolling *guardias*. On the Deyá stretch of coast, the contraband was usually transferred to *Sa Polsimada*, brought ashore and hidden in one of the *secretos* – of which there were two in the Cala and many others along the way to Lluc Alcari. However, thanks to payoffs, it was no longer necessary to carry the sacks over the Teix. Instead, the shipments were taken to one of the *fincas* or to one of the village houses, where they were loaded into a car or a lorry and taken to Palma. Po's father's English BSA motorcycle had been smuggled into the Cala and ridden up Laura and Robert's road.

In Deyá it was one of the *amos* who, on behalf of his masters, made the off-loading arrangements, offered small investments in the shipments, and paid the *guardias* to look the other way. Most young men from the village earned quick money carrying the

92

heavy sacks from the fishing boats to the hiding places. To involve the rest of the village and ensure its silence, the *amo* offered 500-peseta participations. He gave one half of an old torn playing card as a receipt for each, and when the shipment had been safely delivered, paid out 1,000 pesetas to the matching half cards. These stakes were virtually guaranteed. The richer villagers invested small sums in the shipments themselves. Among these was young Gelat, although he dealt mostly with shipments on the Valldemosa stretch of coast.

Wages in the *Guardia Civil* were pitifully low, and only by accepting the payoffs could a member adequately afford to keep his family. The *guardias* patrolled the coast except on the nights a shipment was due. Then they made themselves scarce. However, they could not entirely turn a blind eye. The payoffs were calculated as a percentage of the shipment's value and one member of the garrison was detailed to hide behind a lentisc bush to check they were not being cheated. Every so often, however, a young unmarried *guardia*, bent on promotion, was posted to the village and disrupted the system. An over-zealous *guardia* once shot one of the smugglers and wounded him in the leg – his quarry got away. Another *guardia*, who tried to stop a landing, found himself bound, gagged and taken to Tangier in a torpedo boat, whence he was flown back to Palma on a first-class ticket – only to be posted to some lonely village in the heart of Extremadura.

Father and Mother knew about the smuggling: they could hardly be unaware something was going on, when lorries drove past Canellún at night without their lights on. In Palma there were special houses in the old quarter that sold the contraband – cigarettes, cigars, Zippo lighters, Gillette razor-blades, perfume. It was one of Father's regular stops when he went down town – to buy cigars for himself and mentholated cigarettes for Mother. However, in Deyá villagers took care never to reveal anything to outsiders. Indeed, it is only now, when the heyday of smuggling is past, that my village friends are prepared to tell me the details, knowing that, even so, I would not point out *secretos* or name names.

6

Just as we children were getting more manageable and Mother had a little time to herself, she found she was pregnant again.

Juan, the youngest, was eight; Lucia was nine; I was twelve. At the beginning of 1953, when we returned to Palma after our Christmas holidays, Mother mo ᵈd Martin and Janet from the upstairs flat into another nearby, and installed Maria the Midwife to await the birth. Lucia, Juan and I had all been born in hospital in Devon; the new baby was to be born at home.

Maria the Midwife was a Deyá institution. A plump jolly woman, close to retirement, she had recently buried Don Fernando, a gentleman of means, to whom she had been married in a civil ceremony during the days of the Republic. After the Civil War, such marriages were no longer valid so they had 'lived in sin'. She somehow survived the wrath of the Church, and had attended the births of an entire generation of *Deyanencs*. She was patently left-wing, and must have sensed Mother's sympathy for socialist ideals, for she often came up to Canellún to visit us. On one of her visits Maria brought Mother and Father an envelope which, she said, contained something amusing, and they should open it only when she had left. In it they found a set of French 'art' postcards, verging on the pornographic. Young Gelat's taxi had come to take them to Palma and, in the rush, they left the envelope behind on the dining-room table. As they drove past Maria and Don Fernando's house on the way to Valldemosa, Mother suddenly remembered. Pretending that she had forgotten her purse, she made Gelat turn back, and retrieved the envelope before the maids found it. Had the Carrillo twins done so, they might easily have connected the postcards to Maria; and had our new priest Don Pedro – though not as strict as Don Guillem – heard about it, she could have got into serious trouble.

The baby was born on the twenty-seventh of January 1953. Mother was thirty-seven years old. Maria demanded cauldrons of hot water, and Francisca kept the charcoal stove going once the delivery began. As the water came to the boil, Father and Francisca carried it up from the *primero* to the *segundo*, while we three meekly sat on the sofa, where we had been told to stay and 'read'. The event was so awe-inspiring that we did not even quarrel. Later, when it was all over, we were allowed upstairs and Maria introduced us to our new brother, Tomás.

Whereas with us, Mother had usually followed Father's suggestions, with Tomás she took charge completely – Father rarely even had to change his nappy, as he had so often changed ours.

Mother was determined to bring Tomás up so that he would have
the best possible prospects in life; for, at the time, it must have
seemed to her that neither Lucia, Juan nor I stood much of a
chance. However, I do not remember that she spoiled Tomás as
he grew up. I certainly never felt jealous. The age difference
between us was such that I behaved towards him more like an
uncle than a brother. Juan, at eight, was far more susceptible to
Mother's protectiveness towards the baby. He lost what edge he
had had by being the youngest, and even Lucia, to whom Juan
had been closest, now doted on her new baby brother. Juan's
tantrums increased; his feeling of rejection must have been desperate and it may well have contributed to the eventual crisis.

One of the first problems Mother had to solve with Tomás'
arrival was how to get back and forth from Deyá at weekends with
the three of us and the baby: she bought us a car. Our car was a
pre-War Renault, new cars then being almost impossible to buy.
Mother drove, and she may well have been one of the first women
drivers on the island – especially with a husband sitting by her
side. Father claimed that in 1926 he had driven once around the
block in Cairo and that this had been such a terrifying experience
he had vowed never to try again. This was just as well because,
lost in thought, he would have been a menace on the roads.
However, Father soon became an expert at hand-cranking the
ancient Renault. Having a car meant we could leave the flat early
on Saturday mornings and have two full days at Canellún. During
the holidays, when we stayed in Deyá, it made shopping, and
going down to Palma, very much easier for Mother. It also saved
us a fortune on young Gelat's taxis, and must have seriously
dented his profits.

7

Pedro Pizá, who had first spoken to me at my new school,
became, with Po, my other best friend. Years later, he still tells of
his surprise when the English boy they had been told to expect
spoke Majorcan with a Deyá accent. From that very first day,
Pedro had kept a protective eye on me. His widowed father was
the manager of the best glove shop in Palma, and many of the
gloves he sold were hand-sewn by women in Deyá. In 1952
during the summer holidays, Pedro came to see me, and stayed in

the village with the manageress of his father's sewing ladies. He so much enjoyed his stay, and the company of Po, myself, and the Lluc Alcari group, that the following summer his father rented a house in the village. Pedro's father could only come up to Deyá for weekends; and he and his elder sister, Juana, were looked after by Rosa, their wonderful – but hideously cross-eyed – Valencian maid who acted as a mother to them. During the Christmas and Easter holidays, Pedro often stayed with me in Canellún; I in turn stayed with him in their rambling house opposite the Palma Town Hall. For the following few years we became inseparable.

Pedro, although a shy and somewhat solemn boy, was a natural comedian; one moment serious, the next he was miming a flying bird, a crashing car, a weight-lifter. He picked up English effortlessly and he loved making bilingual puns, and plays on English and Spanish words. He had a genius for timing. I never knew what to expect. He was so funny that he could literally make me laugh until I wet my trousers.

In Palma, Pedro and I went roller skating or to the cinema together. He taught me to jump off a tram while it was moving – the first time I tried I fell flat on my face. Although the amenities of Palma could never outweigh the wellbeing I felt in Deyá, I was slowly getting used to being in town. I could move around on my own, and in many ways not being known gave me a freedom I did not have in Deyá. Once Pedro and I were to meet at the public swimming pool. I was waiting for my tram, smoking – everyone smoked in my class – when a tall policeman, whom we all knew by his badge number as 'One Hundred and Eleven', came up to me.

'How old are you?' he said.

'Sixteen,' I lied, trying to deepen my voice which had not yet broken. That was the minimum age.

'Show me your identity card.'

'I left it at home,' I replied, stuttering and blushing, getting deeper into the lie. As a foreigner I would not have had an identity card even at sixteen.

'Let's go to your home and you'll show it to me.' Just then my tram went by. I dashed after it, hopped on as Pedro had taught me, and left One Hundred and Eleven shaking his fist.

Every summer, Pedro came to Deyá. His father's employment of the glove makers gave him great prestige in the village, and he was known as Pedro Rovira, Ca'n Rovira being the name of the glove shop. Pedro, too, loved the Cala and we ate there almost every day, since the *Patrón*, Toni's father, had begun serving meals on his terrace overlooking the beach. His clients were such summer visitors as the Vidals, Pedro and his sister, and even the rare timid tourist venturing as far as Deyá. The *Madona*, the *Patrón*'s wife, was the cook. She was very thin, and wore her hair in a small bun at the back of her head. She prepared *paella* or a filling fish-and-rice soup on the charcoal stove in the hut, and when it was ready, the *Patrón* blew his sea-conch. Those of us who had ordered a meal dived into the sea for one last swim, put on our shirts, and climbed the steps to the terrace. Joana, Toni's pretty sister, served at table. After lunch Pedro, Po and I walked up to the woods beyond the terrace to lie on the pine needles, smoke a forbidden cigarette, and drowse. Local folk-wisdom had it that, to avoid getting cramp and risk drowning, one should not go into the water for two hours after lunch. The languid surface of the sea, the fragrance of pine resin, and the clamour of cicadas in the midday heat, produced a sense of contentment I would try to recall in later years, whenever I was away from the island.

At our age we loved a good story, and *Patrón* March was a born raconteur. After lunch, when it was windy and we did not go up to the pines, we sat at his feet while he mended his nets. Among the legends and stories he told us was one in which he claimed that Majorca rested on pillars beneath the sea. He embellished it by saying that the long passage into the Font Ufana spring led straight to this underworld. This spring lies below the main road, on the way to Valldemosa. Po and I at once decided to explore it – Pedro, who suffered from claustrophobia, stayed back. We entered a long corbelled passageway carrying candles and, at its end, found ourselves at the throat of a narrow cave system down which water was trickling. We were small enough to squeeze through, and we emerged into a chamber filled with stalactites and stalagmites. We climbed a small cliff-face at the back, and this brought us into a really spectacular chamber with thick, majestic stalactite columns, which glittered in the candlelight. The chamber sloped off to the left and, at the bottom, was a small pebble beach with clear running water. Alas, there were no 'pillars under the sea', but it became our favourite place to smoke.

Pedro was so enthusiastic about the Cala that, one summer, he virtually lived with the March family. Every afternoon, once the midday heat had passed and the beach was in shadow, he would board the *Estrella*, still used for fishing, with the *Patrón*, Toni and Joan, to motor down the coast to the lee of the Foradada promontory where they would lay their nets. The evenings he spent by the light of a hissing *Petromax* lamp while the *Patrón* told stories of his childhood and youth: how fishing boats from Deyá and Valldemosa sailed each summer up the coast to the Pollensa fishing-grounds, and did not return until September; how Mediterranean monk-seals basked on the rocks on the Cala; how, when a cloudburst washed the *Son Al. luny* road away before the War, the fisherman in the hut below had nearly been swept out to sea by the thundering force of the torrent, which broke through his back door and out the front. Pedro slept on a bunk in the boys' quarters and, at daybreak, went out again in the boat to pull in the nets and recover the catch. What the *Madona* could not sell in Deyá or use in the kitchen, they took to the Soller fish market in the *Sa Polsimada* to be auctioned. They would return with a cargo of soft drinks, fresh vegetables and bread for the restaurant. Later, Pedro would join Po and me on the beach for a swim before lunch. The next few hours we spent together. Then, as the sun set behind the hills, and Po and I climbed up the path to the village, dragging our damp towels behind us, Pedro would wave goodbye, and once again board the *Estrella* with his adopted family to set the nets.

8

The combination of an English tutor and a Spanish school proved to be an unsatisfactory preparation for my Common Entrance for Oundle, the school Mother and Father had finally selected. I could not get to grips with my work. I knew I was a poor student and I felt bored, working on my own, for an exam that seemed pointless to me. It would have been fun if there had been someone my age with whom to discuss my lessons, and decide what Martin wanted of me. My friends at *Estudios Universitarios* were as carefree as ever.

'Forget about your exam, Guillem, you can study for it tomorrow. Let's all go to the funfair.'

I went along with them. Father was even expecting me to win a scholarship, just as he had done to Charterhouse. Mother was more realistic. Anxious that I might fail not only the scholarship exam, but also my Common Entrance, she had the former cancelled; as the date of the latter approached, Martin, Janet, Mother and Father all coached me for it as though I were a prizefighter.

The day Martin walked me to the British Consulate, it was pouring with rain. The Consulate was housed in a large palatial building, in the very centre of the old part of Palma, close to the cathedral. Someone ushered me into a huge chilly room, with high ceilings, and tall windows facing the damp stucco wall of the building opposite. I took off my raincoat, sat down on the chair provided, arranged my pencils and rubber on the table in front of me, and waited. I had never taken a proper exam before and hardly understood its bearing upon my future. I did not feel bothered about the outcome – that was Mother's concern. The Vice-Consul, a Majorcan, came in, handed me my exam-paper and left. I looked blankly at the printed sheet, sucked my pencil and wrote answers to what questions I could. I could hear the rain dripping relentlessly on the window ledge. Every once in a while the door creaked as the Vice-Consul checked whether I was all right. Time passed surprisingly quickly, and all of a sudden he came in and took my answers away. I put on my raincoat, and wandered to the tram stop in the still unremitting rain.

After my exam, I continued my lessons with Martin in a desultory way, still going to *Estudios Universitarios* in the afternoon. When I heard the postman shout *'¡Cartero!'* up the stairwell and heard him ring our bell, I went down to see if my results had come. When the letter finally arrived I ran upstairs, and gave it to Mother. After all, it was she who wanted me to go to Oundle.

CHAPTER VI

1

Chiggers – Mr Chignell the Housemaster – was doing his rounds in the junior dormitory trying to make us feel at home.

'Weizmann, everything all right?'

'Yes, sir, thank you, sir, very good, sir.'

'What about you, Graves?'

'Christ, all right, I suppose,' I answered.

Chiggers turned puce and spluttered: 'Tomorrow, after prep. my study!' and stormed out.

I was mystified by Chiggers's reaction, and turned to Weizmann who had come up through the junior school, 'Now what did I do wrong?'

'You stupid Dago, "Christ" is blasphemy; and you didn't say "sir". It looks as if you're in for three of the best.' It was all so confusing. 'Christ' was an expletive both Father and Karl used all the time, and I had never even given it a second thought. Nor had I ever said 'sir' to anyone.

Being Robert Graves's son probably counted more than my Common Entrance results, when I was accepted by Oundle School. In September 1954, I was put on the new regular BEA Viscount flight to London, and was met by Mother's sister Enid. I spent a few days at Heath Drive with my grandparents, while Aunt Enid took me to be kitted out with everything I needed, including my school uniform: a grey flannel suit, white shirt with detachable collars and studs, black tie, grey woollen socks, black lace-up shoes – I still itch when thinking about it. Some friends had driven me up to Oundle and had dropped off at New House.

Nothing I had been told by Father, Mother or Martin came close to the nightmare I found myself living. I had never slept in a dormitory, bathed in a communal bathroom, eaten a school meal, or done my homework at a large table surrounded by other boys. There was no central heating; some winter nights were so cold that the water in the dormitory wash-bowls froze. We had 'fagging' which involved sweeping out the older boys' studies, and cleaning and laying their grates. I had never played any sports, knew nothing of first division soccer, rugby or cricket, nor could I name any of the players. I had listened to only a couple of the BBC shows that could be picked up in Deyá; the Top-Twenty hit-parade songs left me unmoved. If Martin had told me Anthony Eden was Prime Minister, it was a fact for the exam; I did not recognize it when I read the newspaper. My life in Deyá was of no interest to anyone. No one knew or cared where Majorca was; all they knew was that Franco was a fascist dictator. I was called 'Dago' and 'Wop' which, like so many other slang expressions, I did not understand, although I realized these were abusive. I was in a deep cultural shock; and very lonely.

I worried all the next day about my expected caning. After 'prep' I knocked on Chiggers' door. Father had chosen New House for me because Arthur Marshall, the writer and broadcaster, had been housemaster; he left and was succeeded by Mr Chignell the term I arrived.

'Come!'

'Sir,' I said as I closed the door behind me.

'Sit down, Graves.' It was not what I had expected. 'Do you know what blasphemy is?'

'Yes, sir, no, sir, I don't know, sir.' I replied. Chiggers, who was more sensitive than I gave him credit for at the time, proceeded to lecture me on English swearing instead.

Gradually I fell into the school routine. In the Michaelmas term I could not play rugger because the hard football boots rubbed the scar on my foot and made it bleed. The other boys thought it was an excuse, and it did not help me to make friends. In the Lent term, however, I participated in Athletics, and was sent with the others on cross-country runs, which I detested. In the summer term, I avoided cricket, and rowed instead: I enjoyed being on the river although I was not heavy enough to make the house 'four' until my third year. Academically things were bad. Throughout the year I came twenty-ninth in a class of thirty, in virtually every subject. The only name I can remember in that class is Calvert, the boy who came thirtieth and saved me from total ignominy.

After lights-out, the more interesting discussions in the dormitory were about life after death, or the historical figure of Christ, or the existence of ghosts. I had never talked about anything like this with Pedro, Po or Rosito. Other than Weizmann, who was Jewish, my dormitory mates were all brought up in the Church of England. In response to their more conventional ideas – many of which were alien to me – I tried to air some of those I had heard from Father; but I was starting from an impossibly different perspective.

Father venerated the White Goddess. His poems were addressed to her and, every month, when the new moon – sacred to her – appeared, he went outside, on to the *depósito* in Canellún or the balcony of the Palma flat, and bowed nine times. He then turned a silver coin three times to attract fortune. His worship was as familiar to me as church-on-Sundays to my dormitory mates. However, Father's upbringing had been strictly Christian, and he knew his Bible as well as many trained theologians, but he now no longer trusted the transcriptions and translations of biblical texts. The following is an extract from a letter he wrote while working on *The Nazarene Gospel Restored*. It is typical of the sort of explanations I heard at our dinner table.

Why did Matthew X.29 say only two sparrows were sold for one farthing, and Luke XII.6 say that five were sold for two farthings? Once one has solved this problem the sense appears: it is all about the unlucky sparrow (of two sparrows) that got sacrificed when a leper got cleansed (Lev. XIV.5); God wouldn't forget the poor little blighter, though he cost only half a farthing; how much more wouldn't he forget the disciple who lost his life when Preaching the Kingdom of God. Answer: Luke put 'five for a farthing' by mistake; an editor wrote 'no, two' having consulted Matthew; subsequent stupid editors though he meant farthings, not sparrows, and amended it accordingly. I can't make out how Biblical critics have failed to solve potty little problems like this; but I suppose to have DD to one's name is a hindrance not a help. [RG to CG, 31 December 1949]

Father used this form of reasoning to develop his unorthodox ideas on matriarchy, the Creation, or the Virgin Birth, which he published in *The White Goddess, Adam's Rib*, or *The Nazarene Gospel Restored*. For his historical deductions he resorted to a faculty he called 'analepsis', and frequently obtained startling results.

> I read all available contemporary accounts, handle and study whatever objects I can find that survive from that period, throw myself back in time, and go walking the streets of 1st century Rome or Jerusalem, 6th century Constantinople or Antioch, 17th Century Oxford or London, 18th century Dublin or Boston, and wherever else I may require to go. [RG, unpublished article for *Book News*, 1947]

How could I possibly explain his worship of the White Goddess when on the subject of life after death, or his views of the Gospels when on that of the figure of Christ, or his theory of 'analepsis' when on that of ghosts – none of which I understood myself – to the boys in the dormitory?

The first book of Father's I read was his autobiography, *Goodbye to All That*. I broke into a cold sweat of relief that I had been sent to Oundle rather than Charterhouse. How could I have survived the teasing provoked by Father's intimate account of his crush on a younger boy at his school? Many of the same homosexual goings-on were also prevalent at Oundle; scandalmongers whispered that so-and-so had a crush on so-and-so. Yet it all seemed fairly chaste, and I remember no feeling of sexual harassment. Indeed, I found it very childish: Pedro, Po and I already went out with girls, and I was writing letters to a girlfriend while I was still in the fourth form.

My second year at Oundle went slightly better. By then I understood much of the slang, so when boys mentioned George Brown or Stirling Moss I knew whom they were talking about. I was no longer a 'tick', and had a desk of my own. Academically things also improved. Little by little, I worked my way up to the middle of the class. I was preparing for my 'O' level exams, and I found that I enjoyed science subjects. However, I had to take humanities as well. Our Latin teacher, Mr Sutcliff, promised us that if we learned seven simple rules, and we remembered enough vocabulary, we would get through the exam. Thanks to my

Majorcan, French was easy; Spanish was a walkover. My difficulty was with English Language and English Literature. Eventually I managed Language, especially in 'precis' and 'comprehension'; though my spelling was terrible. Literature defeated me. I had read few 'grown-up' books at home other than – at Father's suggestion – Defoe's *The Year of the Plague* and *The Great Fire of London;* I had read no poetry since few poets, other than E.E. cummings and Father's recently deceased friend Norman Cameron, seemed to fulfil Father and Martin's criteria. Though I knew that other boys had a system for writing essays on set books, I never acquired the knack. Yet my English Literature teacher still expected me to show the Robert Graves spark. His was the only 'O' level I failed.

2

Majorcans claimed that, away from home, we all pined for the *Roqueta*, our small piece of rock; and Majorca was then deservedly called 'the island of tranquillity'. Deyá had the added attraction of its majestic mountainous scenery, and the particular pleasure of being cut off from the rest of the world, so much so that even the short drive to Palma was avoided. When I returned to Canellún for my summer holidays, the first thing I did was to tear off the grey school uniform I had arrived in, rush down to the Cala, and take a cleansing dive into the cool water. All memories of school were washed away and it was as if I had never left home; I was once again at peace, under the protection of Father's Goddess.

Quite early in my life I noticed that people tended to behave differently in Father's presence. Perhaps he gave off an aura they reacted to; perhaps he just knew intuitively how to draw them out. He could always find something to speak about which interested him, even when the person he was talking to had a technical or scientific background. He asked a tree specialist details about those trees which formed his 'Sacred Tree Alphabet' on which he based *The White Goddess*; or questioned a physicist about the mathematical thought processes: were they really as logical as the final results led one to believe? He could always discover some common ground unless, of course, the person was so dull or full of himself that Father shut himself away in his workroom, and let Mother get rid of him.

Father's personality suffused Canellún: his worship of the God-dess, his use of 'analepsis', his insistence that everyone who came to the house was someone special. Where else but at Canellún could failing my English Literature exam be laughed at as though this were a clever joke; both a reflection on 'Literature' and its teachers? Where else could Julian Glover, Honor Wyatt's son, have walked through our kitchen door unannounced after ten years' absence, and be greeted by Father: 'Oh, hello, Julian, cut up these cucumbers for me, will you? By the way, have I told you about ambrosia and the nectar of the Gods? No? Well . . . .'

The day at Canellún was ruled by Father's work. By eight o'clock, he was up, and had his breakfast, while preparing Mother's tray of coffee, toast, home-made marmalade – in a small silver cup beaten out of a pre-war 5-peseta coin – and the latest air-mail edition of the London *Times*. After taking the tray up to the bedroom, where Mother was still dozing, he went to his workroom for his session with Karl. He then worked solidly through until lunch. Meanwhile, Mother got little Tomás up, drove to the shop in the village, and then cooked lunch; the Murciana twins, Antonia and Salud, who had taken over from their sister Francisca, did the housework and laundry. The rest of us had drifted downstairs around nine o'clock, breakfasted on the shady landing of the steps leading to the front door, and disap-peared towards the beach. At half-past one, the twins served lunch in the dining room for Mother, Father and Tomás, as well as any one of us not eating at the Cala. After coffee, Father took his siesta.

'William, call me in twenty minutes.' He would pick one of us to wake him and, flat on his back, his arms at his sides – as he had learned to do in the trenches – he fell into a deep sleep. Exactly on time, I woke him and he returned to his desk. After a couple of hours, he went to the village to collect his mail, read it in the café and dropped it on his desk. It was time for his swim. He strode briskly down to the Cala in shorts and *espardenyas*, a large straw hat on his head, his bathing trunks and a small towel over his shoulder, sorting out work in his head as he went. On the beach he changed, climbed around his cliff-face, dived into the clear water, swam to the middle of the cove, and back to his clothes. With his towel draped loosely over his middle, he sat on the shingle, talking to whoever was close, while he pulled off his wet costume and pulled on his shorts. He then hurried back home. Occasionally, someone would ask to walk to the Cala with him but it took a teenager like myself to keep up with his stride. It was some three kilometres in all; two hundred metres down and the same back up, much of it on irregular cobbled steps, but within an hour of leaving the house, he was back, having tea with Mother and anyone else who had called. After a quick gulp he returned to his desk and answered his mail. In the evening, once the heat of the day was past, Mother watered the garden, and Father came out to give her a hand and to check his compost heap. Lucia, Juan and I were up from the beach by seven and, after an ice-cream in the village, we helped lay the table for supper which, if it were fine, we had on the *depósito*.

Though affectionate, we were not an intimate family. We neither kissed nor hugged; nor did we reveal our innermost feelings to each other. We laughed a lot, family jokes tending to be bilingual puns, or clumsy direct translations from or to Spanish. All of us were circumspect with Juan who, though kind and loving by nature, was still liable to throw one of his tantrums if anything went wrong. I still teased Lucia, a reflex left over from when we were younger: she would always cry if I told her – untruthfully – that she had a bumpy nose. The last time Father knocked our heads together, I was sixteen.

3

In about 1954 Father bought the lease of the *escar de Ca's Floquer* – meaning 'the slipway belonging to the house of the ribbon maker'. The last Floquer had died, and his sisters had no use for it. The *escar* lay on a beautiful stretch of coast below Lluc Alcari. It had a small jetty, a pine-log slipway on which to pull up boats above wave height, and a small boathouse at the top.

In the boathouse, we kept a small snipe-class sail boat, the *Pago-Pago*, which had once belonged to Bob Creeley. The Deyá coastline is too sheer and open for safe sailing. Either there is a storm, or a flat calm; rarely is there a suitable breeze without waves. Mother and Father went out a few times with sailing friends only to find themselves becalmed, whistling for the wind. Thereafter the *Pago-Pago* was left to Pedro, Po and myself. We glided for hours under the thinnest of breezes, making long tacks to get into the Cala and often – as with Rosito and our rubber dinghy – had to row back.

Once we acquired the *escar*, it became the custom that, instead of going on Sundays to the Fonda, we picnicked at Ca's Floquer and invited our friends. Pedro would always be there as would any visitors from England. At about one o'clock, we drove to Lluc Alcari, and walked down to the slipway for a swim, before unpacking the baskets with the salads, cheese and fruit, which we ate in the shade of the pines. Father did not like sunbathing. After his swim, when we and our guests were lying on towels getting a suntan, Father went off collecting sea-salt from rock-pools, or picking samphire from rock-ledges for our salads. Immediately after lunch, he walked back to Canellún to get on with his work, while Mother and the rest of us stayed on.

In Spain, the coast below maximum wave height cannot be privately owned, and any rights must be paid annually to the *Comandancia de Marina* – the Admiralty – by the leaseholder. When Father bought the lease he was not aware of this and sadly, after several years of great enjoyment, we lost the *escar* to a man from Palma, who had been paying the rights without his knowledge.

4

As the West slowly pulled out of its post-War trauma – and the Spanish Civil War ceased being such a visceral subject – Deyá once again became, as in the Thirties, a magnet to overseas visitors. Initially it was mostly Americans who could afford to take up year-round residence. Among the first were Jim Metcalf and his wife Tom, who were sent by the Gittes family. Jim was an American sculptor with an interest in Celtic prehistory; Tom a clever jeweller. After the Judith affair, it was Jim whom Father asked to illustrate *Adam's Rib*, and he did so in handsome woodcuts.

Another early American resident was Bynum Green, a Korean war veteran, who would not be parted from his basket in which he carried a four-litre carafe of brandy. He was convinced that he was guilty of losing one thousand Chinese prisoners of war, and he became the subject of one of Father's short stories.

A little later came Alston Anderson, a black Jamaican writer, who lived above the bakery and sat in the café all day. Asked what he wanted to drink, he answered: 'I don't care what – so long as it's a double.' He was a gentle person who had studied philosophy at Columbia University, and metaphysics at the Sorbonne; he lived for his jazz records to which he listened on a wind-up gramophone. Father wrote the introduction to Alston's book of short stories, *Lover Man*.

Bert Morton and Vida Gabriella, both American, were perhaps the most bohemian. They lived in a house on the coast, below the Lluc Alcari road. They swam naked off the rocks, and when Don Pedro went down at Easter, with the collection bowl, to bless their house, they received him – Bert dressed in the briefest of shorts, Vida in a bikini. They gave generously and Don Pedro returned every year.

As had Father and Karl, so other pre-War residents returned. Fräulein Emmy Strenge, who had been Laura and Father's pre-war German neighbour, returned to her house on the corner by Canellún, where I had my accident. Before one of our trips to England, she asked us to bring her back a dachshund. Mother did, to everyone's regret. 'Bobby' barked at anyone who walked by on the road, and we could hear him whenever we sat on the *depósito*.

Another Deyá year-rounder, and one of our best friends, was Jimmy d'Aulignac, a young Anglo-Catalan who had 'retired' to Deyá at the age of twenty-eight to live on his investments. Jimmy sported a beard – one of the few seen in the village since the old *telegrafista* had died – spoke in a quiet voice, and had an imposing aristocratic manner. He had unusually beautiful girlfriends, though he remained a confirmed bachelor for many years. Cooking was Jimmy's hobby, and his gourmet dinner parties took him all day to prepare. They began with a trip to Soller in Gelat's taxi, to buy fresh shrimps, meat, vegetables and fruit in the well-stocked market; they invariably ended in highly alcoholic after-dinner talk around his candle-lit table.

Karl had made it clear on his arrival in 1947 that the basic relationship between the two families was a formal one: we were friends, but our friends were not necessarily his. Though we had many in common, Karl and Rene's circle of friends – some, local Spanish residents – tended to be less footloose than ours. This became increasingly true as more foreigners settled in the village.

By the middle Fifties, tourists and 'artists' were actively seeking new 'unspoiled' retreats in the Mediterranean. Portofino in Italy was already established, and St Tropez in France had been discovered. Deyá became one of the smaller artists' resorts. Those who did not have the means to stay all year spent an extended summer there. Mati Klarwein, an Israeli who lived in Paris, painted intricately detailed still-lifes and landscapes, while listening to one of the first transistor radios hung on his easel, and managed to capture the magic of the olive groves and terraces. Both Po and I, naturally for our age, were more interested in his radio than in his painting, although I was rather jealous of his lovely portrait of Lucia in Majorcan costume. Another talented artist was Bill Waldren, an American sculptor and photographer, who also lived in Paris, and skated professionally in *Holiday on Ice*. The summers he spent in Deyá, with his French wife and baby daughter, surrounded by his Left Bank friends.

Collectively the villagers called regular visitors *estrangers*, to differentiate them from the more ephemeral *turistas*. Each *estranger* had a nickname, mostly conferred at the Cala restaurant by Joana, Toni's beautiful but sharp-tongued sister, as a way to remember who had ordered what. Alston, naturally, became '*Es Negre*'. Some received the name of the house they lived in, and Jimmy d'Aulignac was '*Jimmy de Ca l'Andresa*'. Others were given vaguely approximate-sounding names, and Mati became 'Martin'. Among the memorable nicknames were 'the Eel-man', 'the Devil', 'the Dead Man', and 'the Swineherd'.

Henry Prain, known to the foreigners as Mac, was a large, red-nosed Scot. He became '*El Capitán*' to the villagers the day he tried out his new inflatable dinghy in the Cala. He carried it down in its canvas bag, followed by Jimmy with the Seagull motor. The sea was quite rough when they laid the dinghy out and began pumping it up. I watched from the terrace with the *Patrón*, who was scratching his stubbled chin with a puzzled look on his face: it was the first rigid inflatable with an outboard motor he had seen. Mac fixed the Seagull to its bracket and, during a lull between the waves, Jimmy pushed him out. The little engine fired, and soon the dinghy was just a speck on the ragged horizon, disappearing among the waves. '*¡Está loco!*' the *Patrón* was muttering next to me. The sea was building. Breakers climbed higher up the beach; a bursting wave sent spray across the terrace, wetting us. Mac reappeared around the headland. Blown by the northerly wind, the dinghy skimmed the waves, and was fast approaching the beach. The *Patrón*, who felt responsible for everything that went on in the Cala, looked worried. In *Sa Polsimada* he would have headed for a haven in the Puerto Soller. Mentally we were both preparing to pull Mac out of the frothing mass of water which now filled the cove. Suddenly a giant wave took hold of the dinghy and deposited it, gently, high up the beach. Mac got out, hardly wetting his feet and, turning to us watching from the terrace, made a little bow.

'*¡Molt bé – Capitán!*' said the *Patrón*. It was more than a nickname. It was a title.

The old Salón, now owned by young Gelat, did little business other than sell cups of coffee and tickets to passengers taking the half-past seven bus to Palma. Half-used blocks of bus-tickets covered the billiard table and crates of empty beer-bottles filled the once elegant stage. It lacked a terrace to sit out on. The house next to the Salón belonged to a cousin of the Estanco people. He was in charge of collecting the villagers' olive oil, and delivering it to a central depot in Palma. Obviously, this was lucrative, and he opened the brash bar Las Palmeras – the 'New Café', we called it – with its palm tree, spacious terrace, marble tables and multicoloured painted chairs. Ca'n Pep Mosso, where Father collected the mail, became the 'Old Café' and, with its small pretty verandah and friendly wicker chairs, it remained the favourite haunt of the *estrangers*.

Every summer evening, Mati, Bill Waldren, Alston, Jimmy, Mac and others gathered around the long table on the verandah of the Old Café, to watch the towering sides of the Teix bathed blood-red by the last rays of the setting sun. Mati, wearing immaculate white Indian dhotis, would play the guitar and, from time to time, brought up gypsy girls from Palma to dance. The others listened, and discussed their painting, novels, food and jazz; and planned their next tea with Pep Fondevilla.

Pep Fondevilla was an extrovert whose staid, well-to-do Palma family had exiled him to Deyá before the Civil War. Full of fun and practical jokes, he sang in drag on the Salón Deportivo stage, when old Gelat brought in an orchestra. But Pep also sang in church, and led the processions, thus endearing himself to the villagers. After some time he moved in with a German painter, called Leman, who lived in a house up the hill behind the village. During the Civil War, when the shells from the battleship fell nearby, they both moved into a cave carrying with them blankets, tins of pâté, bottles of champagne and a gramophone. Later, Leman left to fight for his country, but first deeded Pep his house. With Franco's takeover, the Church became all-powerful, and Pep had to be discreet but he still managed to sing loudest in processions. When the *estrangers* returned, they brought some fun back into his life.

Pep the Widow, as we called him at Canellún, was now in his mid-forties. When the *estrangers* climbed the path to his house with pastries, he would first serve a formal tea. Then he would round up the men.

'Now we go make pipi,' he would say and lead them to the edge of his terrace to relieve themselves. As they opened their flies, Pep would skip around with great merriment, spraying them with his home-made, overpoweringly sweet-smelling scent. Later, Pep would vanish into his house and, making loud mewing noises, say in an 'offstage' voice: 'Pussy has been very naughty today.' Suddenly he would reappear, pirouetting past his guests in a cat's costume, to rounds of applause.

Leman did not come back for many years. In the late Seventies, Pep discovered he had been abandoned in an old people's home in Germany, and brought him back to Deyá to die. However, instead of doing so, Leman recovered, and took up painting again; he survived, with Pep, Pep's new friend, and some twenty cats, all sleeping in the one double bed, until he was one hundred and four.

5

Of all the *estrangers* welcomed at Canellún, the one who left the strongest mark was Alastair Reid, then an English lecturer at Sarah Lawrence, a women's college in New York. In 1954 he was staying in Palma with his first wife, Jean, and came to Deyá to visit Father. A quiet, broad-shouldered, athletic Scot, Alastair had played fullback at rugger for St Andrews; this endeared him to Father, who had also been a fullback. But Alastair hit it off with all of us; sandy-haired, heavy-jowled, with a slightly pockmarked complexion, he had a terrific sense of humour.

Alastair was the first grown-up with whom I felt completely at ease. It was he who introduced me to the Dave Brubeck Quartet:

there was one track, 'Audrey', which we played over and over on the record player in our Palma flat; he taught me a haunting French tune, '*L'Amour de Moi*', on my recorder; he told me James Thurber stories. We climbed the Teix together. I had been up before with Po, his Valldemosa friends, and their father, who took us via Valldemosa. Alastair and I took the way straight up the cliff-face from Deyá. We lost the path, but scrambled to the top somehow. It was one of those calm, balmy days when every small sound can be heard for miles. We sat on a ledge, some two thousand feet above the village, and could hear the clink of bottles in the Old Café. Both of us were hot and thirsty.

'A cold beer is what I would most like in the world right now, William. And you?' he asked in his soft St Andrews drawl.

'A Laccao!' He always teased me about my favourite chocolate-milk drink.

Even then, I realized that being Father's son gave me access to interesting people. Had I been a charcoal burner's son, I would surely never have met Alastair. I enjoyed our rapport, but I thought of him as a family friend rather than a friend of my own. My real friends were Pedro and Po, who knew Father, not for work or fame, but as my parent.

Now that Martin had gone, Alastair became Father's closest friend, and a sounding-board for his ideas. During the winter of 1956–7 they kept up a correspondence with a view to getting it published. Father wrote from Deyá, recalling anecdotes and expounding his favourite subjects, while Alastair answered from New York, acting the straight-man and feeding Father questions. *Quoz*, as the manuscript is called, is great fun to read, but it never found a publisher.

If Alastair made a strong impression on me, so also did a wealthy young man from England, Robin Blyth. Dorothy and Montague Simmons, pre-War friends of my parents, who now ran a reform school near Cambridge, had him sent them for a black-market offence. He had been orphaned and, in 1955 on his twenty-first birthday, he inherited £48,000. Shortly afterwards, he appeared at our Palma flat with an introduction from Dorothy. Robin had dark hair, quizzical grey-blue eyes and a large sensual mouth. On the day he arrived, I went with him to tank up our old Renault. We then drove around Palma, exhilaratingly faster than I had ever been before. During the drive, saying little, but concentrating on the traffic and oncoming trams, he made two decisions which were to affect us. The first was that he would buy a house on the island; the second was that he would give us a new car. On Father's advice, he bought Sa Guarda in Lluc Alcari, which overlooked the Deyá coast, and was one of the most beautiful houses on the island. He then returned to England and shipped over two canvas-topped Land-Rovers, one of which he gave to Mother, and the other he kept. He himself drove back through France in a brand-new yellow convertible C-type Jaguar, and at once moved into his new house.

Every evening, wearing a *Cordobés* hat, a Spanish cape, and carrying a silver-tipped cane, Robin drove in the Jag to the Palma flamenco joints, where he mixed with gypsies and the bullfighting crowd. He took lessons in bullfighting and, on the twenty-second of December – the winter solstice – he hired the Palma bullring. He had posters made announcing the event. Some two hundred friends sat on the stone benches, drinking champagne and sitting in the pleasantly warm sun. It was not the real thing: in the audience, Father and I watched as he fought and killed two wretched little calves.

Early in 1956 Robin had an accident in Barcelona in which a cyclist died. With Gelat's help, he had managed to avoid prison, but the cyclist's brothers threatened to kill him. He spent the next six months with a bodyguard, nervously looking over his shoulder. Then he had a second fatal car accident in Andalucia. Returning to Deyá he realized he had to leave Spain before his involvement in the previous accident was discovered. Then one wet night driving back from Palma in his Land-rover with Tom, Jim Metcalf's wife, he skidded, went over a wall and found Tom in his arms. Having by then spent his fortune, he took out a mortgage of £1,200 on Sa Guarda, gave Father a power of attorney, asking him to sell the house, and left Deyá with Tom.

The Land-Rover, which he had given Mother, made us very much more mobile, and even allowed us to drive to England, but the custody of Sa Guarda had almost as great an impact on our lives, in that it changed our weekly routine. Sa Guarda was in Lluc Alcari itself, and on the way to our boathouse. During the period when Father was looking for the buyer that he felt 'the house deserved', we began leaving our baskets of food for our

Sunday picnics there – instead of in the pines – while we went down for a swim. After a hot and sticky climb back to Sa Guarda, Father would give us his 'treatment', which consisted in washing off the sea-salt from our swim with a bucket of breath-stoppingly cold well-water. When Father eventually found Sa Guarda the buyer it deserved, the new owner kindly allowed us to keep using the house for our picnics.

6

I was always back from school for our birthday party. It was usually held on the twenty-fourth of July – Father's birthday – and, ever since 1952 when we stopped going to England during the summer, it had become an annual event. It was supposed to be a joint party – Lucia and I were born on the twenty-first of July – but few guests realized this, and Father got most of the presents. Two casks of Majorcan wine were set on the low wall which surrounds the *depósito*, and Karl was put in charge.

'*¿Blanco o tinto?*' he asked.

A large spread of food was provided by Gabriel the Baker: Majorcan *cocas* – a square pizza-like pastry covered with either spinach or tomato and onion or red peppers – several kinds of *empanadas*, and the largest *ensaïmadas* that he could bake. The children were given fresh lemonade. Mother and Father organized games for Lucia and Juan's friends including an archery contest in which they had to hit a small *ensaïmada*. We launched large hot-air balloons, made of tissue paper, by lighting a wad of alcohol-soaked cotton wool, fixed in the opening at the bottom. The balloon slowly filled and rose in the evening air, becoming smaller and smaller in the sky until the flicker of flame was lost among the stars. Most of the villagers made a token appearance, had a glass of wine and some *coca*. Though they did not approve of extravagance, they came, nevertheless, to see what was on offer. They left soon after Antonio Murciano, in charge of the fireworks, had finished his display. The *estrangers* came, whether invited or not, and stayed until late.

Our birthday party became an event that marked the beginning of Deyá's summer season. Guests increased ten-fold, until over two hundred came, and parked cars by the roadside stretched almost the kilometre back to the village; the barrels of *blanco* and *tinto* wine, which Karl attended to, grew accordingly. Children's events were replaced by the play.

The play, in which the family – except for Mother – and friends acted, was soon the high point of the evening. Father would always take a star part. Local characters such as Gelat, Castor the Postman, Miquel the Carpenter, and the *telegrafista*, appeared in the script, which was written by friends with Father's help. The theme – it could hardly be called a plot – was inspired by the latest village gossip and by whatever Father was working on. We performed the play on the small terrace at the back of the grotto and the audience sat, beneath the walnut trees, on folding chairs brought from the village by Isabela and her cart.

After the play and the food, we danced to Laura's old wind-up gramophone. The Four Aces singing 'Three Coins in a Fountain' was one year's hit. By this time, I was allowed to stay up until the last guest had left. At first I was rather shocked when the *estrangers* got drunk; by the antics they got up to when dancing, by the nonsense they talked, and by the smell of their breath. However, though I got used to their behaviour, I never quite approved of it, especially when they passed out on the *depósito*.

7

In 1956 Ricardo Sicré, a prosperous friend of Father's from Madrid, came to Majorca for our birthday party and afterwards helped him sort out the legal tangle of his houses and properties. He stayed on his yacht, *Anne Marie*, at the Palma Yacht Club, next to Errol Flynn's *Zaca*. Father had met Ricardo in England in 1939, when he heard two young men, playing snooker in a pub, speaking Catalan. One of them was Ricardo, who had been a Captain in the Spanish Republican Army at the age of twenty, and had escaped imprisonment, or worse, by Franco's forces. Having reached England, Ricardo managed to get a job at an army training school for commandos. Later he sailed to America and, having no papers, jumped ship into New York harbour. Dripping wet, clutching his letter of introduction, he appeared on the doorstep of Father's close friend, Tom Matthews, book editor of *Time* magazine. For the remainder of the war Ricardo worked for American intelligence – one of his first jobs was to crack the safe at the Japanese Embassy – and there met his quite exceptional American wife, Betty. Then, having acquired American citizenship, he moved to Tangiers with an import/export firm. In the summer of 1947 we went to stay with him at his father's farm in the French Pyrenees, and met Betty and their children. Betty and Ricardo remained our close friends and later Father helped him write his novel, *A Tap on the Left Shoulder*, about the communists' attempt to take over the French Government after World War II. Ricardo was a sharp businessman and he, Betty and their four children now lived in the most expensive country-club estate in Madrid.

Jöan Gelat, Old Gelat's son, had never denied that Canellún, Can Torrent and the Posada were Father's. Indeed, there may well have been a private contract signed to this effect when, in December 1947, these houses were put back in his father's name. However, the law prohibiting foreigners on the islands from owning more than two thousand square metres of property outside village limits was still in force, and the deeds were in his name. Gelat had agreed to return the land as soon as a solution was found. Ricardo suggested the titles be made over to himself, as the family's Spanish councillor. Although Ricardo was a United States citizen and no longer Spanish, he carried a Spanish identity card. Gelat acquiesced.

Although only vaguely aware of the problem, I too felt relief when the business of the houses was sorted out: Father and Mother celebrated with French champagne on board Ricardo's yacht. But the remaining properties – the land on the other side of the road, the land near the Cala, the orchard at Ca'n Madó, the house in the Vinya Vieja and the land at Es Pinets – also in Gelat's name were not in the deal. Gelat now claimed that, since his father's life had been shortened by being sent to prison for 'owning' the Cala road, what might have been Don Roberto's properties now belonged both rightfully and legally to the heirs. Nevertheless, he offered to sell back whatever properties Father wanted at a 'good price'. Unfortunately, at the time, Father's finances were such that all he could afford were ten thousand square metres immediately in front of Canellún – less than a third of the land he had originally acquired – as a protection against its being built on.

The official signing, in the presence of a Notary Public, of a deed 'selling' Ricardo the houses and the land, eventually took place in 1961. Not being Spanish, Ricardo had conveniently 'forgotten his identity card in Madrid'. Once the three houses and this smaller piece of land were in his name, Ricardo arranged for the Deyá Town Hall to certify that the land, Canellún and Can Torrent all lay within the village limits, thus circumventing the two-thousand-square-metre ownership restriction. Finally he had the deeds transferred to Mother's name, reasoning that, being twenty years younger, she would outlive Father.

Father was hurt, as much by the breaking of Old Gelat's word as by the loss of his other properties.

'May a curse fall on all of you, Jöan.'

Although I do not believe in these things, Father's malediction could be said to have been remarkably effective: many of Old Gelat's offspring suffered dreadful misfortunes. Even Gelat himself died impoverished.

8

My brother Juan was not doing well at school. Since I was four years older, he must have sensed that all the family's efforts were aimed at my education. He was also jealous of Lucia, who got top marks at the nuns' school; and of Tomás, who, as the youngest, received the attention that once was his. Father made things worse by telling Juan that he was a genius and that he should not worry, eventually he would find his vocation and everything would be all right. Juan was sensitive and his tantrums were a display of frustration. As a means of escape, he went with his friends to the dogtrack or to the cinema – he saw *The Greatest Show on Earth* eight times. When the Easter funfair opened, he spent his pocket money in the shooting-stalls, winning glasses of vermouth and jars of olives.

Mother decided that Juan needed a better school. She ruled out England and its public school system as being too rough for his susceptible nature. Instead, she chose the International School in Geneva – recommended by someone she met by chance – where both Juan and Lucia could go together. The problem was money. Income from Father's earlier books and fees he received from other publications including short stories published in the *New Yorker*, *Punch* and the *Saturday Evening Post*, hardly covered my Oundle fees, let alone an expensive Swiss school for Lucia and Juan.

Father refused to write the historical novel 'potboilers' his publishers suggested. *I, Claudius* and *Claudius the God* he had written in desperation, when he lived with Laura, to pay off the mortgage on Canellún. Since then he had vowed, as a poet, to write only on subjects which were of interest to him; and preferably about those which were relevant to his poetry and the theme of *The White Goddess*. Father was then working on *They Hanged My Saintly Billy*, an historical novel about Dr William Palmer, a racecourse doctor of the 1850s, who was hanged for multiple murder, but whom he thought was innocent. Since returning to Deyá after the War, Father had written three other novels: *The Isles of Unwisdom*, which tells of an ill-fated Spanish expedition to find gold in the Solomon Islands; *Seven Days in New Crete* – on which he was working while looking after me in the Barcelona clinic – which describes an Utopia, based on the worship of the White Goddess; and *Homer's Daughter*, which incorporates his thesis that Homer's epics were written by a woman. None of them was the sort of seller needed to pay school fees.

Father could still perhaps have managed had he not spent some four years on two massive but moneyless projects. *The Greek Myths*, which Viking Press in America commissioned and afterwards turned down, was published by Penguin and gained a merited place as a textbook on the subject. But it sold slowly and most of the advance – which Viking expected to be returned – went on paying for Janet's research and Martin's tutoring. *The Nazarene Gospel Restored* – which Father completed before *The Greek Myths* – he wrote in collaboration with Joshua Podro. In it they show that Jesus was a practising Jew, who followed the Torah strictly; and that the Gospels were rewritten by the disciples of St Paul to conceal this. They reinterpreted Jesus' parables, substantiated their conclusions, and added a new historical background. They then rewrote the Gospel itself. When, after two years, Father and Joshua were both finally satisfied, *The Nazarene Gospel Restored* had grown into a thousand-page book. It remains Father's most scholarly work; he held the quixotic notion that it would eventually revitalize the Christian Churches and that his 'Restored Gospel' would eventually supersede the four of the New Testament and furthermore, 'make things right' between Christians and Jews. When it was published in 1953, the book was unfortunately years ahead of its time; it was shunned and restricted to a small print run. Only recently have many of Father and Joshua's ideas been accepted by mainstream theologians.

In his precarious financial state, Father bowed fervently to the Goddess at the new moon, and turned his silver coin with extra vigour. 'Something will turn up' he kept saying, as Lucia and Juan's departure for Switzerland fast approached. He considered the lucrative offers to lecture in America but he felt it poetically unethical to accept. He even contemplated selling his beloved Posada. Father asked me what I thought of the sale – a sign that I was growing up – and I begged him to hold off as long as he possibly could.

Curiously, in spite of his reservations about lecturing and/or writing 'potboilers', he had no prejudices against writing for show business. He judged this akin to buying a lottery ticket, as he did every Christmas. In 1936 Alexander Korda had bought the film rights to *I, Claudius*, and had Charles Laughton play the lead role. Unfortunately Korda's 'Messalina', Merle Oberon, was injured in a car crash halfway through the shooting: the film was first postponed and finally abandoned. Since then, Father had always hoped for a film to be made of one of his books: this would, at a stroke, solve his chronic financial difficulties.

In 1952 Will Price, a little-known American film director, proposed that Father should write a script based on one of the stories in the *Arabian Nights*. Will was in his forties, overweight and with a drink problem, and had been married to the actress Maureen O'Hara. He arrived to work with Father in June, and stayed at the Hotel Costa D'Or in Lluc Alcari with a young English girlfriend. Will knew his job, and kept sober when working: he and Father shut themselves up in the Posada and, between them, they finished the script, called *The World's Delight*, in the allotted six weeks. Meanwhile, his bored young girlfriend ran up a staggering $500 bill in room service and telephone calls at the hotel. Will had to borrow from Father, and gave me his instant-camera, one of the first Polaroids ever made, as a sign of goodwill. *The World's Delight* was never filmed.

The next film opportunity came with *Homer's Daughter*. Roberto Rossellini, whom Father had met in 1954 on a visit to Jenny in Italy, wanted to direct his wife, Ingrid Bergman, playing Nausicaa the heroine. The option was signed, but Rossellini could not find backers, and when he and Bergman separated he lost interest. In

1956 Alexander Korda proposed to remake *I, Claudius*, this time with Alec Guinness in the lead role. However, it was conceived as a 'spectacular', and Guinness refused to participate unless it was rewritten as a domestic drama. Guinness came to Deyá, and worked on a new script with Father, but it too fell through. Almost at once another possibility arose when Will Price managed to retrieve the copyright of *The World's Delight*, and persuaded Fernandel to play the lead. Will also failed to find backers. Although there were several further opportunities, Father had to wait many more years for his film hopes to be fulfilled.

In February 1957 Father finally took up an offer to lecture in America. He had one hundred dollars in his bank there, and another seven pounds in England. With Alastair's encouragement, he had overcome his reservations by reasoning that, having poetry as his subject, he need not alienate the Goddess. Alastair met him in New York. Father wrote to me: 'He ironed my shirts, I washed his socks and we went everywhere together; he as manager, I as star performer.' Father gave two lectures, at Mount Holyoke College and at the YM-YWHA Poetry Center in New York; and also poetry readings at MIT, the Library of Congress and at New York University. His audiences were delighted with him. Such was the ease of his 'grab and run raid' that Father's lecture trips to America to earn the following year's school fees became an annual event. The lectures helped place him in the public eye, and commissions for articles and talks began to pour in, making him comfortably solvent again.

9

At school, I kept the letters that I received. Those I still have from Father are full of vignettes of Deyá and Palma life; how the oranges are ripening, or how many days the 'sirocco' lasted. One of the first adult letters contains a description of the 'suicide episode' in which the grocer on the corner of our street:

> . . . three times tried to kill himself by jumping from the *primero* to the hall down through the well of the staircase. The first time he smashed Juan's (your old) bicycle, the next time I broke his fall from the *principal* and he fell on the bike again; the third time Mother and

> Salud held him while I ran for succour. The spattered
> blood on that staircase! Yet he hardly hurt himself at all.
> [RG to WG, 19 February 1957]

Father's ever-increasing fame meant that more and more people came to Canellún. Some were old friends, some new admirers. Some genuinely wanted to see him to discuss a particular problem; some simply wanted to bask in his presence. Some, like Sir Ralph Vaughan Williams, were probably just curious. I remember Father and Sir Ralph raucously singing the Carthusian school song together – their *paella* getting cold – in a Palma seafront restaurant.

The Posada became the family guest-house and regular visitors occupied it in summer; a few, such as James Reeves, the poet, his wife Mary, who had helped type *I, Claudius*, Honor Wyatt, another poet, and John Aldridge, one of whose pictures hung in my bedroom, had been in Deyá before the War as friends of Laura and Father's. The Posada was a majestic old building on which Father lavished antique furniture, Georgian silver, and beautiful ceramic plates on the walls. However, its amenities were primitive. Water had to be pulled up in a pail from the rainwater cistern. Showers were taken under a blue bucket-like contraption with a spigot and a shower head, previously filled by hand. The only toilet, an earth-privy, was outside in Isabela's stable. The donkey liked the privy door left open, so she could peer in. The diminutive kitchen had only a charcoal stove and a stone sink. The house was looked after by Antonia of the Puig, who spoke French as well as Spanish, but no English; as a special favour she would cook her admirable stuffed aubergines.

As the summers went by, an expanding number of family, friends and 'admirers' asked to be put up in July and August, although most could have afforded to rent a house, or pay for a room in one of the village's four inexpensive hotels or pensions. The fact that some guests had an open account at the Estanco shop, which Father settled when they left, made being 'put up' even more appealing. Soon the pressure on the Posada became so great that Father rented a cottage by the Mirador above the Cala to take the overflow. The amenities at the cottage were even more primitive than the Posada's, and the place had little charm. Yet this was compensated by its being a mere five-minute walk to the beach. For very special friends, Father sometimes borrowed Sa Guarda, Robin Blyth's old house, from Ricardo: for it was he who had paid the £1,200 mortgage when it fell due.

The famous, too, visited Father, and they became a yardstick by which the villagers measured his growing reputation. Alec and Merula Guinness and their son Matthew stayed at Sa Guarda. Father was working on the *I, Claudius* filmscript with Alec, who was quiet, reserved, and a strict Catholic. I invited Matthew, who was my age, to come to the Cala and have lunch with Pedro, Po and myself. When he discovered that all of us smoked and drank wine – both of which he was forbidden by his parents – he became our constant companion. Mother and Father gave a supper for the Guinnesses at the Posada. After the meal, instead of playing 'The Game', we played 'Passengers in the Train'. Each contestant is given a phrase which he must get into the 'conversation' before his opponent. Matthew was given the phrase 'the picture is hanging on the wall' and I was given 'I *do* love pigs'. Being seventeen now, I smoked in front of Mother and Father. I lit a cigarette. The 'conversation' went something like this:

Mother: All aboard, all aboard.
[*Whistle*]
Matthew: Good evening, Sir.
William: Good evening, nice weather for farming.
Matthew: I don't know, I'm a painter.
William: I'm on the way to a pig competition. Would you like a cigarette?
[*Offers cigarette packet*]
Matthew: Thank you.
[*Taking cigarette*]
William: Here.
[*Lights Matthew's cigarette*]
William: I really must go to the guard's van to see my pig.
Matthew: Ah, yes, I have a painting there, 'the picture is hanging on the wall'.

Alec did not say a word: to him, acting was acting, but he was not amused at seeing Matthew smoke. Mother thought it all very funny.

Of the famous who visited Father, however, it was Ava Gardner who caused the greatest sensation in the village. A friend and neighbour of Ricardo's in Madrid, she first came over in the spring of 1956, when we were in the Palma flat. She spent hours with Father in his study, asking him what to read, how to write, and about his poetry. Although she never became a Muse, Father grew very fond of her. In July 1959 she stayed for a couple of days at Sa Guarda. At that year's birthday party, Ava made village folklore by insisting on dancing with the handsome young corporal of the Deyá *Guardia Civil*.

At first he begged off: '*Por favor, señorita, mañana* I will dance all evening with you if you desire, but now I am in *uniforme*, on duty.'

'Don't be like that, corporal,' we encouraged him, 'it's for the honour of Spain!' He did not take much convincing. The *madonas* at the *rentaderos* loved the story, and the next morning demanded to know the minutest details from those who had witnessed the event.

One early evening a telegram arrived for Ava and I went to Sa Guarda to deliver it. Ava was alone. She offered me a glass of wine, and we sat in the garden, under a large pine tree on a small lookout terrace, gazing at the spectacular view of the Deyá coast. The sea was placid and I watched the *Estrella* rounding the Deyá promontory on her way to set the nets; the cicadas had stopped and the scent of jasmine wafted by; the sun's red disc was slipping below the horizon. Ava may have been feeling lonely, and I just a convenient ear, for she began telling me, in her pleasant South Carolina drawl, about her childhood on the tobacco farm. Later, we had a plate of spaghetti and continued talking. The next day, Ava took Mother and Father to supper at an expensive restaurant in Palma. She had too much to drink and, besieged by the paparazzi, who had discovered her whereabouts, she insulted them, and the waiters too; and left Majorca in a fury. I found it hard to believe that she was one and the same Ava who had so charmed me the night before.

10

For years, Pedro and I had ridden my Raleigh together; he pedalled and I sat on the cross-bar. Then his father bought him a moped; Po already had one and, at sixteen, I was given one too. My Raleigh was handed down to Juan. Sadly, I never cared for the moped as I had done for my wonderful bicycle – especially when Pedro was doing the pedalling!

Pedro, Po and I wore some of the first blue jeans on the island, bought by Father from America. We also wore striped seaman's vests bought by Mother in Dieppe on a Land-rover trip across France. Compared to other young Majorcans, we felt very adult and experienced. In fact we were quite naïve. One Sunday morning in Palma, Pedro and I got up very early to meet Po for an outing. We caught the first tram, and we were speaking English, in which Pedro was now fluent. A pretty young prostitute, on her way home, mistook us for American sailors, and came over to us.

'Hey, boys, foki, foki for love, money for souvenir!' We laughed, but we were both really quite upset.

At about this time, I made another close friend in Po's cousin, Teddy Coll. His Swiss mother was Madame Vidal's sister; his Majorcan father worked for the telegraph service. Teddy, and his brother Nene, rarely came to Deyá: their parents had a summer house on the other side of the island. Although we had played together in Maestro Calatayud's guitar group at the Vidals', I first remember Teddy when I was about sixteen. He was in bed with the flu, and Po and I went to visit him in his large mansion overlooking the Palma seafront. Teddy, like Pedro, was two years older than I. Fair-haired, with gaunt chiselled features, he wore glasses and had an infectious smile. He was already a talented painter, and his bedside table was cluttered with watercolours and mugs of dirty water in which he had been dipping his brushes. Teddy's ambition was to become a car designer – sheets of paper, covered with car studies, littered the floor.

'Draw Guillermo,' said Po. I was wearing a peaked sun cap. Teddy smiled and in less than a minute handed me a caricature: he had sketched the cap as large as my body, my face hidden by its peak. Teddy loved an argument for argument's sake and delighted in being the Devil's advocate. He would happily support witchcraft, dictatorship, or even murder, simply to get a conversation going. He could turn any argument upside down and kept us spellbound for hours. We met whenever I was in Palma.

At Canellún we now had a battery driven gramophone. I brought records from England and Po, Pedro and I knew Harry Belafonte's calypsos and Lonnie Donegan's skiffle songs by heart.

124

There were also several records by Josh White, a black blues singer who played the guitar superbly and was Alston's favourite. Knowing the words, Po and I spent hours trying to work out the chord sequence to sing them to on my guitar. However, it was Teddy, the most musical of us, who always had to show us how it was done on the recording. Pedro played the tambourine very well, and he enjoyed singing songs in literal translation into Spanish. 'It takes a worried man to sing a worried song . . .' became *'Se necesita un hombre preocupado, para cantar una canción preocupada,'* and 'Frankie and Johnny were lovers . . .' became *'Francisquito and Juanita, eran amantes'*. He had us rolling with laughter on the *depósito* tiles.

One of Deyá's attractions for Pedro, Po and myself, was the arrival of young foreign girls on holiday with their parents, and we each had a succession of girlfriends. Pedro, having lost his mother early, and being also a little older, took these affairs more seriously than Po and I did. When he was sixteen he fell very much in love with a fourteen-year-old English girl, Carol. Pedro and Carol's idyll lasted several summers, and it was in an early bout of love-sickness, when Carol had returned to England with her parents, that Pedro spent his summer with the fishermen. Mostly our girlfriends were little more than teenage romances; a few kisses under the stars and then a half-hearted exchange of letters for the rest of the year. I was seventeen before I really fell in love.

11

Sometimes Mother and Father drove me back to Oundle in the Land-Rover. We took the night ferry to Barcelona and, by the following evening – the French *autoroutes* were not yet built – had reached Montelimar. The next evening we made Paris, where we spent the night at a small hotel in the rue du Bac and saw Jim Metcalf, who had a studio nearby. Jim had left Deyá after his wife Tom had gone off with Robin. We spent a day sightseeing and visiting other friends and, the following morning, drove on either to Dieppe, where we caught the Southampton ferry, or to Le Touquet, where we took the *Silver City* air-bridge to Lydd. I looked forward to these trips with Mother. She was more fun to be with than when she was running Canellún. She always saw the funny side of things: when we were held up by a village band, or were passed by a Citroën 2CV full of nuns.

When I was sixteen, Mother taught me to drive the Land-Rover, and I began 'helping' her on the road between Deyá and Palma. One invaluable piece of advice she gave me was to expect a mule and cart around every corner. I was still too young to have a driving licence, but Father's attitude towards the law was cavalier and, although the *guardias* all knew I was under-age, they turned a blind eye.

It was not long before I took hourly turns with Mother at the wheel in France. Whichever of us was not driving would sit in the middle-front-seat with the gear-shift between our feet; Father, with his long legs, sat by the door. The Land-Rover's heating could not cope with its canvas roof, so he wrapped himself in a blanket and stuck his feet in a foot-muff. I can still see him in my mind's eye, staring straight ahead, a vacant look on his face, while working through a new conundrum – the occurrence of hallucinogenic mushrooms in the Old Testament.

'That's it, Samson's foxes!' he cried with a smile of satisfaction. Mother and I looked at each other, wondering whatever would come next.

'How could Samson collect three hundred foxes, and send them into the Philistines' cornfields with torches tied to their tails? Impossible! He sent in a battalion of raiders with torches to burn the corn. Why foxes? Because the juice of *Amanita muscaria* could be laced with wine to make the raiders completely fearless, and because this mushroom, when dried, is fox-coloured! So there!' Here was yet another example of Father's way of seeing things. To whom at school could I ever try to explain this?

I was happier now at Oundle and, paradoxically, the more I adapted, the more I behaved differently from my carefree manner at home. I had done better than expected at 'O' level and, no longer having to do 'English', I was occasionally even top of the form. I began looking beyond school. It was unlikely I could get the exam qualifications to get into Oxford, where both Mother and Father would have liked me to go. Father, having been to Oxford himself, had been disappointed that both my half-brothers David and Sam had gone to Cambridge. Had I asked him to, Father might have been able to pull some strings and get me into his old college, St John's, but I was determined to make my own way. I did not really expect to get more than two science 'A' levels, so I picked the most interesting science course that I thought I could hope for. None of the career masters at Oundle had recommended Geology at Imperial College – red-brick universities were regarded with suspicion – but I applied and was called for an interview in November 1957. I was accepted on condition my exam results were satisfactory. This was fortunate because, with the assurance of youth, and having no advice from my parents, who were unaware of how difficult it was to get into university, I had not bothered to apply elsewhere. I was thrilled. It was wonderful to feel for the first time in my life I had consciously achieved something without the benefit of the Robert Graves connection.

CHAPTER VII

1

Sitting down, I looked at the postcard again. Chiggers had put ticks in all the blanks. There was only one explanation: I had passed *all* five 'A' levels. In those days there were no grades, and I may have just scraped the lot of them; nevertheless, I was only the second or third Oundle boy to have achieved five 'A' levels in one go. Greatly elated, I ran out and told Mother who was watering the garden.

'Oh, did you? Well, what'd you expected? Take this over to the compost heap, will you?' I knew it was not Oxford I was going to, but sometimes Mother could be irritatingly depreciative.

2

The Imperial College of Science and Technology was an amalgam of three constituent colleges, the Royal College of Science, City and Guilds College and the Royal School of Mines, which taught science, engineering and mining respectively. Geology was classified as a science, so it came under the auspices of the RCS. However, in practical terms, geology was fundamental to mining, so our department was located in the RSM building behind the Albert Hall. It was through the RSM's massive neo-classical portico in South Kensington's Prince Consort Road that I went every morning to my courses.

I knew nothing whatever about geology but, thanks to the science I had taken at Oundle, I found that I was as well-equipped as those of my fellow-students who had taken the Geology 'A' level. Indeed, my four years at Oundle served me well. Without them I could not have obtained the academic qualifications to get to university; nor the cultural background to adapt to college life. Of the twelve students, the six oldest had done their National Service; for the others, including myself, it had already been abolished and we came straight from school. A wide range of ages was thus formed: the older students relaxed amid us youngsters, while we acquired some of their more mature attitudes towards work. I had little trouble making friends, and I got on well with the ex-National Servicemen. Indeed, I always found it easier to make friends with boys older than myself. Now, for the first time in my life, I was among people who did not know of my relationship to Father and I hoped to keep it that way.

Our year was small enough not to break up into separate cliques. We got to know one another well on our geology field trips. The first trip was at Easter 1959, when we were taken to Dorset and Devon to be shown such classic geological sites as the metamorphic rock outcrops of Start Point, the granites of Dartmoor, and the ammonite-bearing mudstones of the Kimmeridge beaches. Perhaps the brightest and most motivated student among us was David Kinsman, and he had more or less taken charge of the year. A tall, large man with a round face and glasses, David was an ex-RAF officer, very meticulous, with wide-ranging interests from cycling to bird watching. Brian Chadwick was another ex-National Service man: a small wiry chap, with a sharp sense of humour, he was engaged to be married. We met in the pub on our first evening and Chad wanted his usual.

'A pint of Flowers, please,' he ordered.

'Wot d'you want? . . . violets?' replied the publican, who had never heard of the brewery. Chad's fiancée's name was Violet. He collapsed with laughter and 'Violets?' became the catchword of the year.

On a second field trip the following Easter to the Isle of Skye, we stayed in a small inn on the Southern shore, while we mapped low-grade metamorphics. I was down at the bar before the others.

'Where are you from?' the landlord asked.

'Spain, Majorca,' I answered.

'Oh? I know that part of the world. Whereabouts?'

'Deyá, on the north-west coast.'

'Oh yes, that's by the Foradada. I used to skipper my ship around there.' The Foradada is the small promontory with a large hole in the rock, a natural refuge in easterly bad weather, where the *Patrón* laid his nets and where once the *Arxiduc* had anchored his yacht.

'That's right. When was that?' I asked him. He did not reply. Instead he went to the back, and washed glasses. Later I pressed him again but he would not talk. Then it dawned on me.

'Torpedo boats?' I asked him the next evening. He gave me a funny look. I guessed that he had been skipper of one of those ex-Royal Navy flat-bottomed torpedo boats which had worked the Tangiers-Majorca smuggling run.

'Yes.'

'Not the one with the cement?' The ex-torpedo boats were fitted with larger engines than their design allowed and, to stabilize them in the choppy Mediterranean, the vessels needed to be weighted down. Generally, sacks of sand were used as ballast, but the boats were aged, and the continual buffeting of the waves opened cracks in some of the wooden cross-ply bottoms. There was one particular boat with which the *Polsimada* had trafficked: it leaked so badly that its skipper had laid down a layer of cement to keep the sea out. Toni had told me about it.

'No, not that one.' He smiled, and from then on I got free drinks when none of the other students were around.

The College used its first-year exams to cull the weaker students, of which – in spite of my crop of 'A' levels – I was one. Several of the questions required descriptive answers and my poor command of written English, and my dreadful spelling, nearly failed me. The examiner called me in, and I tried to explain – without mentioning Father – that, not having had a conventional English education until I was fourteen, and being completely trilingual, made it difficult for me to express myself correctly in any language. I promised to try harder. Grudgingly, he let me stay on. Of the twelve students who had begun the course only nine of us got through to the second year.

3

I lived in several bedsitters in London's South Kensington, finally keeping one on the top floor of 12, Ashburn Gardens. It was a large, pleasant room with a good view over the trees and lawns of the Gardens. I had a bed, a chest of drawers, a table and chair, and two armchairs in front of the gas fire. A kitchenette and bathroom I shared with an Indian couple, and enjoyed the smell of wonderful curry. For breakfast I made coffee on a hob by my gas fire. Both appliances were fed by a meter, which guzzled shilling coins. Mother had lent me a large painting of Deyá by John Aldridge; and Father gave me a drawing by Ronald Searle of 'Thetis and Neptune'. This was one of the original illustrations Searle did for the American edition of *The Anger of Achilles*, Father's prose translation of the Iliad. I also had a tourist bullfight poster, a gift of Alastair's: my name was printed between those of the *matadors* Luis Miguel Dominguín and Antonio Ordoñez. On my record player I listened to Josh White, Dave Brubeck, the Modern Jazz Quartet. I played Maestro Calatayüd's etudes on my guitar. On those endless dank rainy days so common in London, when I felt particularly homesick, I tried to recreate a Deyá mood by listening to bullfight pasodobles or Majorcan folk-dance music, and by eating the *sobrasada* Mother sent me via friends who had driven back. To remind me I would soon be going home, my air-ticket to Palma was always visible on the mantelpiece. I went to any event in London connected with Majorca, especially if it had any links with Deyá. When *Los Valldemosa* came over, I immediately got in touch.

Los Valldemosa were a singing group from the neighbouring village who had played at our parties in Deyá and who, every autumn, played at the Blue Angel Club off Piccadilly. They sang Spanish, Majorcan, South American and Calypso songs. Rafael, who played the guitar, originally trained as a customs officer – his father had helped finance some of the smuggling in Valldemosa, and thought it would be a good idea to have someone on the inside. His brother Bernardo, who also played the guitar and was the lead singer, had helped to run their parents' small bar and hotel in Valldemosa. The youngest brother, Tomeu, was, at seventeen, already a virtuoso on the recorder. Matias, their cousin who completed the foursome, played the *bandurria* and had trained as a telegraphist. The group began by serenading girls in Valldemosa and playing at village gatherings. By the time they came to our birthday parties, they had already performed at Palma's top night club, where a talent spotter offered them the contract at the Blue Angel. However, it was after Barry Carman, a delightful soft-spoken Australian friend of ours – whom they had met at Canellún – interviewed them on BBC television that they had decided to turn professional.

Occasionally we met in their bachelor flat near Queensway. This was one of my rare opportunities to speak Majorcan and, through their eyes, see London the way I might have done had I stayed at school in Majorca and come over to England for the first time.

'*¡Huep, Guillem!* Today we went on a bus to Kensington, but the conductor couldn't understand us so we ended up somewhere called "Kennington".'

'Matias stopped trying to pronounce things right in English, and asked for a ticket to *Ojos Secos*. It worked – he got his ticket to Oxford Circus.'

'Why do you have these funny little streets called "mews" that don't lead anywhere?'

At around midnight we went to the Blue Angel. I had a drink and watched the floorshow from the bar. Although I knew their repertoire by heart, I never tired of hearing them perform – especially when they sang in Majorcan.

A couple of times a week, to relieve the loneliness of my evenings after I had caught up with my work, I walked along to the Troubadour coffee-house in Earl's Court. Its owner was Mike van Stapen, a burly Canadian who had worked in the Arctic building airfields and then come to Europe, calling in on Father in Deyá during the early Fifties. In 1954 Father was giving his Clark Lectures in Cambridge, and they ran into each other again. Father had lent Mike the money to start up his coffee-house.

The Troubadour was unique at this time. Mike decorated it with penny-farthing bicycles, antique coffee grinders, and old door keys; for colour he had hung turn-of-the-century posters. Mike was a great admirer of Bertrand Russell, strongly anti-apartheid, anti-Bomb, and aggressively environmentalist – long before the word had its present-day connotations. At the counter, which served coffee, milk or water only, he sold *Courier*, the UNESCO magazine. Patrons sat on stools at round wooden tables with cast-iron legs and a candle in the centre – where layers of wax built up every night. While his clients discussed Kant and Sartre, Mike stood watch by the front door, to ensure that there was no unwelcome spill-over from the pub on the corner. Mike served a limited menu from a small kitchen, and I usually ordered steak, corn on the cob and a baked potato, which arrived on trendy wooden plates.

The Folk movement had just begun, and Friday was Folk-Song Night in the basement. There were cushions on the floor to sit on. After my steak, I wandered downstairs to listen, carrying a mug of coffee in my hand. Mike hired a different singer every week, but anyone in the audience was welcome to perform. I rarely summoned up the necessary courage. The evening's highlight was to wait and see who dropped in after midnight. Among those who did were Roy Hall and Jimmy McGregor, who appeared every evening on the BBC's 'Tonight' show; Ramblin' Jack Eliot in his cowboy outfit – unusual in those days – who played Woody Guthrie Talking Blues, and Shirley Collins and Isla Cameron; both with beautiful spine-tingling voices. I wished Po and Pedro could have shared my experience. Instead, I learned to compose and play Talking Blues à la Woody Guthrie, and sang these and other favourites when I returned to Deyá.

Sometimes I took Stella along to the Troubadour. James Reeves's daughter, she had come to the Posada with her parents for a holiday in 1957, and had returned every year since. Stella brimmed over with vitality and was devastatingly attractive, with sparkling blue eyes and a full happy mouth. Whether at the Cala in her bikini reading *The Brothers Karamazov*, or in the Old Café sipping lemonade through a straw, she looked simply stunning. Stella was a couple of years older than I. This age difference seemed to be offset by her fascination with our idyllic way of life in Deyá. I fell in love with her, and was achingly jealous whenever she talked to older men, obviously more interesting and attractive to her than I was. Nevertheless we were excellent friends, and went around Deyá together. We also saw quite a lot of one another in London. When *Los Valldemosa* came over we threw parties at Stella's flat – both Rafael and Matias got married to flatmates of hers. At the Troubadour, Stella looked pensive in the soft light as we reminisced about Deyá, and squeezed the candle-grease into fancy shapes: my heart stopped.

4

Among the regulars at the Troubadour was a young Gibraltarian called Joe. Joe had taken to heart the anti-British *Gibraltar Para España* campaign, initiated by the Spanish government to build up xenophobia, and make the workers forget their low wages.

'How can you possibly live in Spain under that effing dictator Franco?' he snarled. Yet for us, life was pleasant and comfortable. None of my friends on the island was politically active, or even politically aware. I did not know anyone who had been imprisoned for his politics. Nor was I conscious of any feelings of political oppression. Certainly we all enjoyed the latest anti-Franco jokes and everyone grumbled but, like a Spaniard, I thought it facile to say that we lived under a 'fascist dictatorship'.

'Provided you don't get mixed up in politics, it's the freest country in Europe,' I replied. This was the stock answer of most Majorcans I knew.

Indeed, in Majorca political freedom was considerably greater than that enjoyed on mainland Spain. Though the press was censored, we could usually read between the lines, and we knew of the unrest in Madrid and Barcelona and in the Basque country. It did not affect us directly. In Deyá, the villagers were virtually untouched by the regime. In Palma, the economy was improving and beggars, the most evident sign of poverty, had all but disappeared from the streets. There was little petty delinquency, and Palma streets at night were safe – even for young girls. Neither Mother nor Father ever talked Spanish politics. In a letter from Barcelona, getting his visa for the United States, Father wrote:

> Barcelona was fun. No taxis to be had because the trams are being 100% boycotted by the people – against rise in fares – since Monday. Not a soul in a tram except the conductor and the driver, looking very bored, and I saw one *guardia*. Nothing about it in the papers, of course, and no organizers showing themselves – just word of mouth. [RG to WG, 18 January 1957]

This was the closest to a political comment on Spain I remember his making. When he was asked point-blank about Franco, he answered that he was a guest in Spain and thus not qualified to give an opinion.

Tourism was the cause of this relative political freedom on the island. Towards the end of the Fifties, Franco replaced his old-guard Fascist ministers with young technocrats, with orders to bring Spain's standard of living into line with the rest of Europe. The new government decided to make mass tourism the powerhouse of the economy, and have Majorca and the Catalan 'Costa Brava' compete with the French and Italian Rivieras. Before the Civil War, Majorca had been a winter resort: a place to which doctors sent many patients with tuberculosis and other ailments for a 'rest in the sun'. With recently discovered penicillin, these visitors no longer came, and winter holidays in the sun went out of fashion. The island's first post-war attempt at attracting a new breed of tourists had been in the early Fifties, when the Majorcan Chamber of Tourism began advertising the island as a honeymooners' paradise. A remarkably successful poster of the time shows a montage of Palma's cathedral, a sprig of almond blossom, and deserted beaches. The newly formed Ministry of Tourism in Madrid now waged an aggressive international advertising campaign for the island, and opened Spanish tourist offices in the principal capitals of Europe.

From London, for instance, Majorca was in easy flying range. By controlling hotel prices, the government ensured that the island remained cheap. Tourists arrived in droves and, on the Palma beaches, hotels sprang up overnight to handle the influx. If an hotelier found himself overbooked, he put up an awning on the flat roof and made his guests sleep on mattresses there. Staff were brought over from the mainland, and Spanish was heard spoken on the street. At the end of the Civil War, the *Guardia Civil* had been entrusted with 'public morals': they could arrest a girl for wearing a bikini, or fine couples for kissing in public. Now, they were told to turn a blind eye to what foreigners were doing in the tourist areas. Nightclubs sprouted everywhere and the foxtrot and *mambo* reigned supreme.

Tourist complexes developed with little infrastructure and no consideration for the landscape. Planning permission in supposedly protected areas could be obtained, provided a high enough bribe was paid in the right place. Although unspoiled coast still stretched for miles, *urbanizaciones*, chalets and hotels began to crowd the beaches in the more accessible parts. Hard currency, brought in and changed at Spanish banks by tourists, was flown by the planeload to Madrid – to pay for imported steel works, cement factories and the new car-assembly plants.

Karl's means of transport over the previous few years had been typical of the best that was available at an affordable price. After we got our pre-war Renault, Karl bought a Vespa. In the Fifties, motorbikes and scooters, varying in size from the small Moto-Guzzi to the large Sanglas – designed for traffic police – became plentiful, and Karl's Vespa, made under licence in Spain, was the most popular of them all. At about the time we got our Land-rover, Karl bought a Biscuter, Spain's answer to the bubble car. It was a strange-looking conveyance. Indeed, I rode my bike straight into a bramble-filled torrent at my first sight of one. It had been cleverly engineered by the French car designer Voisin. As its name suggested it was a four-wheeled scooter with a bench seat for two, and was powered by a small Spanish-built Villiers two-stroke motorcycle engine with a 'pull start' and no reverse gear. The body was of aluminium with a burnished metal finish. It was fun to drive in the summer when it did not rain. However, its weatherproofing and suspension were poor, and Karl and the new middle classes of the *milagro económico* were ready for the Seat-600. When Fiat announced it, there was an immediate two-year waiting list. Karl's name was also on the list but, after waiting patiently for about a year, he asked Ricardo to pull some strings for him.

Everywhere on the island, there seemed to be roadworks. In Palma, streets were widened to take the new traffic. Tramlines were pulled up, and the friendly squeaking old trams replaced by diesel-belching buses. The road to Deyá was as yet untouched, but ever more cars and buses used it. When we first arrived in Deyá, the occasional taxi – like the one which ran me over – brought tourists to view the coast route. Now, every Monday and Thursday, droves of buses filled with them came up our road. The buses stopped at Valldemosa where the tourists were taken to see two rival cells in the ex-Carthusian monastery, with their respective pianos, both claiming to be Frederic Chopin's abode for the two damp winter months he spent with Georges Sand, in 1838, on a tuberculosis cure. The tourists were then taken to watch the Valldemosa folk-dance group. Afterwards the buses continued through Deyá towards Soller. They were so large they could hardly get round the bends; and slowly knocked over the nice round-backed dry-stone walls on the roadsides. Opposite Canellún they slowed down so tour guides could announce: 'At your left is olive tree of one thousand years old, at your right is house of famous English writer, Mister Robertson, who wrote *Me, Claudio.*'

Outwardly tourism did not appear to affect Deyá. There were, as yet, no package tours and buses did not stop in the village. Indirectly, however, it took its toll. Whereas in July and August the beach and the cafés were crowded, and I no longer knew everyone around, the number of young men living in the village decreased considerably. Some, like my friend Guillem of the Puig, or Toni's eldest brother Pedro, followed the wave of Spanish emigrants to England, Germany or France, to work as waiters and learn a foreign language. Others found jobs in the Palma hotels. As houses became empty, they were rented to *estrangers* who soon wanted to buy or build their own. It soon became difficult even to rent and Mother, when not being begged for a bed in the Posada or the cottage, was asked by friends – and even complete strangers – to find them a place to stay. The drain on Gelat's electric grid at night was such that only a glow now came from the light bulb filaments.

The four village hotels and pensions were doing nicely at the height of summer. An Englishman called Geoffrey Frampton opened a fifth at Ca'n Quet, a farmhouse opposite Ca'n Mado. He made his guests pay when they checked in, and then would not let them leave until their time was up. Someone coined the adage: *Ca'n Quet, Can't Get, Can't Quit*. When Frampton's five-year lease was up, the owners, Monsieur and Madame Coll, who had made their 'fortune' running a restaurant in Lyons, took over. The Colls built a pleasant bar and patio in the garden, served delicious meals in the restaurant and soon acquired a stolid French clientele for the Ca'n Quet rooms. Monsieur Pep Coll, a bald round man with cigar butt constantly in the corner of his mouth and a salacious sense of humour, would hurry and kill a squawking chicken if his pot-au-feu had run out. He drove to the Soller market in his Biscuter and would come back an hour or so later with a load of lettuces, potatoes, ice, and the carcass of a sheep strapped to the top. He had a diesel generator which, though rather noisy, made him independent of Gelet's grid. Monsieur Coll's love was his garden: he had brought his rose bushes from France and every evening he spent a happy hour, hose in hand, watering and pampering his plants. Ca'n Quet was to become very well known to me a few years later.

From the early Fifties on, Deyá gained a reputation for being an artists' colony, with Father as its doyen. Many English and

American writers came and went but, other than Father, perhaps only Alan Sillitoe and Kingsley Amis, both of whom were in Deyá for some months, became household names. A handful of painters and sculptors acquired international reputation. Jim Metcalf, who had just left the Deyá, represented the USA in the 'biennale' of Sao Paulo in 1959; Esteban Francés, a Catalan who had been a friend of Picasso in Paris, designed the set for Balanchine's *Don Quixote* in New York; Joan Junyer, who had spent his pre-war summers in Lluc Alcari, was highly regarded in America; the Italian Domenico Gnoli and the Israeli Mati Klarwein also sold well in New York. John Aldridge, who came for a few weeks every summer, had hung several of his Deyá paintings, including the one I had in my London digs, in the Royal Academy Summer Exhibition. Later he was commissioned by the National Portrait Gallery to paint Father's portrait. On a more local level, there was a group of young abstract artists on the island who exhibited under the name of *Es Deu des Teix* – The Ten of the Teix – about half of whom, including Bill Waldren, lived in Deyá.

Bill Waldren, no longer skating in *Holiday on Ice*, produced low-relief sand-covered canvas collages to which he, very effectively, attached beach flotsam. He began exploring the many caves around Deyá for bronze age pottery and implements. His initial digs were haphazard, carried out with little archaeological background or motivation; they were also strictly illegal. However, by the time the official archaeological body, the *Museo de Mallorca*, heard of his finds and sent someone to Deyá to investigate, the quality of Bill's digs had improved to such an extent that his recovery of artifacts, and reconstruction of pottery, were superior to the *Museo*'s. The *Museo* grudgingly agreed that he could continue his work provided they were given notice of any new discoveries. His digs further enhanced Deyá's reputation as an intellectual centre.

5

It was at Oundle that, for the first time, I became aware how much Father was a public figure: to my amazement, Chiggers offered me a chair in his sitting room to watch Father talk on television about his novel *They Hanged My Saintly Billy*. That same week I listened to him being interviewed on the wireless in

'Frankly Speaking'. I noticed that people I met expected some of Father's aura to cling to me. I would be presented as 'Robert Graves's son'.

'Meet Robert!' said others, anxious to introduce me, but forgetting my name.

'No, William,' I corrected, fighting hard to keep my own identity.

Requests for Father to lecture increased. Whenever it was possible, he took Mother and Tomás with him. In January 1959, the three of them went to Israel as guests of the Israeli Government and Prime Minister Ben-Gurion. In May 1960 they went to the State University of New York at Buffalo for the inauguration of the Robert Graves section in their Poetry/Rare Books Collections. Buffalo's had just bought all Father's poetry manuscripts. He never had any qualms about selling letters or manuscripts – before the War he sold his letters from T. E. Lawrence – and the Buffalo sale helped keep our school and college bills covered for another year.

On their way back from Buffalo, Father stopped off in London to be presented with the Foyle's Poetry Award (£250) at a luncheon at the Dorchester. Lucia, who had left school in Geneva, was now studying for her 'A' levels at the London French Lycée. Both she and I were invited, and were seated among Father's friends and relations at 'Top Table'. My uncles Richard and Charles Graves, and Richard's daughter, my cousin Diana, were there; as were James Reeves, Alan and Ruth Sillitoe, and our friend Kaye Webb, the publisher. Father sat between Christina Foyle – presenting the prize – and the actress Julie Andrews, and was flanked by a brace of ambassadors, Lords and Ladies. The press and lesser dignitaries were seated at other tables. I was next to Diana, of whom I was very fond. She had been an actress and played in the West End opposite the wonderful Peter Ustinov; but she now suffered from chronic bronchitis and emphysema and no longer worked. The food was dull and, as I looked around me, I quite agreed with her when she said in her rasping bronchial stage whisper: 'Darling William, isn't this a fucking bore!'

One Easter when I was at Canellún, Huw Weldon turned up with a BBC television crew to interview Father for his 'Monitor' programme. Unfortunately, the BBC had failed to arrange for the necessary papers, and Weldon's cameras and recording equipment were stuck at the airport, while lawyers and customs officials argued. In the meantime at Canellún, Mother made continual cups of tea for the crew as they crawled all over the house taking notes on the best times of day for natural lighting – Gelat's turbine had not the power to run their lights – and when, where and how they could best use the sun. It took four days for Customs to clear the equipment and, by then, Mother was out of tea.

Weldon decided to shoot one of the scenes – a tree buffeted by the hot summer wind, 'voiced over' by Father reading his poem 'Sirocco at Deyá' – in the village opposite the school. While I fanned dust in front of the rolling camera, Karl had climbed up a pomegranate tree and, hidden by the corner of the house, shook the branches so they swayed as if bent by the wind. In another shot which showed a shutter slamming in the wind, I helped by opening it with a stick, and closing it with a string. Later that morning, we went along the coast to Lluc Alcari to film waves crashing on the rocks; walking along the narrow cliff paths, the cameraman got vertigo, and had to be helped. Most of Father's interview, however, took place in his study. It was the best he ever did for television.

Father's fame attracted distant relations and their companions to Canellún. It seemed as though, all of a sudden, Father was expected to take care of a much-extended family. They wrote to Mother – or sometimes just showed up – demanding to be put up and fed. Often this meant that there was no room for Mother and Father's real friends whom they might have liked to invite. Mother dealt, apparently effortlessly, with the running of Canellún in summer. She still had only the Murciano twins to help, and it was a major task simply to provide food. I would lend a hand collecting people from the airport and driving them back and forth to Palma. At the same time, I thought nothing of inviting Po or Pedro to dinner, if they found themselves at a loose end.

What with all these comings and goings, although not always through any fault of our guests, the front gate was frequently left open at night. Mother and Father and I, with our bedrooms overlooking the vegetable garden, would be woken by the dreaded sound of sheep-bells below our window. Both Father and I would rush downstairs, hurriedly pulling on our trousers, to chase away the sheep before they ate Mother's dahlias and zinnias, or yanked out the peppers and the tomatoes.

Sheep in the garden was a minor crisis. One day my niece Antonia, Catherine's daughter from Australia, caused a fearful commotion. Catherine had recently been widowed, and Father made himself responsible for her children's education. Antonia had gone ahead of us to Ca's Floquer, carrying the basket with all our bathing suits. When we arrived at the *escar*, we found neither Antonia nor our basket. All of us were furious, but then we became concerned and finally extremely worried. Mother and Father returned to Canellún – Mother without having had her swim, Father having swum in his trousers – while Po and I searched for Antonia without success, checking all the ravines and caves into which she might have fallen. Two and a half hours later, she was found in tears, on the Soller road – without the basket. Mother, from whom I had never heard an unkind remark, said, 'Surely, even in Australia, you go downhill to reach the sea.'

Unannounced visitors, well-wishers, and the merely curious, were forever dropping in. We had no telephone, and people rarely bothered to send a note. They just ambled up our drive. If Mother or I were in the garden or on the *depósito* and saw strangers opening the gate, we would cut them off and ask them their business. Karl kept a low profile in Can Torrent, typing away, and would try not to get involved. Generally strangers made it to the kitchen door, and knocked, demanding to see Mr Graves. Mother would tell them to return in the late afternoon or, if she thought they might be interesting, to come back for tea. Indeed, in spite of his fame and the influx of guests, the Canellún routine had not changed significantly. Father still worked the same hours. He took his twenty-minute siesta after lunch, he collected his mail at the Old Café, he rushed down to the beach for a swim, he answered every one of his monumental pile of daily letters the same day. However, in the late Fifties, when Father began striking difficult patches in his work, he often left his study to turn over his compost heap, and think his ideas through.

Father had been introduced to composting by a friend of the early Palma days, Grete Schön, a Canadian anthropologist, and an expert on Eskimos. She had given Father some very special bacteria from Canada and these were still thriving in his compost heaps. He composted mostly with kitchen refuse, vegetable garden cuttings, lawn clippings, and windfall fruit such as tangerines or apricots after a *sirocco*. We kept two buckets under the washing-up sink, one for the compost and one for non-rotting matter such as tins and glass bottles – today's plastic bags and containers were still not around. When the heap was ready it was dug into the garden mixed with Isabela's manure, now her sole *raison d'être*. The compost heaps were Father's pride; each one was given the name of a friend. He brought visitors along to join him while he worked on it, much to their surprise.

One day a telegram arrived at the Town Hall, advising the mayor that His Excellency the Minister of Tourism was coming from Palma to visit *señor* Graves. The mayor, wishing to warn the *senyor*, dispatched the town crier – Guillem of the Puig's father – to Canellún; who found him at the compost heap wearing his downtrodden *espardenyas*, ink-stained shorts, and his shirt-tail hanging out over them.

'So what?' Father said. 'He's coming to see me, I'm not going to see him.' The town crier reported to the mayor that he had left Don Roberto still turning his compost heap with a pitchfork. At that moment, the sirens of the minister's motorcycle outriders shattered the silence, and the two black cars carrying the minister and his entourage sped through the village on their way to Canellún. This affair was later much discussed in the cafés. The villagers were not sure whether Father's reception of Franco's minister, in *espardenyas* and shorts, was a sign of madness; or of seigneurial style approaching that of the *Arxiduc*; or both.

6

In the autumn of 1957 Lucia and Juan were at school in Switzerland and, with all three of us now boarding, Mother and Father and Tomás moved back to Deyá to live permanently in Canellún. Of the Palma flats, they gave up the one on the *primero*, but kept the one on the *segundo* as a pied-à-terre. Mother found it a shock not to spend her winters in the relative luxury to which she had become accustomed. At Canellún, the open fireplaces smoked so badly that a cast-iron Salamander had been installed in the dining room; however, the flue went straight up the chimney and so did most of the heat. Father had his brazier in the workroom; the fumes it gave off could be noxious – in unventilated bedrooms they were a common cause of death. Mother cooked on temperamental charcoal stoves, too small to hold the heat, and forever going out if not kept topped up and fanned back to life. Only occasionally would she get a smuggled bottle of Calor Gas from our yachting friends to feed a two-burner cooker which Father had bought before the War. Our coal-burning oven, which was supposed to heat up the Canellún water, had never worked properly. For baths Father still heated two large cauldrons of water on the charcoal stove – as he had done when living with Laura more than twenty years before – a process that took two hours. In the bathtub, the hot water hardly covered the backs of my knees.

As money at last came in faster than it went out for our education, Mother decided on a few improvements. She had Canellún's chimneys and fireplaces rebuilt so that they drew properly. Instead of the enormous pre-War ice-chest in the cellar, in which we could keep only meat, butter and milk, Mother installed a large American paraffin-burning Frigidaire in the kitchen. Her greatest delight, however, was a coal-fired Aga cooking range, which also provided us with plenty of hot water. Father wrote to me:

> Mother is poised over the Aga which makes the most wonderful sausage rolls in Christendom – Jews and Moslems of course aren't allowed to compete. [RG to WG, October 1958]

She had Father bring back a battery-powered Zenith Transoceanic short-wave radio from America so that she could listen to the BBC World Service every morning. Mother also sold our canvas-top Land-rover, and bought a new pale green hard-top with a better heater.

Now Mother was at Canellún all the time, she had more time to manage the garden. The hardest chore was to prevent our gardener, Castor the Postman, from digging up any young plants he did not recognize and planting potatoes in their stead. One of her achievements was her bermuda-grass lawn next to the *depósito*; it was one of the first on the island. However, Mother's greatest gardening success was her sweetcorn, the seed of which she asked friends to bring over from America every year. To eat corn on the cob was one of our treats in summer.

Blackie's descendants were still about, but Mother also had two pedigree Abyssinian cats, two miniature poodles and, later, a slow loris. Mother had seen an Abyssinian when visiting the Guinnesses in England and had bought one in about 1959. Her first Abyssinian tom was a beautiful creature with a long pedigree, soon to be joined by an equally pedigreed female. These cats produced many litters and, over the years, changed the feline gene-pool in Deyá. Even today Abyssinian throwbacks can be seen roaming the village. The miniature poodles were the result of Juan's love of the Palma telephone – he used to order *ensaïmadas* without Mother knowing. One day in about 1955 some acquaintances rang to ask whether Mother would like one of their puppies, and Juan said she would. Y'Grec was brought to our door. Later Y'Grec had Jotie. The slow loris was given to her by Ken Tynan. Mother kept Ralphie in the room above the kitchen which always had the heat of the Aga in winter; he moved sluggishly around the curtains. Although he was very sweet to look at, he did not like being picked up, so was not much of a pet. Possibly a juvenile when he arrived, the second winter Ralphie became aggressive, and would bite; he tore the curtains to shreds and made a nest out of them; he emitted an overpowering sex-smell. Mother had to give him to the Barcelona zoo; it took years for the smell to go away.

One result of living in a considerably easier-to-run Canellún, with only Tomás to look after, was that Mother once again had time for herself – at least in winter. I had begun learning Russian at Oundle, but had given it up after a year. Mother took my *Assimil* books and records and, as she had taught herself Spanish, she once again got down to it. Mother was always fascinated by Russia, and all things Soviet; and dearly wanted to visit Moscow. She had held strongly egalitarian ideals since she was at Oxford, and was never happy about having servants. Indeed, after the Carrillo twins left, she had her new 'maid' Maria eat at table with us – even when visited by a somewhat perplexed British ambassador.

7

In 1959 Father said I could buy myself a second-hand car in England. I found a 1953 model soft-top Morris Minor. It was black with red real leather seats. In winter, though draughty around the canvas top, its heater kept me comfortable; in summer, especially in Deyá, I drove with the top down. Because of its licence number, YMM 664, Father called it my 'Young Man's Misery'.

In the Christmas and Easter vacations, when I did not have the Morris in Deyá, Mother let me use the Canellún Land-Rover to go down to Palma and see my friends. Po was now training for the Spanish Merchant Navy in the Palma college; Pedro worked in his father's leather goods shop; Teddy was studying architecture in Zurich. We met most evenings at the Bar El Quijote where the barman kept two guitars. Our repertoire now included songs by the Kingston Trio, Spanish *Tuna* songs – those sung by university students in medieval costume – and a variety of numbers Po, Teddy and I had picked up on our travels. We spent more time discussing chord sequences and tuning the guitars than singing. However, the other patrons seemed to enjoy it, bought us quite a few drinks, and did not seem to notice that we rarely finished a song properly.

In summer, Ca'n Quet was our main evening haunt. It had a dance floor, a record player – run on Pep Coll's generator – and we took along our own records. We drank *Cuba-Libres* – rum-and-coke – named after Fidel Castro, or *Lumumbas* – Laccao and brandy – named after Patrice Lumumba, the black-African politician. On weekdays, when fewer people were around, Po and I would play the guitar, and Monsieur Coll would make us his special *Cuba-Libres* with *caña* – the local grape spirit – instead of rum. On Saturday nights the terrace was crowded, especially if Monsieur Coll had hired a band or *Los Valldemosa* came to play. As during the Deyá fiesta, these events were announced by letting off loud fireworks in the sky above the village. On those nights a whole group of us would go, and I would ferry Lucia, Juan and my friends in my 'Young Man's Misery'.

One Saturday, Pedro had come up on his new Vespa and he was in a clowning mood. Staying in Canellún was Cherina, a sixteen-year-old friend of Lucia's from her Geneva school, whose parents lived in Nigeria. Just as we were ready to go to Ca'n Quet, Cherina felt unwell and fainted. She had been laughing with the rest so we thought she was acting and joining in the fun. We loaded her into the 'Young Man's Misery', took her to Ca'n Quet, carried her up the steps to the terrace and laid her on a table. When she came to, we realized it was not a joke, and that she was ill. I drove her back to Canellún – leaving Mother to get her to bed and call the doctor in the morning.

Po and I were always welcome at the Villa Verde, a pension by the convent-school on the Puig. In the 1920s it had been known as the Hotel Turismo but had closed about the time Father arrived with Laura. Nan, a white-haired Scots lady, reopened it and catered for groups of secretaries from Manchester and Birmingham in the summer months. The Villa Verde had a large open terrace, a vine arbour, and a picturesque wellhead surrounded by geranium flowerpots. Nan supplied us with drink if we played the guitar. It was with one of the young English girls – and I regret that I remember nothing about her, except that she was blonde – that I lost my virginity.

In retrospect, Deyá parties seem nothing extraordinary but, in those pre-hippy, pre-drug-scene days, they set a trend. There were no formal invitations. The word got around in the café and people simply turned up with their friends and brought a bottle of wine or Fundador brandy: horrendous sangrias were concocted. Parties generally included food, and began quite early since it was easier to eat in daylight than by candlelight. Gelat's electricity would not run record players, so there was no loud music. Po and I played the guitar and sang; or Mati beat his bongo-drums; or someone else recited poems. After supper on the terrace or in the garden by moonlight, discussions about Eisenhower, the Bomb, the Sputnik or the Pill, were quite coherent until the sangria made itself felt.

The villagers, though often kept awake in summer by our parties, seldom complained about the noise we made. But, listening and watching through the slats of the closed shutters, they knew exactly who was where, and when. They could always tell when I had had too much to drink; or was singing too loudly with Po; or had stayed out until four in the morning with a girl. Next day, when they saw me, I could be sure that someone would make a snide remark:

'That Guillem of Canellún was sowing his oats again last night . . .'

'Just so long as he doesn't have to harvest them!'

Every once in a while, there was a really memorable party. Mati gave one at the Cala. Preparations began early. As the last of the bathers on the beach were gathering their towels, Bill Waldren and I arrived bearing a lamb each on our shoulders, as well as a couple of curtain-rails as spits. Bill's girlfriend, Jackie, carried a basket with the baste – olive oil, brandy, rosemary and bay leaves. Bill and I collected driftwood and soon got the two fires going. While we waited for the embers to form, I had a swim in the calm warm water, now completely in the shade. The beach was deserted and silent, apart from the crackle of the fire. There was not even a rustle of undertow on the fine pebbly shoreline. I swam breaststroke, trying not to leave a ripple on the smooth peaceful surface, on which floated an occasional drift of pine pollen from the woods above. Turning on to my back, I looked up at the Teix, now drenched purple and pink by the setting sun, silhouetted against a blue cloudless sky. With the crowds gone, this was still the paradise I loved.

We stuck the lambs on the spits, set them over the embers and Bill began turning and basting them. Soon others came down the hill carrying baskets laden with wine, salads and fruit. I went up to the restaurant terrace, which Mati had rented for the evening, to help set up the tables. There the *Patrón* lit the *Petromax* lamp, which he normally used to catch *calamar* at night, showed us how to maintain pressure in it, locked his hut, and left for home in the village and an undisturbed night's sleep.

It was now dusk and the aroma of the roasting lamb drifted up to the terrace. Bill moved from fire to fire, dancing among the boulders, turning each spit, basting the meat, occasionally swigging the bottle of brandy. He was a bull of a man with close-cropped hair, broad shoulders, large biceps and slim waist; 'El Capitán', standing on the terrace, remarked that the scene was straight out of Greek mythology. Mati arrived with his bongos, dressed in his usual spotless white. Po came down with Lucia and Cherina. Jimmy d'Aulignac and the rest of the *estrangers* arrived in ones and twos. Mother and Father would have known about the party, but they rarely attended large gatherings. Father disliked late nights, since he was up and at work by eight every morning; and Mother had her hands full with keeping Canellún running, even when fully rested.

We all drank sangria, and waited for Bill to tell us the lambs were ready; then Po and I helped him carry both spits up to the terrace. The meat was so tender it peeled off the bones. After supper, Mati played the bongos and Cherina, now fully recovered from her faint, began a shuffling, foot-stamping, African dance. She went on and on, getting faster and faster, as if in a trance. All of us were moved by the beauty of it: Po thought he was in love. Nothing could follow the magic of Cherina's performance so, the beach now bathed in moonlight, we all went down for a skinny-dip. Po sat close to Cherina, so soon I decided to go home. Taking a bottle of gin, I walked back up the hill, and met the *Guardia Civil* patrol coming down on their rounds. I stopped them and offered them a drink. I kept them talking for half an hour: enough to allow those skinny-dipping time to get dressed.

This way of life I took completely for granted: my birthright, not from being Father's son, but from having grown up in Deyá. An experience similar to living in Deyá during those summers of the late Fifties and early Sixties is depicted in Fellini's *La Dolce Vita*. Ours was no film.

8

In 1958 Margot Callas, a young Canadian divorcée of Greek/Irish extraction, who lived in Ibiza, came to Deyá in answer to an advertisement by Geoffrey Frampton for a barmaid at Ca'n Quet – she gave the job up after a day. Margot was a strikingly beautiful young woman, with a classical profile, raven-black hair, grey-blue eyes and porcelain complexion. The *estrangers* were soon fighting among themselves over her. Mac, 'El Capitán', driving her one day from Palma, made some irritable remark about Mati, and Margot told him to stop the car. She got out, and Mac drove off, 'burning rubber', leaving her in the middle of the road to Vall-demosa. Mac stopped for a drink at Ca'n Quet, then drove on into Deyá, still fuming with rage. Having a drink on the New Café terrace was Margot, smiling serenely at Mati, whom she had seen following them in a taxi.

In September Margot returned to her house in Ibiza but she came back to Deyá the following year, when Mati asked her to star in an 8mm film he was making. The film had a murder plot: Margot was its heroine, and a quiet American writer called Brad Rising was its hero; Bill Waldren and other friends of Mati's were supporting actors. The denouement had Margot, bare-breasted, finding the victim's skull in Father's compost heap. Margot and Mati came to Canellún to shoot her scene with Father. Both

Father. Both Mother and Father liked her at once and, as Father had done with Judith, he began writing poems inspired by her. Margot was full of romantic ideals and aims, and used to being the centre of attention. She projected all the qualities Father attributed to his White Goddess: beauty, intelligence, integrity, humour, independence, disdain for his attentions. But the Muse's spirituality Father provided himself. Some of Father's old friends disapproved of Margot, especially James Reeves, remembering perhaps Father's besottedness with Laura and worrying about the potential disruption of Canellún. As with Judith, the villagers were shocked.

'Did you see the *senyor* with that vixen on his arm? Mark my words, Maria, we haven't seen the last of his little trollops!' was said at the washing-troughs.

I do not know what Mother really felt about Margot as Father's Muse. She knew what Father had written in *The White Goddess*, in 1948, perhaps thinking of her: that something in a poet dies when

> he has lost his sense of the White Goddess: the woman
> whom he took to be a Muse, or who was a Muse, turns
> into a domestic woman and would have him turn simi-
> larly into a domestic man. Loyalty prevents him from
> parting company with her, especially if she is the
> mother of his children and is proud to be reckoned as a
> good housewife; and as the Muse fades out, so does
> the poet. [*The White Goddess*, Faber & Faber (1948),
> p. 394]

By outwardly ignoring the situation, however, Mother allowed Father to have a Muse without 'parting company'. It helped that she both liked and admired Margot. Indeed, when Father received a proposal for making a film version of *The White Goddess*, Mother, who had just seen Mati's film, insisted that Margot should play the Goddess. Mother and Margot remained good friends for many years after Margot's Musedom had ended.

At the time I had little sense that there was anything but a meeting of minds between Father and Margot. I felt no tension. Perhaps there was none. Everybody liked Margot. She had a great sense of fun. In 1960 she acted in 'Lawrence and the Wet-backs, a Musical Farrago', the birthday-party play. Mati played Lawrence of Arabia, and Margot his assistant, *La Dinamitera*. She strutted around the stage letting off firecrackers and sang the Roedean School Song. When Lucia went to the Soller Fiestas, Margot lent her dresses. She now stayed at Ca'n Quet, which had been taken over by the Colls. Margot had a fine ear for languages, and spoke fluent *Ibizenco*, which is very close to Majorcan. She had us all in stitches imitating Mme Coll screeching at her waiter.

In early 1961 the Margot affair, which resulted in a steady stream of 'Muse' poems, took an unexpected turn. Father had arranged for Margot and Alastair Reid to sail back on a liner from New York to prepare for the filming of *The White Goddess*. During the leisurely cruise the inevitable happened and Margot and Alastair went off together to live in the French Basses-Pyrénées. Of the film no more was heard. The sudden desertion turned Father violently against Alastair whom he described in a poem as a

> . . . witty devil,
> The arch intriguer who walks disguised
> In a poet's cloak, his gay tongue oozing evil.
> ['Beware, Madam']

Father's fierce reaction took both Margot and Alastair by surprise. Father did not blame Margot: as a Muse she had behaved in character, and certainly did not allow him to lose his sense of the White Goddess. She was back in Deyá that autumn, and the 'Muse' poetry to her continued for some time. Alastair he certainly did blame. Though Alastair wrote to Father, trying to make him understand that nothing between them had changed, Father never forgave his once close confidant. He forbade us even to mention Alastair's name. Naturally this upset me, Alastair having been my friend for so long. However, when Father turned against someone, he could become quite irrational, and I did not then have the courage to challenge him.

9

In my last year at Imperial College there were not many geology-related jobs on offer. I was invited to join an Imperial and

Birkbeck Colleges expedition to Jan Mayen Island, in the Arctic Circle, led by Dr Frank Fitch of Birkbeck, when the exams were over. My friend David Kinsman was going, so I accepted, hoping that the trip might look good on my CV. I was kitted out with special boots, gloves, parkas and thermal underwear, and bought a seaman's bag to put it all in. The expedition's five graduate students left for Jan Mayen in May; we undergraduates were to join them at the beginning of July, after our final exams.

I scraped a Lower Second and came back to Deyá for a week's break, before leaving for Jan Mayen. I was at Canellún when the news of the accident came over the BBC. Frank Fitch and the graduate students had been motoring in a dinghy up the coast of Jan Mayen when a freak gust of wind off one of the glaciers capsized their boat. They were a couple of minutes' swim from the shore but, in trying to retrieve their gear, all five students got hypothermia and drowned. Only Frank Fitch, protected by middle-age fat, managed to scramble ashore. When the news broke in England, my name was in the *Evening Standard* among the list of those missing. Father's friend Tom Matthews at once wrote a letter of condolence to my parents. He had posted it before my name was omitted in the next edition of the newspaper. Father answered him:

> I'm sorry you had a bad turn about Wm. The news of the Jan Mayen disaster gave me a shock too, although I knew he was safe: I have never got over David's death at the same sort of age. [RG to TSM, 5 June 1961]

Frank Fitch returned to England, and I expected the second phase of the expedition to be cancelled. Instead, it was reorganized under a new leader, whom I did not know. This seemed a sufficient excuse to back out – for I had just been offered by Jake L. Hamon, a Texas oil-millionaire friend of Ricardo Sicré's and a great admirer of Father's, the chance of spending one year in Texas learning the oil business.

CHAPTER VIII

1

I flew down to Dallas on the Monday arranged, took a cab to the Vaughn Building, and caught the elevator to the fifth floor, bags, guitar and all. The pretty girl at the reception desk looked somewhat surprised, but Jake Hamon came out and we shook hands.

'Hi, Bill,' he smiled. 'Come into my office.'

'William,' I said. It had been a constant fight to keep my given name ever since I reached America.

2

In September 1961 I landed at Idlewild Airport, New York: my first impression of the USA was not encouraging.

'Hey, buddy, where're you goin', who're you goin' to see, what for?' demanded the Immigration officer aggressively.

'Jake Hamon, in Texas, for a holiday,' and gave them Jake's letter inviting me. I was on a 'Non-Immigrant' visa, and was not supposed to work. I was held up for a nail-biting hour until they had received a telex from Jake confirming this. Then Customs opened my bags. On trips to Deyá when I was at college, I became used to requests from Mother and Father to bring odd things such as a spare carburettor for the Land-rover, or the latest Shadows record for Lucia, or a Rolls Viscount shaver for Karl, or 2 lbs of Earl Grey tea for themselves; and on my trips back to London to requests to deliver a leather jacket from Pedro's shop, an earthenware cooking-pot, or a bottle of Deyá olive oil. I discovered the best way to get through United Kingdom Customs was to carry a guitar in its bag. It was still a reasonably uncommon sight and when the officer made me open up the guitar he seemed to lose interest in the rest of my luggage. However, at Idlewild this ploy did not work. The officer tried to peer into the guitar's soundbox.

'Hey, buddy, take 'em strings off so's I can feel inside. Or I'll use the scissors.' It was Labour Day weekend and they had to work, but still . . . Then he worked through my other bags, found my precious Deyá *sobrasada* and put it in the bin destined for incineration.

'Raw meat ain't allowed,' he said.

Somewhat depressed, I walked out of the airport building into a grey muggy afternoon and caught the bus downtown. The driver of the taxicab I took at the terminal claimed not to understand my English and then insisted the address I wanted in Greenwich Village did not exist. He grumbled when I showed it to him on his map.

Len Lye opened the door and my spirits lifted. In his sixties, slim and agile, Len had a strikingly bald bullet-shaped head, a pair of wire-rimmed glasses perched on top, and an enquiring smile.

'I'm William,' I announced.

'Come in, Bill. Good flight? How are Robert and Beryl?' Len was a New Zealand sculptor, and a very old friend of Father's. Laura and Father had met him in the Twenties. He had designed the jacket for the first edition of Father's *Goodbye to All That*; and Len's first wife, Jane, had typed the manuscript. Len lived in Deyá while Canellún was being built, and three of his superb silk batiks still hung on our walls.

The two weeks during which I stayed with Len and his second wife Anne were meant by Father to be an 'acclimatization' to the USA. Len and Anne showed me around Greenwich Village, where the first hippies were becoming a tourist attraction. They took me to the White Horse pub, where Dylan Thomas had drunk himself to death – with its cobweb-covered ceilings and sawdust-covered floors, it was not unlike the old *tapa* bars in the backstreets of Palma. We ate at the Museum of Modern Art, and saw Len's 'kinetic sculptures' which were on exhibition there. Len and I drove his VW van to his plot of land in New Jersey and we spent the night in a caravan. The next morning, we drove to a small hardware store to get stakes, wire netting and nails, to build a fence.

Wherever I went – be it London, Paris, New York – everyone wanted to know about Deyá. As we hammered in the stakes, Len talked about the shapes of the boulders on the Cala and the face he had carved on one of them – a face with one ear. I recognized his description at once. It was still in Canellún in a corner of the pressroom. I had not known it was his. Canellún was so full of objects: Len's batiks and stone, John Aldridge's paintings, the furniture we sat on and the table we ate at, even the old Brunswick records we listened to on the wind-up gramophone; each had its place in the Laura-and-Robert history of which I was only vaguely aware. Len began telling me about the beautiful printing Laura, Robert and he had done together on the Albion Press.

'Tell me about Laura,' I asked. For the first time in my life I felt that I should know something about this woman whose presence still seemed to pervade Canellún. Len, however, did not reply; as if unwilling to talk about someone with whom he had broken; as if the very mention of her name would put him back in Laura's power.

In New York I saw several friends from Deyá, including Ralph Jacobs. Ralph, a school teacher and a comedian *manqué* – the privy by the church in Deyá, he called the 'Pope's John' – was more Mother's friend than Father's. Indeed, the slow loris was named after him. Ralph came every summer, and had brought back one of Mother's Abyssinian kittens, now fully grown. In Deyá he seemed so much in his element that I found it strange to see him, wearing a tie, at his school of Puerto-Ricans in the Bronx. To Ralph, and indeed to many *estrangers*, the two-month summer holiday in Deyá was far more real than the life they led during the remainder of the year. It became a drug they could not do without. Ralph spent the winter planning his next visit to Deyá; and remembering past summers. Even his Abyssinian cat gave him a feeling of continuity from one year to the next. We all suffered to some extent from the Deyá syndrome.

3

Jake L. Hamon had left college after the first year, when his father died. The only job he knew was oil-well drilling, in which he had worked during the summer holidays, so he returned to it. He talked to geologists and engineers and, when he thought he knew enough to take the gamble, put all his savings into drilling a well; luckily he hit oil. A pleasant, calm and intelligent man, he had been the youngest director ever of the American Petroleum

Institute. Now in his late fifties, he was a successful independent oil producer, with comfortable reserves of oil in the ground, and much respected in the business.

What made Jake different from the other oil-men was his love of books. He read one a day, and most of Father's were in his library. He and Father had met when Ricardo Sicré had invited them both to the *Feria de Sevilla* for the bullfights. They corresponded, and when Father mentioned I was taking geology at College, Jake wrote back: 'Send him to me, and I'll teach him the Texas oil business!' Father took him at his word.

The evening of my arrival, Jake invited me for dinner at his home on the outskirts of Dallas. We drove in his enormous air-conditioned Lincoln Continental limousine to a district of tree-covered winding lanes, and up a short driveway to the back of his two-storey house.

'Go into the library. I'll call Nancy,' Jake said.

His colonial furniture gleamed; so did the brass reading lamps. The walls were lined to the ceiling with books – far more than at Canellún. Deep in a soft leather sofa, I sipped whisky from a cut-glass tumbler as Jake, a long blond Havana in his mouth, questioned me about life in Deyá; and Nancy, his brunette wife, passed around canapés. Though deceptively quiet, she had studied palaeontology and been in a dance troupe before marrying Jake. I liked her a lot. When we went into the oak-panelled dining room for dinner, what fascinated me was that Jake's bookcase on wheels – holding his *Encyclopaedia Britannica*, *Webster's Dictionary* and *The Times Atlas* – was pushed in with us so that any possible query at table could be solved at once. I thought of the times Father or Mother rose from table at Canellún, and went to the workroom to check on something; or else they sent me to collect a heavy tome of the *Britannica* or the *Oxford English Dictionary*. The polished table was loaded with silverware sparkling in the candlelight. Only once before had I experienced such luxury: when Father had taken me to look at Oundle as a prospective school and we had visited Miriam Rothschild, the entomologist. On that occasion Juan had thrown a tantrum: his under-plate was not gold like ours, but silver; he demanded a *pa amb oli*, a slice of bread and olive oil. Although the meal at Jake's was excellent, I too would have been just as happy with a real *pa amb oli*.

Jake kept me in Dallas for a couple of months and, quite soon, I picked up the oil-field jargon. When he thought I had an overview of his business, Jake sent me to his regional offices in Ardmore, Corpus Christi, Midland, Amarillo and Abilene. I was taught to correlate well logs, read seismic sections, and contour depth-of-strata and thickness-of-strata maps; I was taken to see wells being drilled; I was sent on courses on core analysis and well log interpretation. Slowly I became more than just a trainee: I was beginning to be of some help to Jake's company.

On weekends at the regional offices, I scouted around in my VW Beetle. From Ardmore, a small southern Oklahoma town in the foothills of the Arbuckle mountains, I took a trip through New Mexico to Santa Fé for two days skiing; from Corpus Christi, on the Gulf Coast – it was fearfully cold – I went to a bullfight in Reynosa, Mexico, and admired the pink grapefruit plantations in the Rio Grande valley; from Midland I visited the Carlsbad Caverns in New Mexico; from Amarillo I drove six hundred miles west, stopping only to see the Painted Desert, the Fossil Forest and the Meteor Crater, until I reached the Grand Canyon in Arizona – there I walked the twenty-four-mile trail down to the bed of the Colorado river and back up again. I went to rodeos, college football and drag racing. I learned to shoot a revolver by firing at tin cans while we waited at the oil rig for the drill-bit to reach 'pay-dirt'. I picked pecans, went fishing, saw wild turkeys. I surveyed the ravages of Hurricane Carla, and sheltered in a basement from a tornado. In Dallas I was taken to listen to Andrés Segovia in concert; in Abilene to dance to Country and Western music; in Nuevo Laredo, on the Mexican side of the Rio Grande, to see a mind-stopping floor-show in a brothel – I had not realized the female body was capable of such prowess.

Since I was kept moving from office to office, however, I made few friends, and spent many lonely evenings in cheap hotels, watching television or reading a book.

4

Deyá was never far from my mind. Since there was no telephone at Canellún, we wrote; and on Christmas Day and birthdays we exchanged telegrams. In one of Father's first letters he told me about the drought in Deyá. The oak trees on the flanks of the Teix were turning brown; the springs were running dry. The situation became so critical that Don Pedro the Priest said a Mass for rain and had reluctantly allowed the desperate villagers to carry the statue of Christ in procession to Lluc Alcari. That same afternoon, unaware of the procession and of each other, Bill Waldren performed an American Indian rain dance, and Father opened the water-valve, stood astride the flowing Canellún irrigation ditch, and tinkled his West African rain-bell. All were caught in the thunderstorm that followed.

Lucia took her 'A' levels at the French Lycée in London and did well but, to Mother and Father's disappointment, she decided against College, and went to Madrid to learn steno-typing instead. She and Stella Reeves shared a flat. Stella had taken a teaching job with the British Council there. Lucia wrote how much she enjoyed her course and told me the Morris Minor, which she inherited when I left – now re-christened 'Young Maiden's Modesty' by Father – was going well. But steno-typing must have been boring, for soon Father wrote:

> Lucia is having a shot at Oxford, after all . . . . St Anne's is the choice. Students aren't allowed to marry which may be a good thing. [RG to WG, January 1962]

Lucia was accepted by St Anne's – Mother's former College – and Father was delighted. His disapproval of Lucia's boyfriend Ramón Farrán, a young Catalan jazz drummer, soon passed.

I found the public libraries in Texas excellent and I read a lot. In answer to my query about Freud, Father replied:

> Freud: yes, it is interesting to know what he is all about so that you can laugh at it all. In America he's still current. In England he's exploded (among the top people at least) and gradually vanishing. It was a fad like the 18th century habit of putting cows in bedrooms so that women could be healed by their sweet breaths. To be psycho-analyzed is to have Freud planted in you: and you yourself die. [RG to WG, February 1962]

As a young poet, Father had been interested in Freud's theories, and the result was a book called *The Meaning of Dreams*, in which Father examines the relationship between poetic thought and dreams. He vehemently believed that psychoanalysis destroys poetry. I caught up on some of Father's other books, which I had not so far read, and was rather confused by his *The White Goddess*. With Margot obviously in mind, he wrote:

> *The White Goddess* is a crazy book. She represents the unpredictable natural woman, wholly uninhibited by male honour or conscience or intellect but with extraordinary (call them magical) powers: without whom this world would be a dull world indeed. The poet is the intermediary. Something like that. A Muse is a woman who has these powers; almost always they destroy her in the end, the world being what it is. [RG to WG, February 1962]

At this time Margot and Alastair were living in London. Their situation had not changed, and Father was still 'concerned' about her – willing her to be 'true to herself'.

Having found Father's *Collected Poems* in a library, I tried to read them, but I found that I could not separate his voice from the poem. The poems were mostly about love, and I failed to find in them a disembodied White Goddess; instead I found embarrassingly intimate portrayals of Mother, Judith or Margot.

THE STARRED COVERLET

A difficult achievement for true lovers
Is to lie mute, without embrace or kiss,
Without a rustle or a smothered sigh,
Basking each in the other's glory.

Let us not undervalue lips or arms
As reassurances of constancy,
Or speech as necessary communication
When troubled hearts go groping through the dusk;

Yet lovers who have learned this last refinement –
To lie apart, yet sleep and dream together

Motionless under their starred coverlet –
Crown love with wreaths of myrtle.

It was many years before I could read Father's poems without
wondering 'did they or didn't they?'

5

In June 1962, after the round of Jake's regional offices, I was back
in Dallas. Jake offered me a job after a short holiday. Had I
accepted his offer, I might have stayed with him for a while and
then perhaps joined a larger oil company to work in the Middle
East; slowly making my way up through the company hierarchy.
In short, my life would have taken a very different direction.
However, the novelty of Texas had worn off, and the desire to get
back to my *roqueta* and Deyá was strong.

When I told Jake that I would prefer to find work in Europe, he
was most understanding, and had his secretary send my curriculum vitae to a few oil companies with affiliates there whose main
offices I visited in New York on the trip home. Other than in a
one-room apartment which I rented in Ardmore, I had lived in
cheap hotels, and motels, for almost a year.

CHAPTER IX

1

The Barcelona Ferry docked punctually in Palma harbour at eight in the morning; I folded down the top of my sparkling new cream-coloured VW Karmann-Ghia cabriolet, drove down the ramp, and straight up to Deyá. Rounding the bend above Deyá, where the whole coast comes into view, I stopped, just as we had done on the day of our arrival in 1946. That image of the coast had kept coming back to me while I was in Texas; perhaps Father had held on to the same image in England during the War. I got out of the car, sat on a limestone outcrop, lit a cigarette, and let the silence envelop me. The sea was like a millpond; a slight haze covered the horizon. I could see one of the shrimp boats making for Puerto Soller, the slow thump of its two-stroke diesel quite distinct until it rounded the promontory. Across the valley, a stick-like figure in Son Bujosa, probably the *amo*, was digging the watercourses around the orange trees with a hoe. The metallic striking of the hoe was out of phase with the action: the sound reached me when it was already at the top of its next swing. Sheep bells clanked lazily, somewhere to my right. I could see Canellún – all but the dining-room shutters were closed. Father would already be in his workroom.

Driving slowly downhill, under the large umbrella pine and over the bulge its roots made beneath the tarmac, I could anticipate every bump and hole in the road before I came to it; then uphill into Deyá, the Puig to my left and the Teix towering over me to my right; past the public *rentaderos* – where the women looked up from their laundry and began chattering excitedly among themselves as they recognized me; past the New Café terrace, which was still empty; past the narrow steep stone steps leading to the Fonda; then out of the village through the olive groves, until I reached the green wooden gate leading into Canellún. I opened the gate and drove up the drive, past Mother's

Land-rover and my old Morris Minor, to the kitchen door. Both Mother and Father came out to welcome me. I muttered a greeting, trying to keep stupid tears of emotion back, and carried my bags up to my room.

'Lucia! Juan! Tomás! William's here!' shouted Mother.

Shrieks of 'Where? Where?' and then the familiar hollow sound as one of the Oregon pine doors slammed shut. I lay briefly on the welcoming cool blue cotton bedspread, testing the friendly smells of my room: the linseed oil on the furniture, the whitewash on the walls, the clean starchy bedclothes. In the watercolour of the farmyard, on the wall over my table, the brown and white cow on the yellow hay was still chewing her cud. In the painting of the pink house behind the cabbage patch, on the wall over the chest of drawers, the 'hanging man' I had imagined as a child seemed glad to have me back. I blew my nose.

'Did you find any oil?' asked Tomás, now nine years old, as I gave him the cowboy belt which I had bought in downtown Abilene, and on which I had had his name embossed. We were having breakfast on the front porch. Gabriel the Baker must have just come by, because at the centre of the table lay a plate of oven-warm *ensaïmadas*, and a new loaf of brown peasant bread on the bread board. There was a pot of Father's home-made Seville orange marmalade, with a wasp creeping up towards it, and a plateful of yellow plums from our tree. I could still make out the rhythmic sound of the farmer's hoe which I had heard on the other side of the valley. Did they really want to be told about Texas? What was there to tell, after all? Anything that happened beyond these hills, outside this valley, away from this breakfast table, seemed utterly meaningless – now I was home.

'Yes, I was on an oil rig, and we found oil,' I replied. 'Hold on, while I go upstairs to get some photos.'

After breakfast, I went into Father's study to give him his present. The room had not changed. His table littered with papers; the ink-pot and its special smell; the book-lined walls; the chests full of manuscripts; the Chippendale chair he always sat in. When I had stopped at Albuquerque on my trip to Santa Fé, I had found, among the tourist trash sold by Navajo Indians, a small bear made of turquoise with a leather thong tying a flint arrowhead to it. The figure was worn and slightly chipped, the turquoise a dirty pale green – not the deep blue turquoise the tourists liked – and the leather thong was old and greasy.

'I brought you this, Father. It has *baraka*.'

Baraka is a Sufi concept Father had taken from Idries Shah. In the mid-Fifties, Idries, an Afghan of royal descent, had been studying the influence of Sufic thought during the English Middle Ages and, on a visit to the island, had called on Father. Later, Father had written the introduction to Idries' book *The Sufis*, and persuaded Doubleday to publish it in America. Since Alastair's dismissal, they had become close friends. Now Father bounced his ideas off Idries instead; however, these often came back with a slightly Eastern quality. According to Idries, both people and objects can have *baraka*. In people, it is the supernatural quality they assume, the infallibility they enjoy, if they are 'true to themselves'. In objects, *baraka* is the magical quality these acquire with age and loving use.

I had kept the turquoise bear with me as an amulet these past six months. Father immediately placed it on his mantelpiece with the West African rain-bell given to him by my cousin Sally; the Ashanti animal gold-weights he had bought in London, in 1936, from his antiquarian friend Mr Mills of Paddington Street; the Eskimo soapstone carvings given him by Grete Schön; the obsidian neolithic axe from Bill Waldren; his *baetyl* Earth-goddess stone from Lake Baikal given him by Alan Sillitoe; the now shrivelled sea horse and starfish he had found on the Cala when he was still with Laura. All had *baraka*.

'Thank you, old chap,' he said, giving me an embarrassed hug.

2

I quickly caught up with my friends' whereabouts. Po, now a ship's engineer, had returned to Majorca a fortnight before. He had been on an oil-tanker in the Far East and, after a couple of *Cuba-Libres*, narrated long and elaborate stories about his sea voyages and adventures upriver in Borneo. Teddy was in Palma, wearing a large moustache, and playing wonderful classical guitar.

Stella was in the cottage. She had given up her teaching job in Madrid and had come back to Deyá with Lucia in the 'Young Maiden's Modesty'. She had been helping a group of anti-Franco dissidents – sometimes hiding them in their flat. Fortunately she had not been caught. I sadly found her more distant, as if something had happened; as if her *baraka* had been depleted. Although I was still very fond of her, my infatuation waned.

Ramón, Lucia's boyfriend, stayed with us when he could. He was a year older than I. Since his early teens, Ramón had been playing the drums, and had toured South America with his father – also a musician. Ramón was now playing in the band at Palma's Titos Nightclub, where *Los Valldemosa* also performed. His job left him enough time to write music. When composing, or even thinking about music, Ramón become oblivious of his surroundings, and an angry look seemed to gather under his thundery eyebrows. Interrupt his train of thought, however, and he would break into a bright smile – the same joyous smile he wore when sitting at his drum kit.

Pedro I saw rarely: he lived with Fedora, a tall Puerto-Rican girl of flawless complexion. Unmarried, and saddled with a young daughter, she had been hunting for a husband. Pedro fell for her and, in August 1962, just after I had returned, they got married. It was a small wedding. Pedro's father and sister disapproved and took no part, nor were any other family members present. The only guests were Po and Yancy – Len Lye's daughter – Lucia and Ramón, Teddy's brother Nene, and myself. Nene was their best man, Po and I their witnesses. None of us expected this marriage to last, and we contemplated telling the priest of 'impediments' when asked during the ceremony – the Catholic Church frowned on unmarried mothers – but in the end did not. Lucia was given the bride's bouquet. Once married, Fedora kept Pedro away from the bad influences of his unmarried friends: I had to visit him in secret at his glove shop. When the inevitable break-up came three years later, they had three children – counting Fedora's little girl whom Pedro had immediately adopted – and a fourth on the way.

3

The birthday party for 1962 was only a week away and, on the evening of my arrival, I joined in the rehearsals for the play which was to inaugurate our new theatre. This, my cousin Simon Gough, Diana's son, had built on our land across the road. Though I was sorry the grotto was no longer to be used for our plays, I had to admit the setting Simon had picked was enchanting. The small circular stage stood among the olive trees, at the foot of a low cliff, and some fifty irregular cement seats climbed up the side of the escarpment. The audience watched performances against a backdrop of olive trees, while catching glimpses of the sea beyond. It was perfect for poetry readings and the birthday play.

The year's play was about the building of an hotel above the Cala. It was, as usual, a comment on village affairs, but it bore serious implications.

The Cala 'project' caused perhaps the first real confrontation between the Deyá villagers and the *estrangers*. The hotel and villas were planned on the Cala; details were posted at the Town Hall. Had the project gone ahead it would have meant the end of the beach as we knew it and, indirectly, the very charm of the village itself. The *estrangers* were against it as were most of the summer residents. The villagers, however, felt that boom years of tourism had been passing them by and, on the whole, were very much in favour. Plenty of young men had gone to look for jobs in Palma and abroad, and the idea of an hotel offering employment was very appealing. Indeed, they did not see the Cala as a place of beauty: they saw it only in terms of its slipways, the boathouses, the Marchs' restaurant, and the small temporary bar which was erected each summer, on the beach itself. Not only would an hotel and villas provide more clients for the bars on the Cala and in the village, there would be deck chairs to let and boat trips to arrange. If some *estrangers* left, so be it; other tourists with more money would come. Now, with the plan posted in the *Ayuntamiento*, the villagers assumed the hotel was as good as built. What could the *estrangers* do to stop it? But they had not counted on the *senyor de Canellún*.

Father sent a letter to Don Manuel Fraga, the Minister of Tourism, who, after his visit to the compost heap, was now a good friend. He explained the situation, and suggested that Deyá, and the north-west coast of the island, be declared a National Park, forever protected against high-rise buildings. Already one high-rise hotel, Ca Madò Pilla, had been erected on the road to Valldemosa; and the once pretty Puerto Soller was lost beneath concrete hotels and apartment blocks. Father's letter had its effect: the plans for an hotel were shelved and the villas were reduced to small stone-faced chalets which more or less blended into the landscape. Soon Deyá, and other villages on the north-west coast of the island, came under strict building codes, and the plans of every new house had to be approved by the Fine Arts Council in Palma.

Naturally, the villagers were not too happy about Father's high-handed ways. Indeed, the *Patrón* and his contemporaries remembered how, with Laura and Old Gelat, the *senyor* had made the road to the Cala before the Civil War and had planned to build just such an hotel on his land by Canellún, as well as a university campus by the beach. To pay for it all they were going to sell building plots. The *senyor* plainly had double standards. However, outwardly they remained on good terms with him. A showdown would change nothing since the *senyor* obviously had powerful friends. And who could tell whether these friends would not come in useful some day? Meanwhile plenty of other new houses, mostly stone-faced, were being built by *estrangers*, which provided ample work for those who had not left the village.

The play was a great success. So was the new stage equipment. Hanging from a nearby carob tree was a large sheet of steel to produce the sound of the thunder, which accompanied the torrential rain that washes away the hotel in the final scene. The theatre benches were packed, and late arrivals were forced to sit in the 'gods' on the cliff above. Among the honoured guests were Claire Booth and Henry Luce, owners of *Time* magazine. When I sang a Talking Blues – hurriedly added to the script – about my year in Texas, Mrs Booth turned to Father.

'Say, Robert, who is the American kid?' she asked.

4

With Spain beginning to modernize, Deyá was forced into the twentieth century. Farmers were worried about the low crop prices. Deyá's small terraced holdings were labour intensive and could not compete with large farms on mainland Spain, which were increasingly mechanized. The price of olive oil, Deyá's traditional earner, went down disastrously. The *amos* of the *fincas* found that they could no longer afford to bring over *gallufas* to pick their olives, since these would no longer accept the traditional half-payment in oil. The branches of the olive trees, which should have been pruned every three or four years, were now full and top-heavy, and ugly shoots sprouted around the trunks. Of the twenty olive presses which were working when we arrived in 1946, only a couple were still in operation. Pep Coll, of Ca'n Quet, organized a village co-operative to build a new olive press in the Clot. The press itself was a small, modern machine, sufficient to process the reduced quantity of olives now picked by the village women. However, each co-venturer considered his olives the best, and did not want his oil mixed with his neighbour's. The press never became viable.

Combine harvesters on the mainland also knocked down the price of cereals. In June, the land between the olive trees – once golden under wheat – now was a barren brown. Since the terraces were no longer sown, they were no longer ploughed, and weeds sprouted everywhere. The threshing circles, too, became overgrown. Mules and donkeys, once used for ploughing and threshing, were sold to the knackers. More sheep were bought to graze the terraces. Young men, who might have worked the land, had to find jobs in Palma as waiters, or in Deyá with one of the two builders.

Pep Salas' firm, which had built Canellún, was now run by his son, also called Pep. The new master-builder – an accomplished guitarist – was bookish, but also more business-minded than the old man had been. He enlarged his father's firm so that he could build any new house, or convert any old one, according to the *estrangers'* whims. Every Saturday at lunchtime, his workmen were paid at his house by the Porxo. His workforce had grown, from the three or four masons he employed in the middle Fifties, to the two dozen or so now. Several came from Soller, and their mopeds and motorbikes choked the track. Each worker was given an envelope prepared by Pep's sister Magdalena.

The other master-builder in Deyá was its Mayor, Joan Valentí, a scrupulously honest man. As a boy he had been sent to a seminary and could read, write and keep accounts. A traditionalist, he wore his black beret in winter, his straw hat in summer, and disliked new ideas. Living on the Puig, he preferred to work within the confines of the village. He had no motorbike; if he had to go to Lluc Alcari he grudgingly rode his bicycle. Valentí did most of the villagers' repairs.

As Deyá's Mayor, Valentí was more concerned with balancing his books to the *centimo* than with undertaking new projects. His biggest public work was to re-roof and refurbish the *rentaderos* on the main road – never foreseeing that they would fall into disuse once electricity came to the village. Indeed, Deyá's connection to the Majorcan electricity grid was thought to be imminent and was much looked forward to. Even in winter, while turning at its most efficient, Gelat's turbine at Ca'n Mado was now seriously underpowered and could no longer cope with the demand for electric light. Village women wanted electric irons and to be able to listen to the radio while they worked; men wanted water pumps and cement mixers; the owner of the New Café, a television to watch *Televisión Española*, which had just begun transmissions. In 1960 Joan Valentí had been to see the Civil Governor in Palma, the connection to the grid had been approved, and the first pylons were being erected. Valentí, meanwhile, worried how much the new electricity would cost the Town Hall.

If almost every workman now had a motorbike, some of the better-off villagers were driving Seat-600's. The mule and cart was being replaced by the lorry and, soon, by the ubiquitous dumper. A telephone exchange had been installed at the Lower Baker's and there were a few telephones in the village: Gelat, the two cafés, and Ca'n Quet. Father resolutely refused to be connected. Bottled gas, the revolutionary *Butano*, had become available around 1959, and was distributed by a lorry from Soller. As a fuel, it was used all over Spain for cooking and heating. Without electricity, the coffee machines in the two Deyá cafés had been rigged up to run on it. At Canellún, the *entrada* and the bedrooms were now heated by *Butano* stoves, and the American refrigerator had been converted to run on it. In summer, Mother used a *Butano* cooker, because her coal-fired Aga so overheated the kitchen that she had to let it go out.

After lunch at the Cala, when we could, Po and I sat next to the *Patrón* sipping our coffee and brandy while he mended his nets. It still amused him to talk about the old days. Increasingly, however, he would voice his concern about the way things were changing; about the olive groves – once a sign of wealth – which few looked after, and the many fallen terrace walls, which the *amos*, lacking both labourers and money, were no longer able to repair; about the oak forests, now deserted by the charcoal burners because of *Butano*, and which were becoming a fire hazard with the neglected undergrowth; about the influx of the new breed of *turistas* in his restaurant who, though they spent well, treated him and his family as servants rather than as friends – Joana, of course, got her own back by serving them last.

'You know what?' he would smile, pulling himself together and knocking out his old pipe. 'Things will go the way God wills them to . . .'

Smuggling went on as ever and, if anything, was on the increase. I had certainly become more aware of it. I had gone down to the Cala for a midnight skinny-dip with a girlfriend, and left my car blocking the dirt road to Son Bujosa. On our way back, as we approached the *finca*, I heard a lorry start, and grind its way up the track towards the main road. It did not turn on its headlights: it was obviously a smuggler's lorry. I began to run, wanting to move my car to make room, but then thought better of it: it was safer not to be seen. Sure enough, when the lorry reached the main road, it stopped for a couple of minutes, and then drove off towards Palma. When my friend and I reached the car, we found it had been carefully pushed out of the way.

The smugglers also used large American cars to move tobacco and other light loads, and on another occasion, as I was walking past the Fonda, the steering of one of them broke. It narrowly missed me, and scrunched into a wall opposite the *Guardia Civil* headquarters next to the old doctor's house. The *guardias*, taking stock of the situation, hurriedly closed their door and escaped through a ventilation hatch in the back of their office. Within two minutes, we had transferred the cases of Winston cigarettes from the car into a nearby house. It was then that the *guardias* sauntered over. In emergencies, the village still worked together.

5

After leaving Texas, I flew to New York, where I had the interviews kindly set up for me by Jake Hamon: none was successful. Nevertheless, having enjoyed my summer in Deyá to the full, I needed a job. After some searching, I found a French company called SAMEGA which offered me a post 'mud-logging' on oil rigs. They told me I would be sent to places like the Sahara or the Middle East, and that I would get two weeks' holiday for every six weeks worked on a rig. The life sounded unusual, and the pay good, so I took it. I was trained on a couple of rigs, one in the Spanish Pyrenees, the other in rainy Belgium, after which I was considered ready, and sent to work in the Algerian Sahara.

The French driver who had driven me for an hour through massive sand dunes dropped me in front of the camp mess-hall. '*Allo! Chef?*' he yelled – there were no English speakers. The camp boss appeared. After my flight and the drive I was relieved to be given a room and a bed. Living conditions were spartan: there were communal showers, the toilet was a hole in the ground. However, the rooms were clean, the air conditioners worked, and after school at Oundle I could handle most things. On calm evenings we ate under the stars. The food, as I found in all the French camps, was excellent. I soon became a lover of *Cerveau de Veau aux Capres*, and raw *Artichaux à la Vinaigrette*; apart from tripe, I tried everything. The camp was a small all-male community and, once I had established my position, though low in the pecking order, I became an accepted member of the group.

'Mud-logging' is not a highly demanding job, intellectually. We collected rock cuttings, produced by the drill-bit, analysed them under the microscope, dried them and bagged them. We had instruments to measure the gas coming from the rocks we were drilling. If the bit drilled faster, this might mean we had reached a porous oil reservoir. We would then watch our gas detectors, and search the cuttings for oil staining. Sometimes we took cores. As I began to understand the significance of what I was doing, the job became fun and, where we actually struck oil, flowed it to the surface, and burned it in a massive ball of fire, highly exhilarating.

When my shift was over, I went for walks in the setting sun. Once behind the first large dune, I could no longer hear the rig motors, and delighted in the silence and cleanliness of the desert. I climbed the firm rippled side of a high dune, and followed the razor-sharp undulating ridge to its top, sad that my footprints had spoiled their pristine perfection. For a while I sat on the crest, contemplating the vastness of the sand sea, so beautiful, and yet scenically, nothing could have been more different from Deyá. In common there was the real sense of being cut off from the outside world. It was only when reading a month-old *Time* magazine that I found out about the Cuba Missile Crisis, and how close we had come to a Third World War.

6

The job suited me: the work was new and sufficiently varied; I loved the desert, and my French soon improved. The six-week tour on the rig passed quickly and I usually came back to Deyá for my two weeks' leave. My old friends, however, were elsewhere. I saw little of Pedro now that he was married; my breaks rarely coincided with Teddy's university vacations; Po was back on his ship somewhere in Indonesia. I had no other real friends in Palma. In Deyá, the village boys with whom I had been to school were now fishermen, carpenters, taxi drivers or stonemasons.

'*¡Huep, Guillem!* On holiday again?' they greeted me enviously, unaware I had just worked six full weeks at a stretch, without a weekend off. I had always considered myself as one of them. Now, however, I found myself being drawn more and more towards the *estrangers*; and especially to Bill Waldren.

Bill was building a museum to house his archaeological finds. Having bought the shell of an old flour mill at the top of the road to the Clot, he had already cleared out the debris. When I was back from the desert, I helped to mix plaster and carried it in buckets up the scaffolding, where Bill was spreading it over the rough stone walls with his bare hands. I even donated a few hundred of my Sahara oil-dollars to the project.

The digs were also going well; and I went out with Bill once or twice a week, whenever he wanted a break from his building. He had discovered a new cave, and was unearthing scores of skulls, and hundreds of bones, of what he thought were gazelles. One afternoon, when I was in bed with flu, Bill came over to visit me. I was reading a book about the natural history and geology of Majorca; Bill thumbed through it, and came upon a drawing of the skull of his 'gazelle'. It belonged to an extinct species called *Myotragus Balearicus* – the 'Balearic goat'; only two skulls had previously been found.

On a trip through London I had bought myself a Japanese reflex camera, and had got some good shots in the desert. From Bill I learned darkroom techniques, and I developed, printed and cropped my photographs. Among these were some of the Berber chieftain who often visited the rig on his white stallion; of our cook bottle-feeding a baby gazelle, after its mother was followed and run to death by the pick-up bringing our groceries; of the shepherds grazing their sheep and goats in the grassy shallow depressions in the southern reaches of the Atlas mountains; of Muhammad, our big black 'political adviser', whose job it was to report back to the newly formed Algerian Ministry of Mines as soon as we struck oil, sleeping under a lone acacia tree.

I wrote a short article about my first experiences in the Sahara – Father checked my spelling – and I placed it, and the accompanying photographs, with an agency called Camera Press. They got my article published and paid me ten guineas and the following year I received another six pounds in royalties. However, I still tried to keep geology and Canellún apart, and it annoyed me when I discovered Camera Press had sold one of the photographs of myself – with the rig in the background – to the *Sunday Times*, which captioned it:

> 'William Graves, 22, third son of Robert Graves the
> poet, on his oil rig in the Sahara'.

7

I was becoming an old hand at mud-logging and, at the end of May 1963, SAMEGA decided to send me on a solo job in Greece. The rig was north of Patras, on the northern side of the Gulf of Corinth, on the wild mountain road to the fishing port of Astakos. The drill kept breaking, so I had many free days. Provided I kept in touch with the oil-company superintendent, and was within about three hours' drive, I could go wherever I wanted. I had my Karmann-Ghia with me.

Often I went to see Eleni Dutton, a Greek sculptress and a friend of Father's. They had met in 1961 when Father travelled to Greece for the staging of *Nausicaa*, an opera by Peggy Glanville-Hicks based on his novel, *Homer's Daughter*. Eleni had been very understanding of Father, then in the throes of the Margot-Alastair crisis. She was separated from her English husband, and lived in Athens with her two young daughters and her mother. Every summer, Eleni rented a house on the island of Aegina, which I loved. Aegina was about an hour's journey in the small steamer from Pireus, so I could still get back to the rig in time should they need me. I swam with her children, Davina and

Christina; I posed in front of the rambling house, under the shade of large pine trees, while Eleni sculpted my legs; we ate grilled octopus together, chased down with *ouzo* in the harbour café; she read my fortune in the coffee grounds; in the cool of the evening, we walked up to the temple of Aphaea, and I picked pistachio nuts and figs off the trees along the path. I felt very much at home.

At other times I drove to see the archaeological sites. I visited the early vault graves in the shadow of Mount Pilion, where the mythical Cyclops lived. I watched the sunset from the temple on Cape Sounion, south of Athens. For three days, I drove around the Peloponnese. At Mycenae, I climbed around the vestiges of the city state, and explored the treasure-house of Atreus. At Bassai I went into the bleak grey limestone hills to the deserted temple of Apollo Epicurius, built by Ictinus, the architect of the Parthenon in Athens. Other than its missing roof, it was as it had stood twenty-five centuries previously, when it was reputedly the most beautiful temple in the Peloponnese. Alone I lay on the temple steps and listened to the murmur of the breeze through the columns. In the valley of Sparta I looked at the remains of the fortified city kingdom which had taken on the might of the Persians, and then scrambled around the ruins of the nearby Byzantine monastery village of Mystras. The scale of Byzantine architecture impressed me as so human, so relaxing, that I would have felt content to be a monk there, under the ever-present gaze of the Pantocrator. Leaning against a warm monastery wall, overlooking Sparta, I lunched on goat's cheese and bunches of tiny seedless Corinth grapes, biting into them as though they were soft pears. Then, back in Athens, I spent hours at the Archaeological Museum – with its breathtaking Cycladic figurines, and Mycenean gold.

It was heady stuff. Indeed, I found this sudden exposure to archaeology so stimulating that I began having doubts about my career as an oil geologist. Mud-logging was fun for the time being, but I could not see myself on rigs for ever. To join an oil company as a geologist, and do the job Jake Hamon had taught me, would mean being posted to oil centres such as teetotal Saudi Arabia or malaria-ridden Nigeria, until I was far enough up the professional ladder. Furthermore, I would no longer be able to be in Deyá for more than brief periods – until I retired. Even though I might be ready for what seemed, at the time, a major sacrifice, I knew that I lacked the necessary aggressiveness and determination to get me to the top.

What if I studied archaeology and then worked with Bill Waldren on the island? I saw its drawbacks, but still . . . .

Letters from Deyá did not help. Bill had inaugurated the Museum. The façade of the old mill was unchanged, except for the large glass jars which Bill had cemented where the window openings had been. These gave the building an uncharacteristic New Mexico look. Inside, instead of the usual smooth stucco walls, the rounded boulders were coated with white plaster, smeared on with Bill's fingers, giving movement and life to the surface. His archaeological exhibits were set in niches in the wall, on stands, and in small cases. A reconstructed *Myotragus* skeleton was hung like a painting. Father wrote:

The Museum is staggeringly beautiful: Bill's best work of art ever. [RG to WG, October 1963]

In another letter, Father wrote that he would be coming to Greece at the end of October, to introduce a television programme on Greek tragedies to be filmed in Delphi. It was to be produced by the Standard Oil of New Jersey Company as one of their series on the 'History of Culture'. Would we be able to meet? I thought it unlikely.

However, on the day the shooting was to take place, our rig again had problems. I jumped in the car and drove along the north side of the Gulf of Corinth, through purple heather-covered hills, on dusty dirt-roads, to reach Delphi at noon. I found it to be very like Deyá, nestling beneath limestone cliffs, perched among the terraced olive groves, high above the sea. If not scenically as spectacular as Deyá, the palpable magic of its temple and theatre made up for it. The ancient Greeks considered Delphi to be the navel of the world. Had Deyá been in Greece, it surely could have claimed that distinction for itself.

At the theatre I found the crew setting up their equipment, and Father talking to Alicia Paxinou and Alexis Minotis. Paxinou and Minotis were a legendary duo. Together they had formed the Greek National Theatre and, as Greek classical actors, they had virtually reinvented the art. They divested it of baroque German and romantic French ideas, and insisted that the chorus once again become an integral part of the production. After Father's introduction, I watched Paxinou and Minotis play scenes of

Oedipus Rex and *Phaedra* while the chorus of twelve female dancers moved to the music composed and conducted by Jani Christu. Watching alone, from one of the stone seats – the ruins of the temple of Apollo to my left, the Gulf of Corinth below – it was an electrifying, unforgettable experience.

That evening Father and I went for a walk. He had just bought himself a shepherd's crook with a carved dolphin grip, and he was striding along the road towards the setting sun with it in his hand. As usual, I had to push myself to keep up. I told him of my misgivings about continuing in the oil business, and my thoughts on archaeology. Father was delighted. He had never understood what a Graves was doing in oil – forgetting that he and Jake Hamon had got me into it – and felt that archaeology was just the thing.

'I've got no university in mind yet, Father.'

'Don't be silly. Come to Oxford!' he exclaimed. It was not an idle invitation. Father had been elected Professor of Poetry there, and had been given rooms in St John's College. 'Christopher Hawkes is at the Ashmolean; and you can be at St John's, which is where all Graveses go.' Lucia was at St Anne's, but he meant Graves men.

'It's all very well saying that, but surely I'll have to have an interview or something,' I replied.

'Don't worry, I'll fix that.' He loved 'fixing' things, asking favours from friends in high places. During the First World War, he had fixed things to save his friend Siegfried Sassoon from a court martial for writing a pacifist pamphlet; later, he had fixed things after Laura had jumped out of a window, at a time when, in England, attempting suicide was a criminal act.

Next morning the television crew finished shooting, and we checked out of the hotel – a modern monstrosity more appropriate to a ski resort, built into the hillside with lifts descending from the lobby to the rooms below. Just like the hotel that had been planned for the Cala. Thank goodness, Deyá had no monuments to attract tourist hordes; and it was now protected from the attentions of modern architects. We had lunch in a small restaurant at the foot of Mount Parnassos – Paxinou, Minotis, Father, part of the pretty chorus, and myself. The conversation centred on Greek myths and the theatre – Father was in great form. I sat back, sipped my retsina and listened. I had learned not to join in a conversation unless I had something to add of my own; and what could I add in the presence of these three colossi?

Arriving back at the rig that night was a comedown. They were just getting ready to drill again, and as I switched on the gas detection instruments, I thought about Father's suggestion; the longer I did so, the better I liked the idea of studying archaeology at Oxford.

8

In late January 1964, I returned to Deyá from Greece. The village had, at last, been hooked into the island's electrical grid. Most of the village houses, including Canellún, Can Torrent and La Posada, had been rewired for the new 220-voltage for over a year. The final connection had been held up by an ancient countess in Valldemosa, who refused to have a pylon on her land, because she was frightened the current would set her hay on fire. On their part, the utility company refused to consider an alternative position for the pylon. Meanwhile, Deyá waited. Finally it was Father who got the situation 'fixed' by writing – in verse – to his friend Fraga, the Minister of Tourism. Fraga called the Civil Governor; who called the Valldemosa Mayor; who called the utility company, which agreed to change the position of the pylon. The villagers were duly impressed by Father's influence in Madrid.

'What did I tell you, Maria,' said one of the women washing at the *rentaderos*. 'The *senyor* may be weak when it comes to a piece of skirt, but for the rest . . . I never liked the idea of the hotel on the Cala anyway. Tomorrow I'm going down with my husband, in Gelat's bus, to buy myself a washing machine.'

At Canellún it felt strange to go to bed without a candle. We now had a hi-fi record player, a new fridge, a washing machine, a Kenwood mixer, and electric heaters; an electric pump raised the water from the *depósito* to the header tank. No longer did Father and Karl have to take turns at the pump handle. Father could work past sundown. But some of the magic had gone.

9

Two or three days after my return from Greece we received a telegram saying that my sister Jenny had suffered a brain haemorrhage and was lying in a coma. She had been in Deyá three months previously, working on more changes to a musical about Solomon and Sheba which she and Father had written. The producer had shelved it, but Jenny was a fighter and was determined to get it staged. She had been complaining of bad headaches then.

Of my half-brothers and sisters, Jenny was the one I had always been closest to. After her first husband, Alex Clifford, died in 1952 of Hodgkin's disease, she married Patrick Crosse, the Rome bureau chief for Reuters news agency. Patrick was a Rhodesian, a very cultivated man, who amused me greatly when he asked for a 'disconto' in the smartest shops – and got one. Jenny sold the lovely *castelletto* in Portofino when they married, and they moved to an equally beautiful sixteenth-century tower, the Torre d'Il Grillo, in Rome. Their balcony overlooked the ruins of Augustus' temple. I had stayed with them there on a family visit, and later I went skiing with them in Austria for three years running. It was during the après-ski that I really got to know and love my sister. Patrick had recently been posted by Reuters to London, and they first rented a house off King's Road, and later bought a house in Little Venice. I went to see them whenever I was in town. Jenny was so active, so willing to help others, so infectiously enthusiastic, it was impossible to keep away.

Jenny won an international reputation as an all-round correspondent. After beginning as a war correspondent in the WAAFS, she wrote, as Jenny Nicholson, for several newspapers and magazines – in particular *Picture Post*; she covered anything from Royal Weddings to sex changes, the Vatican, fashion shows, black magic, or political conferences. Her reports were always fun to read. When covering a socialist conference in Venice for the *Spectator*, she jocularly reported that Aneurin Bevan, and two other leaders of the British Labour Party attending it, were drunk. Although accurate, her story resulted in a libel action against the *Spectator*, which it lost. Both Jenny and Father were deeply upset about this outcome. Many years later, one of the politicians involved admitted they had perjured themselves. But Jenny had been professionally winged.

When the telegram from Patrick announcing Jenny's death arrived, I was so upset that on my way to the village with the reply, I passed a camel, and having seen so many in Algeria, never realized it was out of place. Later, I found out that the camel was part of an advertising stunt. Father, curiously, refused to go to the funeral, claiming his passport was out of date. I flew to England immediately. Lucia, who was also very close to Jenny, and I went to the funeral together. As they lowered Jenny's coffin into the grave, I wept. Back home in Deyá, Father promised to write the 'real' story of Solomon and Sheba as a memorial to Jenny. Ten years earlier he would have done so.

10

Father had, indeed, 'fixed' things with Professor Hawkes and the President of St John's College, and I was set to go up to Oxford that October. However, I did not want to hand in my notice to SAMEGA until the beginning of summer. In March I was sent back to the Sahara. The rig was drilling in an area where the undulating sandy surface of the desert was broken, every couple of miles, by chains of high sand dunes. In the corridors between these, changes in the surface texture still showed where lakes had been in prehistoric times, before the desert had formed. At the edges of these lake beds eye-catching circular platforms abounded, some three or four feet across, made up of fire-blackened stones. I combed the sand around these prehistoric hearths, and found shards of incised pottery, and many exquisite flint arrow-heads.

When that six-week tour in the Sahara was over, SAMEGA sent me to a job on the Maas Delta, in Holland. Max, a Swiss geologist, and I were taking twelve-hour shifts each. The site was muddy. The cabin and equipment were brand-new, and full of teething problems. Our American oil-company geologist was being petty and demanding. One day driving back to the rig I crashed my beloved Karmann-Ghia, fortunately landing on a bridge, and not in a dyke. Max and I were staying in a small guesthouse in the nearest village; the food was impossible. One evening – there was a wedding in the main dining room – supper consisted of white bread and butter sprinkled with sugar. It seemed the appropriate moment to hand in my resignation.

CHAPTER X

1

Bill Waldren had built the Deyá Archaeological Museum to exhibit the finds from his digs. Being owner/director also gave him a position from which to approach the authorities since at the time he had no university degree or formal archaeological training. When two houses opposite the Museum came on to the market, Bill suggested that Father buy them, and turn them into a library, laboratory and an apartment. Together with the Museum, they could form an Archaeological Study Centre.

Bill took on the conversion of Father's new property himself, and had *estrangers* to help him. I lent him a hand when I was around. Both Salas and Valentí grumbled that the work was shoddy, that neither Bill nor his helpers had 'work permits', that the *senyor* should know better; but there were no formal protests. As with the Museum, Bill worked to no architect's plans; he rightly trusted his instinct and his sense of space. The doorway to the new Library gave the impression of an entrance to a dolmen, and opened into a high-ceilinged spacious hall lined with shelves. The laboratories consisted of a photography darkroom and a pottery reconstruction room. The apartment on the top floor was small but comfortable. All the walls were finished, like the museum, with roughly applied plaster. Father paid for everything: wages, building materials, and the many cases of beer to quench the workers' thirst. He bought the houses and undertook the conversion as a present for me: the co-directorship of the Archaeological Centre was much more in line with what he expected of a Graves. He had the deeds made out in my name.

Increasingly, I became involved in Bill's digs. He had an extraordinary gift for finding the prehistoric sites – generally in caves with shallow overhangs – and we had two or three digs going at the same time. Much of the work entailed monotonous back-breaking removal of soil and we gathered volunteers from among the *estrangers* to help. However, the tedium was punctuated by the excitement of finding pottery shards, bones, or even artifacts. Then work would stop, and we would gather around to watch the unearthing. If the find was fragile Bill would take over. He would kneel over the object and, gently, with a brush and a small trowel, ease it out. Then, in a votive gesture, he would raise the potshard, bronze needle or skull to the light and exclaim: 'Wow, man, think of it – four thousand years old!'

Later, back at Bill's house, after a shower, and beer in hand, the trophies would be unwrapped on the kitchen table to be admired and discussed. Bill had become a master at piecing and gluing together pottery shards; he also made beautiful drawings of the finds.

Starting my reading on archaeology, I took copious notes – especially on Christopher Hawkes's *The Prehistory of Europe*. I began to realize that Bill's digs themselves were carried out in a haphazard fashion and that much observational data was being lost. I hoped to learn the proper techniques at Oxford so as to be able to work with him scientifically on the prehistory of Majorca. At the time little was known of the relationship between the local *Talayót* megalithic culture and pre-Talayotic cave-culture, and the mainstream European cultures. *Talayóts* were large circular stone burial chambers mostly found on the south-eastern flat part of Majorca and dated around the first millennium BC. Bill's pre-Talayotic cave finds contained 'bell-beaker' pottery and generally dated from the second millennium BC. I was planning to make the relationship the subject of my thesis at Oxford.

In June 1964 Bill and I were invited to the opening of an art gallery at Cala Fornells, in Minorca. The gallery exhibited works by the *Deu des Teix* – Bill's group – and the owner hung several of his own paintings for sale. It was an excellent opportunity to see the archaeological sites on the neighbouring island. We explored the megalithic *naveta* burial chambers and altar-like *taulas*, both of which are much more spectacular than, and quite different from, the Majorcan *talayóts*, and visited the prehistory collections in the Mahon and Ciudadella Museums.

Back on Majorca, we visited a Talayotic village being excavated on the north-east of the island, and were shown around by the Italian professor in charge. We went over to Alcudia on the north of the island and stayed for a week as guests of the Bryant Foundation, which had been set up to fund and provide technical help for the excavations at Polentia, a large Roman town with a well-preserved theatre. Among the ruins we watched archaeologists uncover a fresco in a Roman villa. We, however, were working with Dr Miguel Tarredell of the University of Valencia, on his excavation of a Phoenician necropolis on a tiny islet called Isla de Poros, some 200 metres from the shore. It was a lovely part of the coast: the pine trees swept down to the sand and there was not a building in sight. There were still many such unspoiled beaches on Majorca. Dr Tarradell's was the first professional dig I had worked on. I noted how meticulously the site had been surveyed and how, unlike on Bill's digs, the exact location of every object was recorded on the site plan. I felt I was finally getting my teeth into the past.

2

That summer of 1964, the village was full of new faces: friends of friends, or strangers, people who had heard about Deyá and had come to see for themselves. It was the 'in' place to be. The Cala was packed and the *Patrón* had to turn people away from his recently enlarged restaurant terrace. If I had wanted to buy a second-hand car in New York, or rent a flat in Rome, or get a job in the London theatre, I could have done so sitting on a rock on the beach.

A newer, more affluent breed of 'artists' was beginning to outnumber the original *estrangers* such as Jimmy d'Aulignac, Bert and Vida, *El Capitán*, Mati or Bill. These 'artists' came to Deyá to get away from the 'world', but carried it with them. Each had a novel to write, or a masterpiece to paint; but they sat most of the time on the New Café terrace earnestly debating weighty issues, such as America's new Peace Corps and its Freudian implications. Many became friends of the Waldrens, and I came to know them around Bill's large kitchen table. Apart from our mutual interest in Bill's digs, they and I had little in common: my work in the oilfields can hardly have endeared me to them; even Oxford was suspect. It never occurred to me that they might be tolerating me just to get closer to Father. His presence was essential to them. If a writer of his repute had 'made it' in this out-of-the-way place, so could they. And being able to say 'Hi, Robert' to him made them his confrères. Even so, they borrowed money from

Father and then criticized him behind his back. At first he did not mind, but after one too many bad loans he portrayed them for ever in verse:

WIGS AND BEARDS

In the bad old days a bewigged country Squire
Would never pay his debts, unless at cards,
Shot, angled, urged his pack through standing grain,
Horsewhipped his tenantry, snorted at the arts,
Toped himself under the table every night,
Blasphemed God with a cropful of God-damns,
Aired whorehouse French or lame Italian,
Set fashions of pluperfect slovenliness
And claimed seigneurial rights over all women
Who slept, imprudently, under the same roof.

Taxes and wars long ago ploughed them under –
'And serve the bastards right' the Beards agree,,
Hurling their empties through the café window
And belching loud as they proceed downstairs.
Latter-day bastards of that famous stock,
They never rode a nag, or gaffed a trout,
Nor winged a pheasant, nor went soldiering,
But remain true to the same hell-fire code
In all available particulars
And scorn to pay their debts even at cards.
Moreunder (which is to subtract, not add),
Their ancestors called themselves gentlemen
As they, in the same sense, call themselves artists.

Parties were becoming a bore. The soft flicker of candles had gone and the new discordant brilliance of the mains electricity made people raise their voices. I no longer took along my guitar. I had been replaced by the latest Beatles records. The *estrangers* relaxed by smoking pot. They brought it to Deyá from London or Paris, hidden in their underpants or knickers. We were told that marijuana was harmless and non-addictive, and that users seldom moved on to the harder LSD. Fortunately, heroin was rare then and drugs-related deaths were virtually unheard of.

Father's attitude to hallucinogens was liberal. He had been interested in them since 1947, when we had a short holiday in the Pyrenees with Ricardo and Betty Sicré. There we took walks in the hills and Father carried us across streams and muddy patches. One day, with Juan on his shoulders, he was bitten by a viper, and we had to hurry back to the village doctor. When we got there Father was already pale and trembling, and there was a wild look in his eyes. The doctor did not believe us, saying that he would be dead if he had really been bitten, and gave Father a medicine for food poisoning. Only later, when Mother showed him the fang marks, did the doctor administer the antidote serum; but by then it was not really necessary, and it made Father ill again. While the venom was having its effect, Father claimed that he saw the 'Glass Castle' where the souls of sacred kings – such as King Arthur – are housed after death. This experience made him wonder whether hallucinogenic mushrooms could have a similar effect.

Gordon Wasson, a banker, and his Russian wife had written a book on mushrooms and had asked Father to advise them on the historical and mythological aspects. Father and Wasson began a long correspondence about hallucinogenic mushrooms and their bearing on ancient religions. His thoughts on Samson and the 'little foxes', during our Land-rover trip through France, were typical of the way Father related the two. Indeed, he believed that *Amanita muscaria*, the fly agaric, was the Greeks' 'Food of the Gods'.

At the end of 1959 Father went to New York to receive the Gold Medal of the National Poetry Society of America and stayed with Wasson, now a vice president of the J.P. Morgan & Co. bank. Wasson was just back from an expedition to the mountains of Mexico, where he had attended a religious ceremony in which the local *curandera* gave her followers a powerful hallucinogenic mushroom so as to experience 'Heaven'. Gordon invited Father and some friends to test it with him, while others stood by in case of problems. With doused lights, and to the sound of the tape-recorded chant of the *curandera* performing her ceremony, they took the 'sacred mushroom'. This is an exceedingly powerful drug – considerably stronger than LSD, which was later synthesized from it – and perhaps the amounts they took were high. For not only did it produce ecstatic hallucinations, it also induced in Father priapism – a painful erection – lasting several days.

Father did not consider marijuana any more harmful than

alcohol. Nor was he against drugs such as LSD provided they were not used indiscriminately. He felt that if these were to be taken, it should be done in a 'state of grace' similar to that insisted upon by the *curandera* before administering the 'sacred mushroom'. Perhaps my attitude towards marijuana was pompous, but I found that once joints were handed out at a party, conversation became dismal and repetitive. Whenever that happened, I left. If people wanted to 'blow their minds' that was their own lookout; I just did not want to be involved. LSD, on the other hand, frightened me. I had seen the effect it had on people's minds. One promising young French painter arrived in Deyá in 1960; he had started by smoking marijuana and was soon taking LSD. Four years later he had 'flipped' and was in a mental institution.

3

Ralph Jacobs, whom I had visited in New York, had been on a TV Quiz programme in the late Fifties called 'The $64,000 Question', and had won a trip to Europe for himself and his 'wife'. He was homosexual, so he took his friend Cindy Lee. Cindy's estranged husband, Owen Lee, an aqualung enthusiast, had stayed in our cottage above the Cala, and Ralph and Cindy naturally gravitated to Deyá. They now returned every summer and Mother always found them a house in exchange for the hybrid sweetcorn seed which Ralph sent her from America. I liked Ralph, but I never cared for Cindy.

Cindy was in her mid-thirties, a small, slender, dark woman, with a large nose, and a Brooklyn drawl. A painter, she formed part of the group of 'artists', some of whom hung around the cafés all day and smoked marijuana at night, and about whom Father had written so scathingly in his poem. From what little contact I had with her at parties, I found her a loud-mouthed, unattractive character. Father first mentioned Cindy to me in a letter when I was in Greece, and I recognized at once the signs of an imminent Muse:

Cindy is now becoming Émile [sic] Laraçuen again: her real name. I never knew she was half Mexican – family fought against Pancho Villa, who crucified a lot of them – and half French-Italian. Idries said to her one day: 'Why do you always disguise yourself? Let's see your real self.' She said: 'Very well', and that's how it is. It's staggering what lies behind that fun and games façade. [RG to WG, October 1963]

As Muse, Aemile was Father's creation. He believed in the magical powers he attributed to her 'behind that fun and games façade'. But then Father once told Rene that he could will himself to be in love with his own big toe. What made things difficult was that he expected his friends to feel the same about his Muse as he did.

Aemile has too good a heart, rather than too grudging a one, is about 8 years older than Margot, and Mexican-Italian-Basque. Makes no plans, has lived for several years in Greenwich Village, from hand to mouth: numerous talents, no careerist ambitions, an extremist, no children. Is embarrassed, annoyed, surprised and infuriated sometimes by finding that she and I both get sick and paralysed and psychosomatic whenever we try to break this fatal bond between us – which is rarely sexual and then only because one can't cheat the body, and which has to do with a common huge compunction to think in a region of thought where practically nobody else visits. Her contribution is a fantastic delicacy of moral judgement. [RG to SJ, October 1963]

However, the 'Aemile' alter ego was unstable, and 'Cindy' kept re-emerging. Father saw this as two aspects of the Goddess. But her changes put Father on a switchback of euphoria and despair. He would go to the café a couple of times a day – unheard of even a year earlier – to look for 'Aemile' and, if she was there, walk back with her to Canellún. If she was not at the café Father would summon up his courage and go to her house in the Clot to see if she was painting; and would often find 'Cindy' and not 'Aemile'. When 'Cindy' told him to go to hell, he would return dejectedly to his desk and write a poem. When later 'Aemile' begged his forgiveness, he would write another.

I wrote to you a couple of days ago prematurely, before a general enlightenment and clearing of the air: everything's clear and secure again, and the poems confirmed as true. [RG to SJ, November 1963]

Margot had been sensitive and kind to Father until he had tried to direct her life. The same applied to Judith. Both were on good terms with Mother and the family during their Musedom and remained so after it ended. Cindy treated Father as the sixty-nine-year-old man he was, and seemed indifferent to his feelings. She made no effort whatsoever to endear herself to the family and openly told her friends that it was all a big joke.

At Oundle I had had some rough moments, and I was often homesick in Texas, but I knew that once I returned home I would feel fine. Now, what with the ever-widening drug scene and the Cindy affair, I began to feel uncomfortable in Deyá. I was especially embarrassed by Father's behaviour, although I tried to hide it in front of him. Down at the Cala the *Patrón* had sat down beside me on the terrace.

'Your father seems a little tired this summer, he is always going backwards and forwards,' he sighed, using the Majorcan term *trescar*, which is what bloodhounds do when they follow a scent. I knew Father was making himself ridiculous, and it was hard for me to understand or accept his new behaviour. But I assumed this would soon pass: was it not just a case of male menopause? I had always considered him prudish; or was it I who had changed and was the prude?

4

Towards the end of that summer, as I was getting ready for Oxford, I met Marie – this is not her real name – on the Cala. A French painter and a friend of Mati's, she was staying in the Mirador, the box-like stone studio overlooking the beach. She had wide-set, melancholy blue eyes, high cheekbones and a wide quizzical smile. With her straight blonde hair, broad shoulders and slim waist, she cut a rather boyish figure. She was extremely photogenic and had played supporting roles in two or three low-budget French films. She and her husband were separated and their young daughter was being looked after by the parents-in-law.

She invited me to a party at Mati's. I respected Mati and admired his hyper-realistic paintings. He was becoming well known in the art world, and had his own circle of mostly French friends and acolytes. The food was good and the sangria better than usual. His house next to the Mirador still had no electricity, so there was no record player. Marie and I relaxed in the atmosphere of an earlier Deyá. She told me she was amused that I spoke French, and that I had made a pass at her. Then Mati began playing the bongos and joints were handed around. I told her this was not my scene.

'But William, you are too narrow-minded! How can you pass judgement on others? Who do you think you are?' she said, having a small French *crise*.

'I'm sorry. Stay if you want to, but this is when I leave.'

However, Marie left the party with me. We spent a memorable week together swimming in the quiet coves below Lluc Alcari, driving around the centre of the island away from the tourists, and looking up at the brilliant star-filled sky from the Mirador roof. I knew the Deyá night sky well. Pedro and I had spent hours after suppers, stretched out on the car-less road, smoking, and tracing the Great Bear, the Pleiades, Cassiopeia, the mantle of the Milky Way, and watching out for shooting stars. Those were the nights when the moon was less than half full and hidden behind the hills. The full moon in Deyá was just as spectacular. The stars disappeared and its silvery light could be so bright that one could read by it and even make out colours. Each night I left Marie before dawn, and crept away from the Mirador to keep up appearances with the fishermen in the cottage opposite, although they knew – and I knew that they knew – perfectly well what was going on. When Marie's week was up, she had to return to Paris and her daughter. I decided to put forward my trip to Oxford, pick her up in Paris, and make a detour with her to Brittany, where she was invited to visit friends.

In Deyá I threw my things into the car and headed for Paris, stopping near Perpignan to see a prehistoric cave, similar to some of the cave-tombs on Majorca, and again at Les Baux, near Arles in southern France, to admire the Saracen castle. I ate the *menu économique* in small restaurants and slept in a sleeping bag in the car. Having been accustomed to the hotels SAMEGA put me in, it felt a little strange to be roughing it and living off my savings. These were fortunately relatively substantial because, although my salary had not been over-generous, SAMEGA had paid for all my expenses when I was away on a job, and at Canellún board and lodging were free.

The next day I arrived in Paris and stayed in a pension on the rue du Bac, where Marie joined me. This was her home ground, but having eaten at the same table with French drillers for two years, I knew about French cars, cheeses, pop records, film actors and President de Gaulle; and enough of the *argot* to blend in quite convincingly with her *copains* at La Coupole.

Marie's friends in Brittany had a house on the coast. When the tide was out we climbed over seaweed-covered granite boulders and I took black-and-white photographs, trying to capture the 'texture'. Unfortunately the artistic talent that Marie was determined to find in me remained stubbornly elusive. We visited prehistoric dolmens, menhirs and the stone alignments at Carnac, which I had been anxious to see. On the way back to Paris, Marie decided that she would like to come with me to Oxford. She would do textile designs while I was doing my thesis; her child would stay with the in-laws.

I had already met Professor Christopher Hawkes – a small thin man with ruddy lips, wispy grey hair and thick glasses – at a conference in Zaragossa to which he had invited me. We had empathized at once and had discussed what I should be doing at Oxford and how I might get the most out of it – I was worried having hardly opened a book in three years. I went every morning to the Institute of Archaeology next to the Ashmolean Museum. Christopher gave me a reading list for my thesis subject, 'The Balearic Bronze Age'. After the oilfield workers my fellow students seemed immature and I found Oxford's public school atmosphere stifling. I ignored the rule of displaying a green light on the front of my car to show that I was a student; nor did I volunteer that I was living with Marie.

I bought Marie paints, brushes and a large artist's portfolio. She made me wear a tweed sports jacket, lace-up shoes, knitted ties – and had me grow my hair longer, so that my appearance fitted more with her concept of an 'English gentleman'. We visited *les pubs anglais*. Once a week she went up to London to sell her textile designs, but had no firm offers. This would bring on a *neurasthénie* and, for a couple of days, she would become positively difficult. However, as soon as Marie's depressions lifted, she was again great fun to be with. I suppose I was tiring of the continual stream of girlfriends, and was ready for a more stable relationship. I had been streetwise since I was twelve, and I had not needed Father to tell me the facts of life. Only once did he give me any advice: 'Before you sleep with a girl, ask yourself first, "Would I marry her?" ' I might have proposed to Marie had she not been married already.

I was trying to work and wanted to get the most out of Oxford; I was spending my savings – I had no grant – and the fees were fairly steep. However, in the evenings when I should have stayed at home and studied, Marie wanted to go out, having been shut in all day painting. The friction between us increased, her *neurasthénies* lasted longer. In mid-November she decided to return to Paris to see her daughter and suggested we meet there on my way back to Deyá at Christmas.

It was a great relief to be on my own. I got rooms in St John's College so that I could concentrate entirely on my work. I had read the basic textbooks and was beginning on the papers in academic journals. Discussing my thesis with me, a fellow student asked whether I knew of the Spanish chap at London University who was doing something on the same lines as I. Checking on it I found that a Majorcan had just completed his thesis on the Balearic Bronze Age: my own subject. My plans crumbled and so did my enthusiasm. Christopher Hawkes gave me a new subject: 'The Provenance of Bronze Age Metal Artifacts from Spectrographic Analysis'. He thought that with my geological background, it would be ideal. However, the prospect of working in a laboratory, rather than doing fieldwork in Majorca, did not appeal to me at all.

5

By Christmas, I was back in Deyá. I did not bother to phone Marie on my way through Paris. Our affair was over. However, it was my thesis which really depressed me. I now considered chucking it all in and badly needed someone to help me think it through. I had never been able to talk things over with Mother or Father. Mother was so very private I could never get through to her on any but a superficial level. And Father's mind had until recently always been on his work; now, however, he thought only of 'Aemile'. Nor did I want to disappoint Father by leaving Oxford – unless I had to. Of my close friends, Po was in Sumatra, on his oil tanker, and Pedro was held on a short rein by Fedora. Fortunately, Teddy returned from Zurich and we met every evening in a new Palma bar called the Saddle Room.

Drink in hand, we talked it over. When it was noisy inside we sat on the pavement. If I felt like continuing at St John's, Teddy tried to dissuade me, and if I felt like giving it up, he tried to persuade me to stay on. He gradually brought me to a decision.

Teddy's father had just been elected Commodore of the Club Nautico and was organizing a New Year's Eve party. Teddy thought it would be fun to have his friends come along to liven things up, and he sold us tickets. It was a black-tie affair with drinks, dinner, and dancing. I went with Marisa, an Aviaco air hostess whom I had met a few days previously at the Saddle Room: she was already becoming boringly possessive. The menu was pretentious and the food – when it finally arrived – cold. The speeches, with in jokes about the Yacht Club, were fortunately cut short by the broadcast of the carillon from the Puerta del Sol in Madrid. In Spain it is the custom to welcome in the New Year by eating twelve grapes to the chimes of midnight. Usually I get the giggles halfway through and choke on my grapes. That night, however, I did not miss a beat. Everyone toasted the New Year 1965 with not-the-best Spanish champagne, kissed or shook hands. I tried to look jolly. I knew I was not being nice to Marisa, but I found that we had little in common. I was wondering what I was doing there wearing a silly hat and how soon I could reasonably go home. The band played 'Let's Twist Again', which I had no intention of doing. Marisa, understandably, got angry. Staring across the dance floor, I became aware of a petite brunette in a tight-fitting pale pink Chinese dress, dancing with Teddy's brother Nene, laughing and smoking a large cigar. She had been sitting at the opposite end of the table, and I had not noticed her earlier. My low spirits suddenly lifted, and I danced across with Marisa to get a better look. Perhaps I had seen her before – she was a friend of Teddy and Pedro's – but I had always steered clear of Spanish girls. I asked her for the next dance. Her name was Elena.

From the Yacht Club, Teddy and the rest of us went to the popular Indigo Jazz Club, run by Lucia's fiancé, Ramón. Father had paid for its lease in Lucia's name, and had gone out of his way to help his future son-in-law. When Ronnie Scott, on holiday in Palma, had visited us shortly after the Indigo opened, Father persuaded him to stay for another week to 'play sax every night in return for the hotel and fare'. Ramón had his own three-piece combo in which he played the drums. When Ramón could not get a permit to stay open after midnight – the hours when people are in the mood for jazz – Father had meetings with the Governor General in Palma; and even contacted his friend Manuel Fraga, the Minister of Tourism. The coveted 3 a.m. licence was at last 'fixed'. Lucia, home for the Oxford vacations, lived with Ramón in the Guillermo Massot flat, and, at the Indigo, helped Ramón's domineering father behind the bar.

There were no free tables, so we got our drinks and sat on a wall outside in the street listening to the beat of the music. I looked around for Elena but she had gone. So I took Marisa back to her hotel, and drove back to Deyá.

My mind was made up to chuck archaeology. What I had wanted was to study Majorcan prehistory. Metal spectroscopy merely took me back to the laboratory. Indeed, in my heart of hearts I knew that I was not really in love with archaeology at all; it was its link with Deyá and my desire to return to live there that had lured me into going to Oxford. If archaeology was to lead me away from Deyá, I was not interested. I felt I was letting Bill down, and I knew my decision would hurt Father.

Back in Oxford, I collected my things and sorted out my affairs with Christopher Hawkes and the college. On my way home I stopped in Paris, not to see Marie, but to talk to SAMEGA, who proposed that I help them get into soil analysis measurements for the building trade. They already had contacts with a laboratory in Madrid. In Spain, architects mostly planned conventional foundations for their buildings, and it mattered little whether these were laid on rock or sand. Houses collapsed frequently, and there was a building opposite our flat in Guillermo Massot which was still shored up with telegraph poles ten years after it had failed. I read a book on soil mechanics and drove to Madrid, where I talked to the laboratory about the services SAMEGA could offer. Almost at once, though, I got SAMEGA a contract for work on the east coast of Majorca. We were asked to study the feasibility of drilling a set of barrier wells along the beach to stop sea water from encroaching landward into the fresh water aquifer. Soon I was measuring and mapping the salinity of water wells in the area. Although it was a stop-gap solution, I had managed to return to the island on a SAMEGA salary.

However, I still had ideas about how to earn a living in Deyá itself. If I could not work as an archaeologist, then perhaps I could live off the land. At the turn of the century, the *Arxiduc* had won prizes at international exhibitions for wines he made from his vineyards above the Valldemosa coast. His vine stock was still around. On my way to Oxford I had called in at the *École d'Agriculture* in Montpelier to make enquiries on how to start a vineyard in Deyá. I was planning to lease Father's land across the road from Canellún. On their advice I had the soil analysed by the local Chamber of Agriculture, and I fetched an aged Majorcan vintner, who had worked as a boy on the *Arxiduc*'s vineyards, to look at the site. All agreed that vines should do well. Nevertheless, I was also considering alternative crops that might be better money-earners than vines: the pistachio nuts I had seen in Greece or – if I could find water on the land – the pink grapefruit which I had admired in southern Texas. Meanwhile I was helping Bill on his digs at weekends, and wondering if perhaps there was a living to be made from the now almost completed Museum-Library complex.

Marisa had temporarily been posted by her airline to Madrid. One evening, when I was having a drink on my own in the Saddle Room, in walked Elena. I had not seen her since New Year's Eve.

'Oh, Guillermo, it's you,' she said, sitting down. 'Do you know La Mona?' It was our nickname for an intense young man who had been to school with Teddy and Po.

'I know who he is. What's he done?'

'He invited me for a trip around the island in his new car. I tried to leave the house this morning before he arrived, but he got there earlier than I expected and I was caught.'

'So . . .?'

'So I've had a hell of a day. We've even driven through Deyá – he gave me a ten-minute talk on what good friends you are . . . .'

'Where is he now?'

'Just parking the car. Please, think up an excuse so that I can get away from him.'

La Mona came in. Just as I was saying hello and thinking up a tale, Elena interrupted.

'Juan,' she said, 'look, I'm feeling a little tired and Guillermo was just going to see my brother-in-law so I'll drive home with him. Thank you for a wonderful day.' I had no idea who her brother-in-law was.

'Good to see you again, Juan, see you soon,' I said, and held the door open for Elena and a new life.

CHAPTER XI

1

It was April 1965. I let the bucket down the well on the end of its rope, let it fill, drew it up, and poured the water into labelled plastic bottles – later I would measure its salinity, and plot the seawater encroachment on a map. It was simple enough work for SAMEGA. I went over and sat next to Elena on a low rough wall of rocks, next to the well, overlooking a stony field covered in yellow daisies, bright red poppies and wild peas.

'Don't you think we should get a place so we can live together? It seems ridiculous you living with your sister and I with my parents.'

'I don't know,' she replied, 'I don't think it would be a good idea here on the island. Not unless we were married. You know what people are like.' In the warm sun, bees were buzzing about. I plucked a couple of pea pods, shelled them and popped the tiny peas in my mouth. They were sweet and crunchy.

'Well, let's get married then.'

2

Antonio Lambea, Elena's father, came from a religious Basque family – of his six sisters, four had become nuns. He had studied engineering at the Military Academy in Madrid and graduated top of his class. Commissioned in 1928, he was posted to Spanish Morocco, where the Rif War was being fought against the Moorish insurgents, and acquired a useful reputation among his superiors for being an excellent, if short-tempered, sapper. Elena's mother, Maria-Luisa Hugas, was born of Spanish parents in Argentina. The father had died of the flu when she was a child. The widowed mother returned with three children to Madrid, where Maria-Luisa grew up. She met Antonio in 1930 on his return from the North African campaign, and fell for the intelligent young officer. Having no father for comparison, she thought that his short temper was a sign of virility. On their honeymoon, when a door slammed downstairs, she realized her mistake.

'Antonio,' she asked drowsily, 'won't you go and shut it?'

'Go yourself, woman, I'm tired,' he snapped.

From the beginning of Franco's uprising in 1936, Antonio's regiment was under Nationalist command. He followed Franco's advance, surveying and repairing damaged or destroyed hospitals, factories and bridges. After the Nationalist victory of 1939, Antonio, an unusually young lieutenant-colonel, found himself in charge of building council houses, an artificial-silk factory and a large stadium in Burgos. There he moved Maria-Luisa and the two children – Marta, born in 1932, and Alvaro, in 1934. On the fifth of July 1941, their daughter Elena was born.

For an officer in his position just after the Civil War, Antonio was exceptional: he refused kick-backs. He and the family lived exclusively on his army pay. When speculators asked him where in Burgos the stadium would be located, not only did he not divulge the information, but he took a perverted pleasure in misleading them. This made him enemies and his superiors were pressured into placing him, as a disciplinary measure, in charge of a transmissions garrison in Seville. Antonio, however, was too valuable an engineer to be squandered on garrison duty. Continually reassigned to larger and more complex projects, he and the family moved twenty times in fifteen years.

Antonio worked mostly at home with draughtsmen, whom he had picked and trained from among young army recruits. His temper had not mellowed with age. When she was eight years old Elena saw one of her father's draughtsmen wet himself with fear when being yelled at by the angry *coronél*. His hobbies were carried to extremes. In those days in Spain most books were published in soft covers. He bound his volumes in exquisitely embossed white or light brown vellum covers. Whenever he decided to do this, the dining-room table was out of bounds to the family for the ten days it took. He never chose the simple option. In Burgos where the ground was waterlogged or frozen in winter, he grew a cactus garden; in Seville where there was no water in summer, he planted an 'English' garden. Despite his Catholic upbringing Antonio was an atheist. One day, tired of having nuns call at lunchtime asking for charity, the *coronél* opened the front door to them in the nude.

In 1950 Antonio passed into the reserve as a full colonel. Taking a rainfall map of Spain, he picked on the wettest spot of all: Vigo, in Galicia, in the north-west. There he rented a house and laid out a vegetable garden and built a chicken run. His tomato plants were given the optimum manuring and he was furious when a self-seeded plant below the kitchen window, which received the coffee-grounds and tea leaves, did twice as well. Every morning before school, he made Elena, now eleven years old, check which hens were about to lay by sticking her finger up their behinds, and record the result of each against its name on the board.

Elena began her schooling in the kindergarten at Burgos, where Antonio trained their Alsatian dog to accompany her. Thereafter, because of the constant moves, she never went to the same school two years running. In Vigo she attended the state *instituto*, run on university lines, where the teaching was excellent. Antonio believed that education began at home, and he encouraged her to use his well-stocked library. She did so on long wet winter evenings and was soon well-read in medicine, philosophy and Spanish literature. One of Antonio's army assignments had been to catalogue every bridge in Spain for its load-bearing capacity; he sometimes took Elenita with him, pointing out the different engineering solutions and explaining why Roman bridges were, for their size, stronger than their modern equivalents.

Antonio's ideas were ahead of his time, and it was unfortunate that he was such an unstable character. In Vigo, without a superior officer to hold him in check, he became increasingly despotic.

'Elenita, go to my study and, in the left-hand drawer, towards the back, in a lacquered box, is a ball of string. Fetch it and hurry!' In her anxiety to get his instructions right, so that he would not be angry with her, Elena failed even to see the box – which was exactly where he said it would be. Breaking the lead in one of his pencils was a major catastrophe: he would pace up and down raving at her carelessness. The whole family suffered. Marta left home to become an air hostess; Alvaro volunteered to do his military service the day he became eligible. Only Elena and her mother remained, until one day in a fit of temper Antonio threatened them both with his handgun and they had to flee through the neighbour's maize field.

In 1954 on a trip to Majorca, Marta fell in love with Steve Kusak, an American who had helped form the 'Flying Tigers' in China and had been Chiang-Kai-Chek's personal pilot. He was about to invest his savings in a large *finca*, Son Vida, on the outskirts of Palma, which he planned to turn into a luxury hotel, golf course and housing estate. Steve and Marta decided to marry but, by law, she needed her father's permission to do so. Antonio's condition was that Maria-Luisa, now in Madrid with her sister, must return to him. Maria-Luisa agreed – provided that Elena, now in her early teens, was looked after by Steve and Marta. They sent Elena to a French convent school in Lyons, and she spent her holidays with them in Palma, three blocks away from where we lived in Guillermo Massot.

The following year, Elena, now fluent in French, returned of her own accord to her parents' home in Vigo, wanting to be with her mother. There she was befriended by some of her teachers at the *instituto*, and by local intellectuals who visited her father. When he wanted to, Antonio could be a charmer. However, alone again with his wife and daughter, Antonio still resorted to violence, and after yet another flare-up they fled again, this time arriving on Marta's doorstep in Palma. Elena now went to school in England, at Richmond, to learn English, and then worked as an au pair in London. Maria-Luisa, never knowing when Antonio might send the *Guardia Civil* to bring her home to Vigo – as was then his legal right – escaped beyond his reach to New York, where her sister was now living.

In 1959 Elena took a job in Palma, first in an antique shop, and then in a jeweller's. Majorca became Elena's home. She knew Pedro and Teddy; they had long philosophical discussions on the tram, while they saw her home at night. For a time, Teddy's younger brother was her boyfriend. However, Elena's circle of close friends were *pieds-noirs*, who had come to Majorca during the Algerian war of independence. Though our paths touched, they did not cross. Elena and I had both been in London at the same time – living fifteen minutes' walk from each other. She had come to a birthday party at Canellún with Teddy. I had even driven her in Mother's Land-rover, when Teddy and Pedro and I were taking the guitars to a club where we were due to play. But, until that New Year's Eve, we had never consciously met.

After the La Mona incident, I picked up Elena every evening after work at the jewellery shop. Occasionally, we would spend the night together at our now empty Guillermo Massot flat. On weekends, she came to Deyá. A fortnight later Elena took a week off and accompanied me while I sampled the water wells.

Elena was one year younger than I, with strong Mediterranean features, brilliant white teeth, deep brown eyes, full black hair. She was exquisitely slim and small boned, with a diminutive behind and a firm, well-endowed front. Occasionally she modelled for one of the best designers in Palma. Never satisfied, she complained that her legs were too short. She was a shrewd judge of character, remembering what people had said and how they behaved; she saw situations develop long before the participants did. Her ability to notice minute details in her surroundings was exceptional: once she joined a mycological group and within weeks could distinguish dozens of varieties of mushrooms and toadstools, remembering the characteristic features of each. She spoke excellent English and French. She would have liked to have studied medicine; her medical knowledge was prodigious and so was her diagnostic eye. It was unfortunate that, due to the family situation, she was never given the opportunity to go to university. All these talents contrasted oddly with an unwarranted lack of self-confidence, which stemmed from an unawareness of how special her gifts were.

3

At Canellún, Mother, Elena and I were sitting around the *depósito* table having tea. Mother's Abyssinian cats were sunning themselves on the ground next to us; the poodles kept begging me to throw them their ball. As ever, I found it hard to broach matters that might upset Mother. Her apparent unemotional acceptance of all things was what I found so daunting: I never really knew what she felt.

'Mother,' I finally stammered, 'Elena and I have decided to get married.' There is nothing like jumping in at the deep end, I thought.

'Oh, have you? How nice . . . .' A tense silence followed.

'. . . As soon as we can arrange it.' I persisted.

'Catch, Jotie, good dog!' cried Mother, changing the conversation. Though I was used to this, it did not make talking to her any easier.

'Do you think Father would let us use the Posada until we get straightened out?'

Mother never vouched for Father, even though at the time he was with Cindy in Mexico.

'You'd better ask him,' she said, getting up and walking to the kitchen for some more hot water.

At Christmas when I was having my doubts about Oxford, Father had become increasingly obsessive about Cindy, to whom he wrote constantly. For days he would get no letters in reply and this affected his health – he suffered from nose-bleeds and stomach upsets. When a letter from Cindy did arrive Father would be ecstatic. In February he visited her in New York, where he was giving a lecture; from there both went to Mexico. Mother did not know when, or even whether, he would come back. With his previous Muses, Father had always kept one foot firmly in the domestic fold. Now, however, he had been absent for two months, the longest he had ever spent away from his beloved Deyá since our return in 1946. It appeared as though Father's poetic obsession with his Muse, as it had done with Laura, might force him to leave his family once more.

I cabled: 'MARRYING SOON STOP IS POSADA AVAILABLE STOP LOVE WILLIAM.'

He cabled back: 'WHOM TO STOP CERTAINLY STOP FATHER.'

4

I had always loved the Posada and in 1956, when money was tight, I had pleaded with Father not to sell it. Father still housed his guests there. The Posada abuts the church and faces north, looking from the top of the Puig, over the olive groves, to the Mediterranean. Parts of the house date from the fifteenth century, parts from the seventeenth. Squat and malproportioned, it shares a wall with the church, and another with the rectory. At one time it had been a convent and – before Laura and Robert bought it in 1935 – Sunday School was held there, the children entering by a connecting door from the rectory.

I fitted the large old-fashioned key into the lock, turned it, and swung back the two heavy wooden leaves of the main door, letting Elena in; I then closed the external glass door, to keep out the cold. The *entrada* was large. The closely spaced beams holding up its high ceiling were adze cut. The walls were uneven from countless layers of annual whitewash. The floor was paved with square blocks of limestone, the joins grouted with smooth light-brown cement; in one corner, bedrock showed through. It was rather overfurnished with two large tables, a dozen odd chairs and a bench, all products of Father's forays into the shops of his antiquarian friends. The wall the house shared with the church was covered by a vast *tapa* from Tonga, made of pulped Pacific mulberry wood, and patterned with a brown design. It had been given to father by Queen Salote's niece. The other walls were mostly decorated with old ceramic plates, but above the large door at the back of the *entrada* hung a carved and gilt red-and-yellow Spanish royal coat of arms. This door led, up two wide steps cobbled with smooth rounded stones which Father had carried up from the Cala, into the dining room on the right, to the garden door on the left, and to the kitchen door ahead. The minute kitchen, with a shallow stone sink, charcoal stove and cupboard – but no running water – was about the size of a ship's galley. The dining room had yet another set of table and chairs, and a large corner-cupboard which stood out from its corner because the walls were so crooked. Above the table were hung the two splendid oil paintings of Majorcan dance-costumes by Joan Junyer. A low door at the far end of the dining room led to the foganya, the 'chimney room', with its fireplace and whitewashed benches surrounding the burnished floor of what once had been the hearth of a large open chimney. Upstairs were the bedrooms, and a small washroom, water for which had to be carried up in buckets. On the far side of the small garden, with its almond trees and picturesque wellhead, was Isabela the donkey's stable, with the 'privy'.

Elena was enchanted with the Posada and we moved in for the Easter weekend. We slept in the front bedroom and were woken by the shuffle of feet, the coughs and the intermittent low chants of the Easter Sunday procession which circled the Puig, and passed beneath our window.

5

Marta, Elena's older sister, had been trying for years to arouse her interest in Palma's more eligible bachelors, and had been concerned when Elena took so little notice. When we announced we were getting married, Marta was delighted. It seemed, thus, that I was a satisfactory match. What she did not know was that I had no idea of how I would earn a living. Still, I had savings to last us for about a year; and hopes that something would turn up. Elena showed no signs of being bothered.

We went to the Saddle Room and found Teddy.

'Teddy! Elena and I are going to get married!' I said, slapping him on the back. I was taken aback by his reaction. The colour drained not only from his face but almost, it seemed, from the walrus moustache he sported. He ordered two double gins, one for himself and one for me and, leaving Elena on a stool at the bar, steered me outside, and sat beside me on the pavement.

'Guillermo, do you know what you are doing? You hardly know Elena! I have known her for years. She is wild, that one. She'll have you for breakfast! This is just love on the rebound, after Marie.' He took a slug of gin; I sipped at mine.

'Maybe so,' I said. 'But I love Elena. Anyway, if things go sour, there's always divorce. That's why we're getting married in England.'

'But, but, but . . . .' Teddy realized that, for once, his logic was of no use and that nothing would budge me. He finished his drink, and for a while we sat silently; then we went back to join Elena and celebrate.

Both Elena and I realized that a mere three weeks' acquaintance was a feeble foundation for a lifetime. However, being very much in love, there seemed little point in waiting. As I had told Teddy, we planned to head for England. In any case, it was most unlikely we could ever get married in Spain: when Elena had last seen her father he had threatened her, 'Someday, you'll want to marry and then you'll have to ask my permission!' Elena had no intention of doing so.

Unfortunately, our trip to England had to be postponed: we discovered that Elena's passport could not be renewed. Unmarried women in Franco's Spain were required to do six months' 'voluntary' social service, the equivalent of the military service for young men; and one of the means by which the government ensured a regular quota of 'volunteers' was to refuse passports to women over twenty-one who had not complied. We therefore decided to go to Madrid to seek the help of a friend of Elena's family, who had contacts in the government, and could, we hoped, get us over the passport hurdle.

In the meantime, Father had returned to Deyá, ostensibly for our wedding. He arrived in poor shape: he had lost weight and suffered from chronic indigestion, nausea and nosebleeds. In Mexico, Father had not managed to keep up with Cindy and she had then gone off to live with another man. Father thought he had broken with Cindy, yet by his rules she remained his Muse, and he could talk of nothing else.

'You see, Elena,' he said. 'Aemilia's problem is that she suffers from hypoglycaemia. If she does not eat regular meals, she goes crazy. Otherwise she is the best woman on earth.'

Never having met Cindy, Elena reserved judgement, but she was puzzled by Father. The ramblings and preoccupations of the man she faced did not seem to correspond with the works of his she had read. Was something wrong with him?

The evening before our trip to Madrid, Marta and Steve gave us a farewell party – a substitute wedding feast – at their house in the chic Son Vida estate. Among the hundred or so guests were Pedro, Po and Teddy, the Waldrens, Elena's *pieds-noirs* friends, Steve and Marta's local and expatriate circle, and of course Mother, Father, Lucia and Tomás. Juan was in Australia. It was a lavish affair: waiters served canapés and champagne. Watching Elena move in and out of the throng of guests with such assurance, I wondered whether she would ever be satisfied with the kind of life I was likely to provide her with.

6

We loaded the Karmann-Ghia on to the Barcelona ferry, drove to Madrid, and went straight to see Nini about getting Elena's passport. Nini Montián, an ex-actress, earned a comfortable living by doing what were termed *favores* for people. In her sixties, and of aristocratic background, she knew everyone of importance in Franco's government, as well as their peccadillos . . . It was her custom to arrange quiet dinner parties for ministers and their mistresses. In exchange Nini got introductions and audiences – sometimes with Franco himself – for Spanish and foreign businessmen, and took a commission on whatever contracts they obtained.

Elena and I were ushered through the luxurious main room – hung with chandeliers and a large portrait of Nini's father, the count, on horseback in full Hussar regalia as King Alfonso XIII's aide-de-camp – into a smaller sitting room. Nini, heavily rouged and made up, wearing a loose-fitting silk housecoat, looked at me appraisingly as we sat down around a table in the corner. We explained our difficulty and how we wanted to get out of the country to be married.

'Elenita, are you . . .?' she asked.

'No,' Elena replied.

'What's your hurry, then?'

'We want to get married, but we also want to be able to get a divorce if things don't work out.' We were interrupted by Nini's senile mother, the countess, asking when they were going to the Palace.

'Later, Mama, later,' Nini said gently. 'But why not get married in Spain? An annulment is better than a divorce, and I can always arrange that. As for your father, Elenita, he need never know. Now let's see . . . Guillermo, in what Church were you christened – Anglican?'

'I never was,' I replied, unhappy at the turn our conversation was taking. An annulment presupposed a Catholic marriage.

'Well, you'll have to become a Christian if you want to get married quickly. Never mind, you can get yourself christened at the British Embassy, their church is just across the road. If they make a fuss, we can always make you a Catholic. I've friends in the cloth.' And, without giving me time to protest, 'Now, Elenita, tell me about Marta and her children.'

Nini could easily have arranged a passport for Elena. However, her solution to our problem had its merits. A register-office marriage performed in England was not valid in Spain. Legally Elena would remain a spinster unless she took British nationality. Finding we had begun something not easily stopped, we went to the British Embassy the next morning to enquire about a minister.

'Ah yes,' the girl behind the counter said. 'The Archdeacon Basil-Ney, that's whom you should see. Let me see, I have his phone number somewhere. . . .'

'¿*Oiga*, Hello? The Reverend Basil-Ney? My name is William Graves and I need a baptism certificate to get married.'

'Er . . . where were you baptized?' said the voice on the other end.

'Well, actually, I'm not,' I replied brightly.

'Er . . . I think you had better come around to see me. Would next week be all right?'

'Couldn't you see me now?'

I drove at once to see him, a comfortable-looking chap.

'Well now, Mr Graves, you do realize that I shall have to prepare you, before we can receive you into the Church of England?'

'Oh? I went to a public school for four years. I have a pretty good idea of what it is about. I thought one just got christened and that was that. I don't really want to become a Roman Catholic, but I have a priest laid on who will do it right away.' I explained our predicament.

'Well, I suppose in that case. . . . But I can't perform the ceremony for another ten days. I'm repainting the church.'

'It'd just be Elena and me,' I said: I did not want to hang around in Madrid for ever.

The following afternoon, Elena and I walked into the British Embassy church. It was lit only by the evening light coming through the high stained-glass windows; it took a while before I discovered the Archdeacon up a ladder at the far end of the apse, paintbrush in hand. The altar was covered by sheets.

'Ah, one moment,' he said. 'Just coming.'

When he came over I introduced him to Elena. I caught his eyes going to her waist. His surprise at not finding her noticeably pregnant was obvious. He first filled in the forms.

'Father's name?'

'Robert Graves.'

He raised his eyebrows. '*The White Goddess*?'

'Ah,' he said, as I nodded, as if that explained everything.

The ceremony was short. He poured holy water out of a bottle into a pyrex bowl, read a lesson about it being better late than never, had me recite the Lord's Prayer with him – although my mind went blank and I could remember only snatches of it – and finally gave me the blessing. I thanked him, made a small donation to the church, and we stepped into the evening sun, the baptism certificate in my hand.

Next morning we went to the bishopric of Madrid, and were ushered into a large bright study. Years before, Nini had introduced her friend Don Abel to his future mistress.

'Ah, yes,' he said. 'Nini told me you would come. What a wonderful lady! How is she? Now, what can I do for this young couple?' When we explained that we wanted to marry, he called one of his assistants, a priest with that typically ecclesiastical smell of musty clothes and incense, to take our particulars. Nini had warned me that if the form was not filled in too truthfully it would make an annulment easier to obtain. Her chauffeur, who had come with us, swore that he had known me for ten years and vouched for my good character. Elena assured the priest that her father had given us his blessing but that he was in South America. For my permanent address I gave Nini's; Elena, that of her aunt's flat, where she and her mother had once fled, and which was now let. The banns had to be posted in our local parishes but, by special dispensation, this period was reduced to a week. Since we needed two witnesses, I went out into the street and conscripted a couple of passers-by.

'If it doesn't take too long,' they both said.

In front of them I swore I would bring up our children in the Catholic faith. The marriage was set up for the following week in the church of Chamberí, the parish for the address Elena had given. The priest closed the folder: on it, beneath our names, I read 'Friends of the Director of Diocesan Tribunals'.

Instead of staying in Madrid while the banns were posted, we went to Galicia where Elena had lived with her parents. This was partly a pre-honeymoon trip, and partly for me to get my own passport stamped at the Portuguese border. At the time I had no residence permit, and I had to leave Spain every three months. We drove to Vigo, battling to keep the car on the narrow main road as the massive refrigerated fish-lorries swept past us on their way to the Madrid markets. So when Elena asked me to pull over, and she got out of the car and was sick, I thought nothing of it. In Galicia we stayed close to the Portuguese border in a small hotel overlooking the port of Bayona, where Pinzón had docked the

Pinta, after his discovery of America with Columbus. We dined in pantagruelian fashion on octopus, shrimp, prawns, crabs, oysters, mussels, clams, goose-barnacles and scallops, helped down with chunks of the doughnut-shaped Galician bread and young, slightly fizzy, Ribeiro wine. While getting ready for bed, Elena suddenly pushed me out of her way, ran into the bathroom and was sick again. I thought it must be food poisoning but Elena knew better. She was pregnant.

It changed nothing. We drove to the Portuguese border and I had my passport stamped. We then walked the long windswept sandy beaches; visited Galician dolmens; and ate more wonderful seafood. Taking the tram along the coast to Vigo, we visited friends of Elena's, asking them not to tell her father of our presence: she had no intention of letting me meet my future father-in-law. She was very funny when she told stories about the *coronél*, as she called him.

'He had lost an eraser. I might have taken it to do my homework. Anyway he lined us up in the garden, standing to attention: Mother, Marta, Alvaro, and myself. Pacing to and fro, he harangued us about not taking things without his permission. He was in full regalia on his way to a parade. Behind him was a white bench made of slats which our gardener had just painted. The *coronél* sat down and glared at us. When he got up, his backside was covered with white stripes. Mother looked at each of us and put her finger to her lips. He left for the parade in his striped uniform.

'My mother was like that, a natural subversive, and she kept us sane. Afterwards, of course, we were all punished, but it was worth it.'

As we came to know one another better, Elena succeeded in getting me to be more open about myself. At Canellún, I had never told Mother and Father what I did during the day. By Canellún standards, 'Went to Palma,' was a long statement. She made me give her a chronological account of everything I did, and then fill in particulars as she asked for them.

'Tell me the sort of things you tell your "inner self",' she said.

'What do you mean by my "inner self"? I don't have one.'

I was unused to talking about myself in the intimate way Elena expected. Previously, I had never had a heart-to-heart talk with anyone, even my parents. Mother shied away from any intimacy; and the age difference with Father made him emotionally inaccessible. Though I loved them both, we rarely kissed or hugged one another or had any physical contact. Not until I met Elena had anyone ever scratched my back; I realized how many years of pleasure I had missed.

Our wedding was set for the sixth of May 1965. The night before we both lay awake in an hotel on the granite slopes of El Escorial, outside Madrid: each wondering whether we were doing the right thing. However, Elena's pregnancy helped remove any doubts. We arrived at the church in Madrid half an hour before the ceremony – Elena wearing a brown suit, I, a sports jacket – to find that, although secular weddings were forbidden in Franco's Spain, all the legal documents must still be filled in at the church. So I rushed to the register office for the necessary papers, and got back to the church just in time to welcome our handful of guests.

Nini, in mink though it was already the sixth of May, had offered to be our 'godmother'. Irakly of Bragation, 13th Prince of Georgia and married to a member of the Spanish Royal Family, was our best man. Nini claimed that having a best man of high social standing would make an annulment easier; she was calling in a favour the Prince owed her. The British Consul-General, Mr Sedgwick-Jell, expecting a large formal gathering, came to register the marriage, wearing his cousin's Stowe School morning coat and a silk carnation in his buttonhole. Nini's chauffeur made up the group and, with Mr Sedgwick-Jell, acted as co-witness to the ceremony. It was held in the vestry. The six of us emerged to find the Prince's long pearl-grey Mercedes in front of the church steps. The Prince left in it, after the briefest of handshakes. The Consul, with the Register under his arm, took the *Metro*. We kissed Nini goodbye, thanked her chauffeur, and drove towards Barcelona. The church photographer, deciding perhaps that we could not pay, never even sent us the pictures which he took during the ceremony.

CHAPTER XII

1

When Elena was still working at the jeweller's, her boss, Miguel Miró, told her jokingly that the day he got rid of her, he would make a pilgrimage to the monastery of Lluch. Now he decided to keep his word. Steve Kusak, Elena's brother-in-law, having had her on his hands for ten years, offered to join Miguel. Elena and I, with Mother and Father and the Waldrens, drove to Lluch and prepared a picnic for the pilgrims' arrival after their fifteen-kilometre walk.

'You may be happy to be rid of her,' Father told Steve and Miguel after lunch, 'but to show you how delighted I am to have her in the family, I will walk from Deyá to Palma, and cook lunch to boot!'

A week later, Father – then almost seventy years old – Bill Waldren and I walked the thirty kilometres to Steve and Marta's house and there barbecued a calf.

Before Elena and I had left to get married, I had finished the job for SAMEGA and once again resigned. Meanwhile, waiting for another job to turn up, I worked with Bill at the cave from which he had recovered a great many bones of *Myotragus Balearicus*, the extinct goat. In the same layers as the bones we found pre-Talayotic tools. We organized a symposium to discuss these finds. Several professors and experts attended and we presented to them our novel conclusion: that man had hunted the *myotragus* to extinction.

The symposium meetings were held in the newly completed Library, an addition which gave the Museum even more prestige. The Complex was now called the Deyá Archaeological Museum, Library and Gallery Teix and, together with its archaeological functions, was also used for the *estrangers*' cultural events. Villagers, regrettably, did not join in, but I could understand their reticence. I could even foresee future trouble with them, since Bill and I were hoping to add a shop to the Complex, to sell paintings, sculpture, photographs, ceramics and jewellery produced by *estrangers*. As ever, I kept looking for a niche to make a living in Deyá.

The Complex was impressive and Bill enthusiastically showed visitors around. One American was so taken by the project that he promised Bill $20,000 in support, unaware, perhaps, that we had no tax-deductible nor even legal status. That evening, in the Library flat where the Waldrens were now living, Father, Elena and myself and a few others met to discuss the 'donation'. It soon became plain that I was not the only person who was clutching at straws for ways of staying in Deyá. Within half an hour we had budgeted the full sum. When Elena suggested that maybe we should ask our Maecenas for a pledge in writing before we went any further and actually began spending his money, Bill's wife Jackie snapped at her, saying that being pregnant gave her a jaundiced view of life. As usual, Elena was proven right: the donation never materialized.

In the mid-Fifties, Alastair Reid had joked that Father should have his own Book-of-the-Month club. However, after Father began lecturing in America, his output slowed down, and he concentrated on his first love: poetry. Since 1957 he had published some essays, two translations and several children's books. His only substantial major work was a collaboration with Dr Raphael Patai, *The Hebrew Myths*. With this scaled-down literary production Father could hardly justify having Karl's full-time secretarial help. Nevertheless, he would doubtless have kept him on, had it not been for Karl's strong dislike of Cindy.

Unforgivably, Father sacked Karl by letter from Mexico, probably at Cindy's instigation. It was a shameful way to break up their thirty-five-year partnership. What Karl did for Father can never be fully appreciated. Without his editorial help, Father could not have produced half the voluminous works that came out of his Deyá study. Karl had been as loyal and as industrious an assistant as anyone could ever hope to have.

When Father returned from Mexico and Elena and I were leaving to get married, Karl was winding up his affairs. During his three months' wait for a US visa, he never once set foot in Canellún. It felt strange in the house without his presence. I was concerned with how Mother would cope on her own: over the years she had relied increasingly on Karl to change fuses, organize plumbers and carpenters and keep Gelat's water flowing. Karl, though, had often made Mother face up to things she would rather not, for he was never one to keep quiet when he objected to something or someone. What had upset Mother most was his disapproval of Ramón, Lucia's Catalan boyfriend, and she now looked forward to Karl's departure with relief.

Happily, Karl had secured, with no help from Father, a position as reference librarian in the University Libraries of the State University of New York at Buffalo. Later he became the curator of the Twentieth-Century Poetry Collection – where Father's poetry manuscripts were held. For Karl, leaving Deyá at that moment proved to be a blessing. He, thankfully, missed the worst excesses of Father's later behaviour. He also missed a general disintegration of the village society as he had known it.

That summer Lucia and Ramón got married. Lucia had just come down from Oxford, having earned a brilliant First Class Honours degree in Modern Languages. She had worked hard for it. She never went to parties or out with boys: as she was engaged to Ramón, Oxford to her was simply a place of study. Like me, Lucia had not been baptized, but in her case there was no need: Ramón had time to get the Vatican's dispensation to marry a non-Christian. The birthday party was cancelled even though it was Father's seventieth – he celebrated it instead with a poetry reading at the Museum – and all efforts at Canellún were directed towards Lucia's wedding and reception.

The ceremony took place in the rectory, bedecked with flowers and with sweet-smelling myrtle shoots covering the path leading to it. Lucia, in white, was given away by Father. At Canellún the hundreds of guests swarmed up the drive towards the *depósito*. The reception followed the same pattern as our birthday parties: the play, food, champagne and wedding cake, and then a dance-band. Karl was conspicuously absent at the wine barrels.

2

In asking Father for the Posada, I had come, quite unwittingly, between Father and his Muse.

William . . . cabled me to Mexico for the Posada which I'd promised Aemile. Aemile had gone off to a place where there was no mail, and did not answer my letters when she returned and had decided to marry another, rather sweet man (but another *perdido*) – who promptly went off elsewhere with someone else's wife. So I cabled William letting him have the Posada. I also wrote to her and told her what I had done.

Eventually I got a vague, but most loving letter, which showed she hadn't even troubled to pick up my letters from the P.O.; so that's how it is or isn't. [RG to RF, May 1965]

That had been in May. By July Cindy was back in Deyá. Father now wanted the Posada for her. He thought up an arrangement which he considered perfectly reasonable: the Posada would be Cindy's, and Elena and I could live there as her guests. Father imagined that Elena and I would love her because 'whoever loves me, loves her'; he could not conceive that anyone might not. This was the attitude he had held with Laura Riding, and because of it many of his close old friends had abandoned him; he had made the same assumption when Judith and Margot were Muses except, perhaps, that Judith's Musedom was too brief to break up any friendships, and Margot never seemed to take her Musedom as anything but a compliment and, indeed, was generally loved by all – even Karl. When I told Elena of Father's proposal she was furious.

'I'm not staying in this house if I have to have your father's mistress here!' she cried. 'What happens if I open the door and find them in bed together? What do I say then? . . . I'm sorry? I'd be having your own mistresses in the house next!'

Father got into a great frenzy over our refusal, and insisted that we change our mind; but he would not tell us outright to leave. This was my first confrontation with him, and it both confused and distressed me. But I dug my heels in. As I saw it, Father had lent us the house, and I was determined not to move until our baby was born. When he realized we would not leave of our own accord, Father banged on our door at eight the next morning: he wanted a painting which he said he had given Cindy. The following day he woke us up again: he demanded a table which he said was hers.

Elena was livid. 'What else in this house belongs to that woman?' she yelled at him. 'This table? Well take it. I prefer not to be in the same house as it.'

I helped her carry it outside. Father went off sheepishly, not used to being shouted at, the table too heavy for him to carry on his own. It rained all day, and the table-top, which we had lovingly polished, had begun to warp before someone came to pick it up. A couple of days later, when Elena and I were sitting on the verandah of the Old Café with some friends, Cindy came up to me, looking for a fight.

'You bastard!' she said, fury in her eyes.

I just stared coldly back at her and said nothing. Cindy went away swearing under her breath. Later, Father marched up to the Posada wanting me to apologize to her for being insulting!

Elena convinced me that Cindy was trying to take over Canellún. I was determined that this should not happen even if it meant further confrontation with Father. We went over to Canellún almost daily to see Mother, who appeared unmoved by Cindy's return. Mother smiled, did the gardening, made tea, and cooked for everyone. She allowed Father to keep up his pretence that life was normal. I doubt that she ever took him to task about Cindy. She knew him well, and to force a break could have unforeseen consequences. Indeed, she must have been upset at the way Elena and I were confronting him, unsettling him and making matters worse. But her apparently calm acceptance of the situation did not mean that she enjoyed it. When Cindy came to the house, Mother would retire to her room while Father's Muse strutted around as though she owned it. Mother suffered from terrible stress-migraines and, when she thought no one was looking, she would often sit holding her head with her eyes closed.

I do not believe that Father ever thought he was doing wrong or might be hurting those that truly loved him. He may well have imagined his Cindy affair as a new 'Trinity' such as that which he, Laura and Nancy had lived in the Twenties. Nevertheless, it must have been obvious, even to Father, that there was not the communion between Cindy and Mother there had been between Laura and Nancy.

That September Selwyn Jepson came to Deyá with his wife Tania, and stayed in the now empty Can Torrent. Mother and Father had met Selwyn, a thriller writer, and Tania, an antiquarian book specialist, in 1951 when they visited my sister Jenny in Portofino just before Alex's death. All of us had read and loved Selwyn's books. A small bird-like man, he was a splendid organizer – during the Second World War he had recruited agents for the French section of the Special Operations Executive. Over the years he had become a kind of godfather to the family. He arranged for Mother's Aga cooker to be shipped over from England; he watched over Tomás who was now at Bedales School in Petersfield, a five-minute drive away; he advised Father on financial matters. As early as 1955, Father had dedicated *Homer's Daughter* 'To Selwyn Jepson, of course'.

Selwyn realized that challenging Father directly about the Cindy situation would not work. Nevertheless, he was the first family friend to make Elena and me feel that we were not wrong to make a stand. Selwyn told me that Jenny too had been furious at Father for taking up with Cindy. This news made me wonder whether Father had not stayed away from Jenny's funeral because of her attitude towards Cindy. Nevertheless, Selwyn assured us that the Cindy affair had almost run its course; that Father and she were quarrelling ever more frequently; and advised us to be patient. I believe he saw parallels between Father's present infatuation and his earlier infatuation with Laura, and felt that, once the affair was over, Father would again become considerate towards his family and friends. Indeed, Selwyn was much less concerned about Cindy than about the real reason for his visit to Deyá.

In order to avoid paying American tax, Father had assigned all the copyrights of his works to a Curaçao offshore firm called International Authors N.V. of which Roturman S.A. was the Swiss holding company. Several other authors had also done this, including Graham Greene, T.H. White and Professor Parkinson, who had formulated the humorous Parkinson's Laws. The arrangement worked well for a while, until the director, a financier called Roe, was caught and jailed in Switzerland accused, among other things, of passing counterfeit $100 notes. International Authors was investigated and found to be bankrupt. Not only did Father lose the $30,000 that was owed to him but, because he no longer officially owned his copyrights, he could touch none of the royalties that were accruing at his publishers. Until the copyrights could be restored to him, no more money would come in.

It was to sort out Father's finances that Selwyn had come to Deyá. Selwyn had him list his assets, and found there was only one which could be realized without affecting the Canellún way of life. This was the Library, the deeds of which were in my name.

'William, would you mind if we sold it?' asked Selwyn.

'The house was never mine,' I replied.

If Father wanted to sell the Library I would gladly do so. However, Father had allowed the Waldrens to live in the Library flat and he could not face having to evict Bill, knowing how much Bill advised him. He asked me to explain his position to the Waldrens myself. My close friendship with Bill had been cooling since Jackie Waldren's remark about Elena's pregnancy, which had upset us both. I now had little involvement in Bill's projects and digs.

When I told the Waldrens – perhaps over-directly as was my way – that the Library was to be sold and that the flat would no longer be available to them, they would not believe me. They thought the story about the loss of Father's royalties was simply a ploy to make them leave 'their' house, and accused Elena and me of wanting to destroy the Complex for our own gain. Indeed, it must have seemed inconceivable to them that Robert Graves, the great man of letters, who was so generous with his money, had no investments to fall back on. They refused to move, and lawyers were called in on both sides.

If I was hoping that by helping Father our relations would improve, I was badly mistaken. Cindy was delighted with this turn of events and spread word among the *estrangers* that Elena and I were indeed the real villains. Father, naturally, would not contradict her, and he referred to the situation as the 'Bill-William imbroglio'. But even Father got angry when Jackie Waldren claimed that he still owed them money for work done building the Library. Every week he had given them whatever sums of money were asked for, and demanded no accounts. The 'imbroglio' had made me realize that not only Elena and I, but also Father, had few real friends among the village *estrangers*. We settled out of court and the Waldrens received ten per cent of the sale price 'in compensation' when the Library was eventually sold in February 1966.

3

When Elena and I first moved into the Posada, Father allowed us to make a few improvements. It was one thing, on a two-week stay in July or August, to shower in the garden with a bucket of water, and to use the 'privy' in Isabela's stable; it was quite another to await a baby in December without proper plumbing or any hot water. We enlarged the bathroom and put in a tub and a lavatory. An electric pump drew water from the cistern to a header tank; a *Butano* geyser heated it. The tiny kitchen remained as it was except for a necessary sink, fridge and *Butano* cooker. Both bathroom and kitchen were behind closed doors and did not change the character of the old house. We stored some of Father's furniture in the attic and the rest we rearranged so that the rooms no longer looked cluttered. We waxed and polished tables and chairs and dusted pictures and plates. Whitewashers added yet another coat to the hundreds of ancient layers covering the walls. Though Elena disliked sewing, she made curtains from traditional patterned Majorcan cotton to help keep out draughts. She was relieved to find that it was not a catastrophe when we broke a glass. I just swept up the splinters, put them into the rubbish bin and bought a new one if needed. However beautiful, however much *baraka* or patina things had acquired with age, they were still just things, and were not worth getting upset over.

Antonia of the Puig, who had always taken care of the house, came in every weekday morning to do our housework and laundry. She was more than a domestic help: she looked after the Posada key. Every householder in Deyá had a neighbour to whom he entrusted his spare key. This was especially true for *estrangers* who might go away to foreign countries – Old Gelat had looked after the Canellún key during Father's ten-year absence – or for people who moved to Palma and used their house on weekends only. The key-holder was responsible for visiting the house every few days to check that the shutters were sound, that roof tiles had not cracked, that the well was filling with winter rain, and that there were no rat-droppings. Antonia, however, appeared also to feel responsible for what went on in the house, as though we were mere temporary visitors. She somehow always knew when we had guests, and would appear in the kitchen with a pile of clean dish-cloths – which she kept for this purpose when doing our laundry – to check who they might be.

If Antonia ruled in the house, Castor reigned in the stable. He had retired as village postman, but continued to look after Isabela, who was now getting on for twenty years. Antonia complained constantly about them both; and not without reason. The house was invaded by flies from Isabela's droppings, and rats thrived on the alfalfa Castor fed her. For his part Castor did little to keep the stable clean. There seemed to be nothing we could do about it. Isabela provided Father with manure, essential for digging into the garden with his compost, and was untouchable. We had to put up with the smell and her early-morning braying. We could not grow flowers beside the path to the stable because Isabela pulled them out by the mouthful as Castor led her through. Castor collected her every weekday morning, slipped on the halter and took her to graze on some terraces he owned near the Mirador. In the evening he brought her back. On fiesta and Sunday mornings Castor called in to water Isabela after Mass, dressed in his Sunday best. From our bedroom we could hear the performance: the creak of the garden gate, the clatter of the chain as the bucket dropped down the well, the thump as the bucket hit the water, the slow squeak as the full bucket was pulled out, the splash of water being poured into Isabela's shallow drinking pan, Castor's footsteps as he carried it over to the wall by the stable; the clack of the wooden bolt sliding back . . . .

'Isabela my love, good morning, look at this lovely water I have brought you.' But the old donkey had bad teeth, and it must have hurt her to suck the cold water out of the pan on the floor; we could hear her sniffing.

'Come on, don't make me take you to the *rentaderos* to drink.'

Then more plaintively: 'Isabela? . . . Oh, all right . . .!' And the clip of Isabela's hooves as they left together.

After Castor's retirement, the post was once again delivered by old Jeroni, who had taken over from Castor while he was in prison during the Civil War. Officially, Jeroni's son had been appointed postman, but he was a mason. Jeroni was some eighty years old, far older than Castor, and he hobbled around the village carrying the mail in a basket. If we were at home he would hand ours to us; if we were out, he would hide it. When we returned, we sometimes found letters behind the shutters, or under a rock, or in a crack in the dry-stone wall. Occasionally, if he had seen Antonia, we might find our mail in the house. Twice we found it in our car and once it was returned to us by the owner of another car which happened to be the same colour as ours.

Elena had her first real contact with the village when we made the improvements on the Posada. We naturally used Antonia's husband, Joan Valentí, for our master-builder. He was also the Mayor, which put us in good stead at the Town Hall. Valentí was a lovely man but he had only one way of doing things: the way he had been taught. The kitchen sink had to be installed at seventy centimetres from the ground and neither Elena nor I could get him to fix it a centimetre higher. She also came up against the eternal water problem. The cistern remained full of rainwater during winter months, but with the new pump it would not last through the dry summer: we had to have it topped up by hosepipe from one of the springs. When Toni of the Puig, Antonia's neighbour, overcharged us, we went to Gabriel of Son Bujosa. When we discovered that Gabriel was charging us more than our neighbours we arranged for a water-lorry to deliver it. I was not being bankrolled by Canellún and could not afford to pay above the market price.

Although Elena understood Majorcan, she claimed that she could not get her tongue around the guttural vowel sounds, so she did not try to speak it. The villagers addressed her by the formal *usted* in Spanish, whereas they still addressed me by the familiar *tu* in Majorcan. Among themselves, Elena was referred to as the *senyora de sa Posada*, while, for the time being, I remained *Guillem de Canellún*. The conversation at the *rentaderos* must have gone something like this:

'She looks about six months gone already,' said one. 'I bet she was pregnant before they were married and therefore the rush.'

'They wouldn't be the first,' said the other. 'Anyway, the boy hasn't done badly for himself. According to *madò* Antonia of the Puig, the young *senyora*'s clean and can cook, and I never see them in the café. A pity she is not Majorcan, but at least she understands us.'

'I hope he doesn't start messing around like his old man.'

'He won't. She's got plenty of character and she won't let him get out of line, you'll see!'

4

Elena was an excellent cook and enjoyed eating. She was never too tired to produce a meal and did so quickly and effortlessly. All she needed was a saucepan and a wooden spoon, never measuring anything. She made a large variety of dishes, from paella to roast beef, from curry to Chinese 'chow' which her brother-in-law had been taught by General Chiang-Kai-Chek's staff. My task was to run down the hill to the Estanco for anything she needed, lay the table, and do the washing-up.

We liked having friends to meals and, as winter approached, sitting with them around the fire in our *foganya*. Pedro and Teddy came up; as did the few *estrangers* with whom we had not quarrelled, and Elena's *pieds-noir* circle. We found that a language common to everyone present – be it Spanish, English or French – was essential if there were to be sensible conversation, and we made our invitations accordingly. I still felt self-conscious about joining in, and tended to stutter; so I usually let Elena, who was a great conversationalist, do the talking for both of us. When something occurred to me, I would prompt her, and she would take up the thread. Being so well read, she had an encyclopedic knowledge, and I felt quite uneducated compared to her.

I came into my own when it came to repairing taps, getting the carpenter to paint the shutters, or handling village situations. On one occasion, my knowledge of the way disputes were settled locally enabled me to help out my brother Tomás. He had a dinghy with an outboard motor with which he sailed from Ca's Floquer to the Cala. In winter he left the motor in the Canellún garage from where, one day, it was stolen. We reported the theft to the *guardias*, and for three years nothing happened. Then one summer at the Cala Tomás saw a villager return from a fishing trip in a boat with an outboard motor like his stolen one, but painted in a different colour. Tomás went to check its serial number, as he was wont to with all motors he saw of his model, found it was indeed his own, and ran along the beach to tell me. I followed him back, removed the motor and climbed up to the *Patrón*'s terrace.

'Toni,' I said, 'if so-and-so of the Clot asks where the outboard motor is, tell him he only has to come to see me.' I was not surprised to find out who the thief was. He had been caught stealing a pencil when we were at school together and Don Gaspar had left him standing in the square outside the school all day with his face to the wall. As far as I was concerned that was the end of the affair. Elena could not understand it.

'Why don't you go to the *guardias*?' she asked. 'It's stealing. It's a crime. He should be punished!'

'What will the *guardias* do?' I replied. 'It would just put the whole village against us.' Toni and the other villagers of course would have known, or suspected, that the engine was Tomás's all along and any official inquiry would have forced them to lie. 'This way he'll lose the trust of the village, and that will hurt him much more. It's best this way.' Elena shook her head in bewilderment.

Elena had a volatile temper which she could lose easily if patronised or spoken down to. Garage mechanics and officials were guaranteed to cause an outburst. She had a swift rapier-like tongue which would cut to the quick, in short lethal thrusts. Fortunately it was rarely directed at me. Losing her temper affected her physically and she would even come out in a rash. Perhaps her most momentous rage was directed at an official in the Passport Office who would not issue her a new passport on the grounds that, being married to an Englishman, she must therefore be British. Elena dragged me straight to our solicitor, and had him read us the pertinent article and paragraph in the latest civil code book. This stated that a wife lost her Spanish nationality if her husband's country automatically gave her his – not the case with Britain. She grabbed the solicitor's copy and stormed back to the Passport Office, almost rubbing the official's face in the law-book.

'Read what it says!' she yelled.

'Take her away!' he pleaded with me, 'or I'll have her locked up.'

Elena got her passport.

My own temperament was more passive. We were taking our siesta one hot afternoon in August. Elena was about five months pregnant and beginning to get quite large. We no longer walked down to the beach every day.

'*¡Ave Maria purisima*! Guillermo?! Elena?!' It was Brother Rafael's voice. Brother Rafael was of the La Salle order and an expert in micro-mammals. We had first met him at the *Myotragus*

Balearicus symposium, which Bill Waldren and I had organized, and where he had given one of the papers. On the day of the symposium he had dropped in to our house on his way to Mass later in the day. Although we had running water in the new bathroom, the connecting arch between the lavatory and the cesspool had not yet been built. He used it, flushing the lavatory all over the garden. To begin with we had shown an interest in Brother Rafael's tiny rodents and he came to see us at least once a week, until both Elena and I came to dread his visits. I now suspected that he was trying to convert me, and get Elena to go to church.

'That's it!' I told Elena. 'I've had enough. I'll get rid of him!'

'But how can you?' She could not imagine me ranting and raving like the *coronél*. She followed me to the top of the stairs and listened. I went down to find Brother Rafael beaming from the frame of the *entrada* door.

'Hermano Rafael, good afternoon. I'm sorry, but I must ask you not to come to this house again,' I said quietly and formally.

'But, but . . . .' he stammered.

'I'm sorry.' And I closed the door behind him.

Elena was waiting for me at the top of the stairs with a look of astonishment on her face.

'How can you do that without losing your temper?' she asked.

5

Elena broke waters on the sixth of December 1965, in the middle of the night. I helped her down the Posada steps to the car, and we drove to the hospital in Palma. It was a beautiful night with bright moonlight. We listened to the French general election results on the car radio. General de Gaulle was getting re-elected. We arrived safely at the hospital only to find that the midwife had no telephone. I found her house and drove her to the hospital. She looked at Elena and called her gynaecologist at once.

We were prepared for a difficult birth. The baby had turned feet-first, and the problem had been exacerbated by Elena's blood which had tested Rh-negative – common in persons of Basque descent – and could set up a fatal allergy in the infant. After some probing the doctor decided on a Caesarean section. I was allowed to watch the operation through a window in the operating theatre door. I sat reading Richard Hughes' *High Wind In Jamaica* and, every couple of pages, I would look through the window. I was not unduly concerned. My confidence in Elena was such that I knew all would be well. It was only when I saw our baby boy – there was no doubt about the gender – and could see Elena was fine, that a lump finally rose in my throat.

Philip was an ugly baby with an enormous mouth and an insatiable appetite. The following day Mother came down to the hospital to see her first grandchild.

'Don't be alarmed, Elena,' she said, 'they all look like that when they are born, but they don't turn out badly in the end.'

With Philip safely in the world, I began to fret about not having a job. I wanted to remain in Deyá if possible. Indeed, Cindy had returned to New York to over-winter, and for the time being the pressure was off the Posada. I reconsidered my ideas for vineyards or a grapefruit farm on Canellún land, but even I could see they both required more capital and expertise than I had. The Museum Complex venture was dead. I could have gone back into the oil business and continued mud-logging – but that would mean being away from Elena and the baby for six and seven weeks at a time. Elena kept assuring me something would turn up; but the uncertainty made me restless. I needed a goal to work towards. I tried setting up a mobile grocery business, on the lines of Migros in Switzerland, and contacted Migros, looked over vans, saw ministry representatives in Palma about permits, and even consulted a lawyer about legal aspects. I wrote to Selwyn Jepson asking for advice. 'Call yourself "William, the Grocer on Wheels",' he wrote back. I had no business training but it seemed feasible. Father, however, was horrified. 'No Graves has ever gone into trade!' he wrote to Selwyn, forgetting that when in Boar's Hill at my age he and Nancy had run a grocery shop. However, my plans came to nothing, and Father wrote to Selwyn, overjoyed:

> Your worry about William's van business has proved unnecessary. The government is already planning a similar service to keep prices down in the villages, so he can't get a permit! [RG to SJ, April 1966]

Selwyn's worry was, not unreasonably, that I had no business experience; he felt that I should be looking for a job where I could put my training as a geologist to some use.

By Easter 1966, my savings were running low and I was getting desperate. I sold the Karmann-Ghia and bought a second-hand Seat-600. I had Elena and Philip to think about; but I could not break away from the sense of security Deyá gave me. I was deeply depressed, beat my head with my fists and wept in Elena's arms. When I heard at the café that Father had been to a marijuana party, I stormed into Canellún and accused him of corrupting the village. My Deyá dream was coming to an end. Elena calmed me down and talked things back into perspective. If Deyá was out, then perhaps we could both find jobs in Palma: it would not be so bad, and we could come up to Deyá on weekends.

I was finally coming to terms with the idea of moving to Palma when someone mentioned that the then tenants of the hotel Ca'n Quet were starting their own restaurant. As ever clutching at straws, I rushed down to Palma to see Monsieur and Madame Coll, who had retired but were still the owners. Yes, Ca'n Quet was available. I asked for a day to talk it over with Elena, but I knew at once we would take it.

CHAPTER XIII

1

'¿*Oiga? Mr Graves?*'

'¿*Sí?* Yes?'

'I work for the *Daily Express* and I understand you have just taken on a hotel in Deyá.'

'That's right . . .'

'Would it be convenient if I came up with a photographer to do a short piece about you?'

'If you don't mind my painting the garden chairs while we talk.'

I knew that running the hotel was not going to be easy and that we would need all the publicity we could get. A short article in the *Daily Express* could do us some good – even if it were only 'Robert Graves's Son William, 25, Opens Hotel in the Sun'.

Ca'n Quet was a small pension with thirteen rooms. Geoffrey Frampton had not spent much money when he converted it from what had once been a farmhouse. Partitions between the rooms were flimsy, doors closed badly, plumbing was sub-standard, and the roof leaked. However, for every three rooms he had built a bathroom and he put in plenty of extra lavatories; best of all, there was an ample supply of water from the Es Molí spring. When Monsieur Coll had taken the pension back from Frampton, he had added a large dining room, which could cope with both his guests and casual trade. Though the kitchen was somewhat primitive, it did have an industrial refrigerator and a large coal-fired cooking range which, while it would not produce the intended hot water, at least removed the chill. As a pension, open mostly in the warm part of the year, it was adequate.

Ca'n Quet was built on one long narrow terrace. Its drive led up from the main road, through a small parking lot, to the lobby door. In front of the lobby stood two spectacularly tall date palms, one of them clad halfway up its trunk with a mantle of native ivy. Next to the lobby was a covered and tiled patio, with a

221

marble wellhead in one corner, and a collection of potted aspidistras and philodendrons around the walls. It formed the entrance to the dining room, which had been built out at right angles to the original farmhouse. Beyond the dining room, tables and chairs were set out on a paved patio we called the *terraza*, its bar hugging the rear wall. A circular pergola, hung, in summer, with bunches of juicy green grapes, their massive vine forming a canopy over a dance floor, separated the *terraza* from the garden. The garden was full of fruit trees: orange, tangerine, fig, cherry, apricot and loquats. There were two narrow herbaceous borders at the front and rear of the terrace, which ran the length of the garden past the pergola and around the *terraza*. In them Monsieur Coll's French roses vied with daisy bushes, lilies, sweet-smelling philadelphus, geraniums, dahlias and nasturtiums in providing colour and greenery for the guests. Next to the bar, deep blue morning glory rampaged up the wall.

The Ca'n Quet sat wedged in a small depression near the bottom of the village. It looked up at the church on the Puig and at the towering Teix behind. In the foreground was the picturesque old stone mill-house of Ca'n Madó, with its green wooden shutters standing out against the white window edgings. In its shed, Old Gelat's *turbina* now sat rusting from disuse, and much of the spring water that had once turned the generator was lost – we could hear it cascading into the cane-filled torrent below the *terraza*. Above Ca'n Madó was the four-star Hotel Es Molí, newly enlarged and converted from the *finca* which Old Gelat had sold to the doctor's cousin. The main road from Palma, flanked by plane trees, ran below the hotel, over a bridge across the torrent, and then climbed, past the entrance to the Hotel Es Molí, into Deyá: a pleasant ten-minute walk to the cafés.

The Ca'n Quet lobby had originally been the *entrada* of the old farmhouse, and had been enlarged by removing the wall of the adjoining room. It had little charm. Its walls were panelled in shoulder-high, dull brown, slate-like agglomerate, to guard them from being scratched by the backs of chairs. A set of dreary green velvet sofas stood around a wood stove, for out-of-season use. By the staircase, which led to the guest rooms, was an unattended counter with cubbyholes for the room-keys. The guest rooms were, thankfully, not at all bad. Frampton's furnishings – a bed, a chair, a small wardrobe and a sink – were so spartan as to offend nobody. On the other hand, Monsieur Coll's dining room certainly offended Elena's sense of taste. Its plywood furniture was early-Fifties 'modern'. China swallows flew in formation up the wall, through a motley collection of landscapes left as payment by various 'artists'. Mme Coll's prize chandeliers hung from the ceiling in the corners of the room: each had, extending from a central matching vase, six S-shaped, frosted and gold-painted glass arms, with a candle-shaped bulb at the tip. One of the chandeliers had received a knock from Mme Coll – when trying to hit her husband over the head with a chair – so that two arms had broken out of their cement fixing and hung limply to one side.

Elena and I gave ourselves one month to get organized before we opened. In the dining room we took down the china swallows and removed the chandeliers; we put in indirect lighting, made curtains and brightened the room up with red-and-white checked tablecloths. We repainted the *terraza* furniture. In the lobby we covered the slate-like panels with strips of bamboo awning. Our cook and his assistant came from Palma and our waiter and two girls from the village. We advertised Ca'n Quet in the *Lady* and the *Sunday Times* – the article about the pension in the *Daily Express* duly appeared. We ordered drinks for the bar and food for the kitchen. A laundry service in Soller offered to take care of our sheets, towels and table linen. We employed a business administrator in Palma to pay the staff's social-services quotas, to keep our dance-permit valid, to get our room and bar tariffs approved by the Ministry of Tourism, and keep us out of legal trouble in general. On the fourteenth of May 1966, we opened for business.

2

Although we had inherited Monsieur Coll's mostly French clients, we slowly replaced them with more spendthrift British guests who had been attracted by our advertisements. Whereas the French sat in the bar for hours nursing a single *pastis*, the men hidden behind a newspaper while their wives knitted – Elena likened these to *Les Tricoteuses de la Bastille* – the British knocked back several 'rounds' before dinner, a bottle of wine with their meal, and then a brandy before walking into the village. If our bar was still open when they returned, they had a nightcap before turning in. They enjoyed their stay and presently the word got back to England. Soon we were paid a visit by a manager of Erna Low Travel, who sold away-from-it-all holidays, and Erna Low became our main agents.

The Ministry of Tourism regulated our room prices. These were set so low that the only way to make a profit was to have our guests on full board and keep to a tight food budget. Since the Ministry allowed us to charge for extras, we provided a strong house wine at a reasonable price, which made our guests mellow and less exigent about their food. Picnic lunches were far cheaper to prepare than the three-course meals the Ministry made us provide, so we tried to persuade our guests to take these and spend their day down on the Cala.

At the height of the season, both Elena and I worked some sixteen hours a day. It began at breakfast: guests needed postcards, stamps, picnic lunches, cigarettes, Tampax, mountain guides, bus timetables. They enquired so often about the weather that we felt responsible when it rained. As soon as it became warm, we served breakfast on the *terraza* so that they could look at the scenery. Still they asked questions.

'Mr Graves, on my way up from the Cala I heard a gorgeous birdsong, what bird was it?'

'That'll have been a nightingale, Mrs de La Brown, there are lots of them down there in May and June.'

'Mrs Graves, what is the tree with bright leaves and the long green pods?'

'That's the carob tree, Mr de La Brown, the pods turn dark brown in September and you can buy them for a-penny-a-piece in England. They're called St John's bread.'

'What is that?' asked Mrs de La Brown, pointing to a large rat making its way from the torrent, along the telephone line, to its nest underneath the dining-room roof.

'Oh, that! That's the Majorcan squirrel which loses its tail-hair in summer. It stores up almonds in September and lives off them all winter,' Elena interrupted sweetly. She taught me to lie: in Ca'n Quet we often had no option.

'Mr Graves, may I make a call to England?'

'I'm sorry, Mr Brown, our phone's out of order at the moment.'

Our hand-cranked telephone was connected to the switchboard at the Deyá bakery which Magdalena the Baker's twin daughters operated. As a rule, the guests wanted to make their calls at breakfast time, which was the bakery's busiest moment selling bread and *ensaïmadas*. When we thought that the rush at the bakery had passed, our telephone suddenly 'worked' again. Putting a call through was always time-consuming. One to England could take an hour or more to be connected, and Elena or I had to be around, first to ensure the call came through – and complain if it did not – and secondly to find out how much to charge. A call to America could easily take half a day and if it had not been put through by ten in the evening, Magdalena would ask us to cancel it, as her twins had gone to bed. Elena tried to explain to her that it was still early afternoon in New York.

'That's not our fault, *senyora*, let them change their time to ours!' she snapped, disconnecting us.

Three times a week, at dawn, I drove to the Palma market. I bought artichokes, runner beans and potatoes by the sackful; cauliflowers, lettuces and melons by the dozen; green peppers, aubergines and tomatoes by the crate as well as apricots, plums and grapes. Pork, lamb and beef I bought by the side; fish by the box. I loaded the supplies into my little Seat-600 from which I had removed the front passenger seat, and inched my laden way to Deyá in low gear. When I arrived back, most of our guests were out. It was time to look after accounts, stock-taking or maintenance. Elena looked after menus, laundry, and staff. Both of us took turns with Philip.

At six months old, Philip's insatiable appetite had made him so fat the doctor put him on a protein diet. Even then, a little naked Buddha, he crawled around the *terraza* with a perpetual crust of bread in his hand, which we replaced every so often with a clean one. When we were both busy, we sat him in his pen where he would play contentedly on his own, oblivious of the hotel guests.

Our lunchtime casual trade was especially heavy at weekends. Monsieur Coll had given Ca'n Quet's restaurant an excellent reputation, and whole families drove up from Palma for a Sunday *paella*, mother-in-law squashed in the back seat of the car with the children. When trade was brisk, both Elena and I would help our waiter. Weekdays were quieter and at times we even had the dining room to ourselves. After lunch, we tried to have a rest or went up to the Posada for a much-needed break. We had little time to go to the beach: because of Philip, we could not walk down for a quick dip the way Father did.

In the evening we had to perform again. Supper was served at eight so Elena and I were down by seven to mix with the guests at the bar, and be on hand for more phone calls, postcards and questions. In the dining room we sat at a table from which we could ensure that the waiter was doing his job, and again help out if necessary. On summer evenings I took a quick bite with Elena and Philip and then, while she put him to bed, went out to the *terraza*, turned on the illumination, put candles on the tables, and lit the charcoal in the barbecue.

The barbecue pit was made of an oil drum cut lengthwise. The charcoal sat in the bottom half of the drum with a grill placed over it. The hinged top half of the drum had a chimney, and closed over the bottom. In this manner, the drum also acted as an oven. When it was alight, our chef's assistant put foil-wrapped potatoes inside to bake. He then laid out, on a table in front of the barbecue, steak, shrimp, fish, kebabs and mushrooms to be grilled, and the salads and sauces to go with them. As the customers arrived, I took orders and waited at tables, while Alfonso the Chef, who had now finished with our regular meals, broiled the steaks with panache on the now open fire, and dramatically tossed flaming mushrooms and shrimp in the air from his frying pan.

When I had cleared away the last of the plates, Elena and I sat with our guests again. Often Elena told stories about the *coronél* and had everyone rolling with laughter. These could be magical evenings: on nights of the full moon we put out the lights and let everyone watch its silver disc skim across the top of the Teix, one moment basking us in its full rays – bright enough to observe one another's bewitched expressions – the next, just an expectant glow behind a jutting peak. Often our Palma friends came to see us. When Pedro and Teddy turned up, we got out the guitars and sang *Tuna* songs, and Belafonte calypsos.

Running Ca'n Quet put me in touch again with my old Deyá school-friends. Toni March brought us fresh fish; Xesc Burota, now the carpenter, fixed our shutters; Pere of Son Beltrán, driving Gelat's taxi, collected our guests. In my friends' eyes I was now doing a 'proper' job and my relationship with the tourists, and even the *estrangers* who came to the restaurant, was more businesslike and comprehensible. They seemed to accept me, once again, the way they had when we were children. They often called in for a drink after supper and to check what was going on. Together we reminisced about Don Gaspar or about stealing myrtle berries on Son Bujosa land. Toni showed me the *secreto* in the back of the building, where contraband used to be hidden before the farm had been converted and, from then on, our waiter used it for the black-market cigarettes he sold. If the young English secretaries belonging to the groups staying at Villa-Verde were on the *terraza*, my village friends would linger for a second drink.

By midnight most clients had left the *terraza*. Our waiter closed the bar but Elena and I stayed on and joined those of our guests who remained and seemed to want our company. When, in utter exhaustion, I got what Elena called my 'blank look' or when I was not quick enough to stifle a yawn, she would lovingly kick me under the table. Rarely did we get to bed before one o'clock in the morning.

3

The long hours and the exhaustion of running Ca'n Quet we could cope with, and enjoyed. However, our first season in the pension took on a nightmarish quality, the memory of which still sends shivers down my spine. Indeed, Deyá ceased to be a paradise for me, and turned into a kind of hell: outwardly perfect and beautiful yet inwardly flawed. Now, when I drove back from Palma with the groceries and rounded the corner where the Deyá coastline comes into view, I no longer felt the magic; instead, a sense of foreboding. As if a major tragedy was about to take place.

Father's attitude towards me was now openly hostile. He would barely talk to me, let alone to Elena. There appeared to be more to this than simply our opposition to Cindy. Fortunately, she was in Mexico, and did not show up that year, so we were not actively confronting Father over her as we had during the previous summer. Perhaps our taking on Ca'n Quet without consulting him, and without asking his help or advice, had something to do with it. He loved to arrange things for his friends and family, but demanded complete subservience and agreement in whatever he said. Other than poor Jenny, I was the only one of my siblings to stand up to Father: this did not endear me to him. Whereas he had been so eager to help me and 'fix things' when I had wanted to become an archaeologist, now he seemed to think Elena and I were 'in trade' in Deyá simply in order to undermine his position. Nor did his health help matters. He felt rotten and was living on a diet of rice, shredded apples and milk of magnesia. I was not very sympathetic, believing that this was psychosomatic, brought on by Cindy's letters – or lack of letters – which continued to upset him. I felt sorry when it turned out to be a gall-bladder stone which needed removing.

Father's money problems, at least, were over. Not only had he sold the Library in Deyá for £4,000 – a good price at the time – but he also sold a large number of his manuscripts to the University of Southern Illinois for $37,000, which was then a very substantial sum. From this windfall he paid the remainder of Karl's severance fee, bought Cindy a building site in Mexico; and a house in Deyá, the Torre, to tempt her back to him. His royalty payments were reinstated at about the same time.

In spite of Father's coolness, Elena and I visited Canellún two or three times a week, at teatime, to take Philip to see Mother, and to get away from our hotel guests for a while. Having cleaned up both the Posada and Ca'n Quet, I began to notice how run-down Canellún was becoming. The garden paths, which were so neatly trimmed when we arrived in 1946, were overgrown; the shutters needed painting; the cat door – a piece of cloth over a pane removed from the French windows in the *entrada* – was torn. For help Mother had the daughter of the eldest of the Carrillo girls living in, but Encarnita was still in her teens, so Mother now had to cope virtually single-handed with the house. Father did little more than make jam and jelly and turn over his compost heap. It was a pity that he did not invest some of his windfall money in Canellún.

Afternoon tea at Canellún had turned into an open house, and there was always a cake, or a large cream-filled *ensaïmada*. Sometimes, when Lucia and Ramón were over on holiday from Madrid, or there were other family or friends, it was a pleasant and relaxing break for us. Increasingly, however, 'friends' of Father's, with whom I had absolutely nothing in common, came to tea. Then Elena and I left as soon as possible. Indeed, Father had gathered around him a group of hangers-on, people for whom, only a few years previously, he would have had no time at all. All claimed to be friends of Cindy's. Admittedly, many were genuine admirers of Father and expected pearls of wisdom in his every statement; but others were professional spongers.

The village had become, like parts of the neighbouring island of Ibiza, increasingly a centre of hippie culture. Deyá's attraction to hippies had little to do with Father's presence – although *The White Goddess* made him a cult symbol to some, he was no Beatnik guru; it was more the feeling of being cut off from the outside world, which Deyá and its surrounding valley had always imparted. The drugs scene now moved centre-stage, and although there was still little junk, pot and acid were readily available in the cafés. Lacing people's drinks was common and was thought to be a great joke. Joachim, a German fashion designer and a friend of ours, was invited to a party, offered a drink and soon found himself hallucinating. Terrified, he just managed to get home before losing all touch with reality.

The villagers were confused. They had never really made much of a distinction between one foreigner and another. *Estrangers* were regulars, *turistas* stayed for a couple of weeks at one of the hotels or simply came for a day visit in a rented car. The hippies were also regulars, but were something new. They took drugs, played loud music and made a mess of the houses they rented. At the end of the season, the house owners spent so much time and money scraping grime off the floors and furniture, and white-washing the walls, that their rental hardly paid for it. What upset the villagers most about the hippies was the way they treated their children. Nicolás, who now ran the Old Café, often threw a blanket over the five-year-old boy and his three-year-old sister, forgotten by their unmarried mother, sleeping underneath one of his tables. Older children were openly handed marijuana to share with their friends. A group of twelve- and thirteen-year-old boys and girls used to party in a house opposite the Museum. Walking past one night, I saw them through the open window: drugged out of their minds, crawling naked around the room, rubbing against each other, and laughing themselves silly.

Since the hippies seemed to be friends of Father's, the villagers blamed him for the invasion. Father's ambivalence about drugs – especially when with Cindy – meant he was not averse to sharing a joint at a party, much as he would take a glass of wine if he was offered one. Whereas a few years previously he had rarely left

Canellún without Mother, he now put in solo appearances at his new friends' parties. This caused consternation with the local authorities. At Ca'n Quet we had daily visits from the *guardias* making their rounds.

'Don Guillermo,' they said, 'your father mixes with the wrong people. They make use of him at their parties knowing we can't touch them when he's there. But one day we'll have orders from Madrid and we'll have to pull him in. Please tell your father to be more careful when choosing his friends.'

'I've done so,' I replied, 'and I'll try again. Thanks for your warning. Another brandy?'

I knew it was only a matter of time before this happened. There was a move afoot to get the drug situation under control and Father's presence at these parties made it awkward. The *guardias*' normal procedure was to raid a party, round up everyone in the village schoolroom for questioning, and deport those who had overstayed their three months in the country without an extension permit. Merely taking a statement from Father would have caused an international scandal. And this nobody wanted, least of all his friend Manuel Fraga, the Minister for Information and Tourism.

Knowing of the rift between Father and Elena and myself, and our dislike of drugs, his hangers-on had as little time for us as we had for them. One evening they sent a gang of their children – the oldest about seventeen – to sit on the Ca'n Quet *terraza* and smoke pot. As manager of the pension, I was legally responsible for everything that happened on the premises. Therefore, I phoned the *guardias* telling them that I had a small problem and please to come at once. As I expected, when the children saw the *guardias* climb the steps from the road, they fled past the pergola into the darkness of the garden.

'I'm sorry to have bothered you,' I said as I poured each a double brandy. 'A drunken foreigner. Fortunately he's left.'

A few days later Father's hangers-on again tried to get us into trouble. Would it not be great fun, and bring us down out of the clouds, if some pot were found at Ca'n Quet? They discussed possible ways of doing this with Father around the Canellún kitchen table. Staying as a guest at Ca'n Quet at the time was Isobel Stuart-Wortley, a cousin of Father's first wife Nancy. When she called in at Canellún, she was let into the 'joke' and, sad to say, Father gave her a packet of marijuana to plant on us. In a state of shock and disbelief, Isobel handed it straight to Elena who burned the packet in the kitchen stove. Two days passed and then the *guardias* came snooping.

We were so involved in running Ca'n Quet we hardly had time to analyse what was happening. My sense of foreboding persisted. We were so busy we could not attend the joint birthday party. When I found there had been several digs at us in the play, I felt quite sick. Everyone seemed to be against us. Fortunately we had our Palma friends, and we began collecting new ones from among the guests. We made one excellent and dear friend: Henry Prain, who had been coming to the village for years, and who was known to us as Mac and to the villagers as *El Capitán*. This large kindly Scot was profoundly disturbed by the goings-on in Deyá. After our brush with the hippies, Mac became our eyes and ears in the village, and kept us posted as to what was being said about us.

In these upsetting circumstances, therefore, it was with a tremendous sense of relief that I welcomed Selwyn Jepson's second visit, when he came that September to check out the financial situation at Canellún. He once again brought with him a breath of much needed sanity. He had seen from Father's letters that the tension between us persisted and, thinking that this was entirely due to Cindy, he advised us to be patient.

'The Cindy/Aemile thing has just about finished,' Selwyn said. 'You will see that Robert will then behave as if it never happened. Just forgive him when he does.'

'That's a relief and of course I will,' I replied. 'But Cindy is at present the least of our worries. . . .' Elena and I went on to tell him what we had been through and about Father, the *guardias* and the drugs. Selwyn blanched. He knew that Father's reputation was at risk, especially when he discovered that one of the main culprits, an American called David Solomon, had boasted that if he were caught and gaoled, Father would go with him. Selwyn went at once to Canellún to ensure that Father had no marijuana in the house: when Father owned up to having some, it was put in the centre of the hottest compost heap.

Selwyn then summoned Solomon and lectured him on the dangers of getting caught. However, like many other foreigners in the village, Solomon felt he could do whatever he liked in Spain with impunity. That winter he was arrested: fortunately, Father was not present.

> That fool David Solomon whom you lectured at Can Torrent on security moved to Palma with his hash smoking teen-age daughters, threw a party (for their friends at the local school) and passed the reefers around after drinks. One of the kids had a *Guardia Civil* father; so Solomon's in jail now for some years with a crippling fine added. This really proves that pot *is* dangerous in its accumulative effects on common sense ratiocination. [RG to SJ, March 1967]

Solomon's lawyer bailed him out after a couple of months, and he returned to Deyá.

Selwyn's second visit was a watershed for us. The nightmarish quality of the summer subsided and normality seemed to return. In opening Father's eyes to the nature of drugs and to the fickleness of his 'friends' such as Solomon, Selwyn also made Father realize he had behaved unfairly to Elena and me. Although he still did not approve of our hostility towards Aemile, nor of our running Ca'n Quet, at least we were back on speaking terms. However, something was not quite the same. He no longer seemed to have that incisive interest in things he was working on, which so fascinated me. He was more distant. Again I ascribed it to worry about Cindy.

4

At the end of October, we closed Ca'n Quet for the winter. We returned to the Posada, took up our life where we had left off in May and gave Philip, now almost a year old, our full attention. I worked on the house and in the garden, and answered Ca'n Quet letters. When Mother accompanied Father to England for his gall bladder operation at St Thomas's Hospital, we looked after their cats and dogs at Canellún, and collected their mail.

Financially our first season at Ca'n Quet was no worse than I had expected, but there was no money in the bank at the end of it. Already my attitude towards Deyá was changing: I decided to work on an oil rig for part of the winter to keep us in funds until the summer months, when money from the pension would come in. After Christmas I went mud-logging in the Libyan desert, and was away for three months.

In February, when Mother went to Madrid after the birth of Lucia's first baby – a girl, Natalia – Father was becoming so absent-minded that she asked Elena to move into Canellún with him. Elena did so for Mother's sake. Father now wrote to me in the desert as though nothing had ever come between us. Indeed, there were occasional glimpses of the father I thought I had lost forever:

> At the moment I'm alone at Canellún with Elena & Philip; and it's remarkable how little housework we cause each other, although Philip gets more and more adventurous each day and just now (when he thought I wasn't watching) he did three solo steps along the table without clutching it. He's an extraordinarily good baby – as you were too – not I think merely because you were first-born. [RG to WG, February 1967]

That spring, Father was awarded a plaque by the local government for his contribution to the island. Mother, who disliked formal events, asked Elena to drive him there. Father was seated at the side of the Civil Governor's wife, Elena at the side of the Governor himself. The food was late in being served and Elena watched, speechless, as Father ate the bread off everyone's plates. On the way home, our Seat-600 broke down and Elena and Father had to walk the ten kilometres to Valldemosa to find a taxi.

> Getting stranded . . . that night . . . .with her was a great experience: the long walk to Valldemosa and the three hours at the Hotel Artista waiting for a lift. I wouldn't have wished for better company than Elena and was really glad it happened in a way. [RG to WG, March 1967]

The hatchet was finally buried and, although Father could never ask Elena's forgiveness – Cindy was still Muse – he began buying her presents for the Posada: a chair, a brazier, a vase.

Elena reopened Ca'n Quet in mid-March and I got back from the desert a month later. We were now listed as one of the special hotels in the Erna Low Travel brochure, and our clientele included doctors, architects, TV producers and writers. We were written up in glossy magazines such as *Cosmopolitan* and *Nova*. On my desk I found a flood of letters to answer and, by mid-June, we were fully booked. Erna Low charged £50 a fortnight, full board, including the flight: we had become the 'in' place to be. Girls wearing the latest Carnaby Street mini-skirts and white knee-high boots graced our *terraza*. The new clients impressed even Father, and he and Mother began to bring their friends to us to dine. When Father was interviewed by the BBC, the crew stayed at Ca'n Quet, and some of the exteriors were shot there. In one, Philip is sitting on his grandfather's lap.

5

Ca'n Quet now went from strength to strength. We were 'discovered' by young British actors, who found it far easier and more pleasant to spend their summers with us on their Equity money. Some even managed to pick up work on films being shot on the island.

'Haven't you got a sleeping bag?' asked one of the actors who wanted to stay on when his booking ended.

I set up a tent at the bottom of the garden and charged him one peseta for the lodging; he paid full board for his meals.

Guests were a continual source of wonder. The – to us – elderly matrons, Delia and Lisa, were of Empire-building stock and became a yearly fixture. At four in the afternoon Lisa would lean out of her window.

'Delia,' she shouted. 'Tea's ready!'

'Coming!' replied Delia who had been snoozing in the garden. They brought with them a kettle which worked on solid fuel and which, for all I know, was designed to work on camel-dung in Outer Mongolia. For many of our guests Ca'n Quet was becoming like a club in which they had a vested interest. One day Elena heard shrieks from the bathroom, next to Room 12. She rushed up to find Delia with her hand over the pipe fitting, the tap lying on the floor, and water spraying everywhere. Delia determinedly held back the flood until the 'natives' turned off the flow at the mains.

A fifty-year-old woman checked in accompanied by a young man in his early twenties. I put them in a room with a double bed.

'But they are mother and son!' said Elena angrily. 'How could you do such a thing?'

'Not in their passports they're not,' I replied. 'Nor by the hungry looks she gives him.' I was right.

After a few amorous days the young man had an epileptic fit. We called the village doctor, who gave him some pills. The following day the boy had another fit, and the doctor increased his dose. But his epileptic fits persisted and Elena, worried, called a doctor friend for a second opinion.

'Get him to hospital at once, or you'll be taking him out feet first,' our friend advised. 'And you cannot imagine what paperwork that involves!'

Elena drove the couple to the hospital. The young man was found to have an infected appendix, which was poisoning him and was causing the epileptoid fits. He was operated on at once. Five days later the couple was back in Ca'n Quet, he looking drawn and in need of rest. That evening Elena was sewing some knee-patches on Philip's trousers when the 'mother' sat down by her.

'When do you think we can do it?' she asked.

'I'm sorry?' said Elena, thinking her English was failing her.

'You know, do it.'

'Oh, forty days,' replied Elena with biblical firmness.

Although Deyá had fortunately lost the nightmarish feeling of our opening season at Ca'n Quet, it had not fully recovered its magic. Outwardly it was as beautiful as ever, but even on the bright crisp mornings when the nightingales sang, I felt a certain heaviness. Just as the father I remembered of my childhood seemed to be changing, Deyá was also undergoing a metamorphosis. The outcome of both was uncertain.

6

My brother Juan's crisis came to a head at the beginning of the summer of 1967, when he was twenty-three years old. In 1962 after his schooling in Geneva, where he did poorly academically, Father found Juan a job with Camera Press in London where he could learn about photography. According to Father, Juan was bound to become a 'top photographer' since he had all the necessary qualities and knew how to 'melt' into the background.

As an initial part of his training, Juan was put to work in the darkroom but, being young, he missed the sun and his Deyá friends. After a few months he left and returned to Canellún in a fit of depression. In 1963 Mother persuaded him to attend a crammer in London to retake his 'O' levels. These he passed, to our astonishment, but his depression persisted. Father was unconcerned: 'Juan is a genius. Like all Graveses he is just a late developer.'

Father assumed that his family and friends, almost by definition, would be top in whatever they did. He never for a moment considered the pressure this put us under. Of the four of us, only Lucia had so far lived up to his expectations: getting a First at Oxford and marrying – according to Father – Spain's top jazz drummer. Fortunately, by opting for science, I had avoided Father's attention during my formative years. Tomás was still at school and was, to some extent, protected by Mother from Father's enthusiasm. Juan, however, suffered the full force, and knew he could never fulfil Father's hopes.

Selwyn Jepson, aware of the pressure Juan was under from Father, suggested that he should go as far away from Canellún as possible in order to build his self-confidence. In 1964 he went with a former school-friend of his to Australia. They landed in Sydney and worked anti-clockwise around the continent doing odd jobs, and even felling timber. For a year or so, all was well. Juan missed Lucia's and my weddings, and he must have felt as homesick in the outback as I had in Texas. Then, in late 1965, he caught a liver infection, was hospitalized in Darwin, and came home to recuperate in Deyá.

Almost at once his depression reappeared in an increasingly acute form. He would not leave Deyá because, he said, all shoes other than rope-soled *espardenyas* hurt his feet. He complained of severe migraines and had his sinuses operated on in Palma. In early 1967 Mother insisted that he go to England to see a specialist, but nothing was found wrong with him 'that he would not grow out of'. Juan came back to Deyá.

Father had just finished 'Englishing' *The Unquiet Mind* by Dr William Sargant, English psychiatrist and ardent proponent of chemical cures for neurological disorders. At Selwyn's suggestion, Father now wrote to Sargant describing Juan's symptoms. Unfortunately, Selwyn failed to appreciate that Father's description would be, naturally, highly subjective; and Sargant, unforgivably, did not have Juan come to England to see him. Instead, Sargant sent Father a large jar of pills intending, perhaps, that Dr Darder, his close friend and Palma GP, should administer them. Father, however, handed Juan the whole jar.

Initially the pills seemed to work. For most of the day Juan stayed in his room listening to records. He seldom came down for tea at Canellún, and he rarely visited Ca'n Quet, so Elena and I saw little of him. At night, however, he would take Mother's car and drive to the Palma discos with his friends. There, as he was very good-looking, girls flocked around him. Then, one evening in June, the crisis came.

Carlos Navarro, a boyhood friend of mine and part of our Lluc Alcari group, told me that he had seen Juan the evening before in the café, and that he was acting strangely. At the time, Mother was in England staying with the Jepsons, and attending Parents' Day at Tomás's school. Juan was alone in Canellún with Father. I at once drove over and, though it was late, found Father by the Aga, stirring a copper pan full of apricots.

'Is Juan all right, Father?' I asked. I could not count on him: Father would deny anything was wrong, because Juan was under medication prescribed by the 'world's greatest psychiatrist'.

'I suppose so,' he said, still stirring his jam. 'I haven't seen him today. He's probably in his room.'

I found Juan upstairs, hyper-excited, hallucinating, and every so often throwing himself on the floor. He had obviously not slept for a couple of days. He seemed glad to see me. He was talking non-stop and had lost his voice.

'Aeroplanes, grey aeroplanes, going at Mach II,' he kept repeating in a hoarse whisper.

I wondered whether he had been given a drink laced with LSD at one of the hippie parties. Perhaps it would pass. Carlos kindly offered to spend the night with him in Cannelún.

The next morning Juan was no better. Carlos and I, having convinced him we were going to Palma to hear a group of black American singers, drove him straight to Dr Darder's surgery. When Dr Darder saw Juan he was shocked at his state, and said that he saw no alternative other than to put him in the Palma psychiatric hospital and see what could be done.

'But what about Dr Sargant, in England?' I asked. 'Surely . . .?'

'Ah, my friend Dr Sargant! Well, perhaps, if you can get Juan to him . . . .' Dr Darder sent us to a clinic where Juan would be kept under observation until I could arrange for his transportation to England. There were moments when Juan was quite lucid. When we arrived at the clinic, a nurse, syringe in hand, asked who the patient was. Juan pointed to Carlos and it took some time before we could persuade her otherwise.

The clinic kept Juan heavily sedated and, two days later, I saw him off, stretcher-bound, on the BEA flight to London, and Dr Sargant. My main problem had been to find an English registered nurse that BEA insisted must accompany him. I enquired all around Palma, only to find one among our guests at Ca'n Quet. She kindly offered her services and returned the following day to complete her holiday.

Whatever the reason for Juan's breakdown, whether the uncontrolled swallowing of Sargant's pills, or a drink laced with LSD – even a combination of both – his eventual cure and convalescence took months. After his release from hospital he stayed in London with friends, continuing his treatment as an out-patient until, eventually, he was allowed to return to Deyá. Here, indirectly, he was helped by Margot Callas.

During Margot's reign as Muse, Father had given her a beautiful but semi-ruined house on the old mountain footpath to Soller, with a large orchard and a spectacular view of the coastline. When the International Authors affair tied up Father's money, and Margot's Musedom was ended, Father demanded the ruin back so as to obtain some ready cash. Margot refused but, no longer wanting the house, deeded it to Juan for whom she had a soft spot. Once Juan regained his health, he began taking an interest in his house, and finally rebuilt it. Having a house of his own, for which he owed Father nothing, played a fundamental part in his recovery.

7

Shortly after Juan's crisis, Elena got word that her father was in hospital in Galicia with throat cancer. She and Marta decided that, in spite of everything, they should see him and, perhaps, bring him back to Majorca to take care of him during his last days. They arrived at the military hospital in Vigo and asked for his room: the fear in the nurse's eyes was like that which Elena had seen when her father's draughtsman had wet himself. As his daughters entered the room, Antonio yelled: 'Shut the door!' Looking around they saw the reason: some two dozen budgerigars were perched on the furniture or flying free and bird droppings covered everything. Antonio was propped up in his bed and glared at Marta and Elena as if he had seen them only the day before. Obviously he had not changed.

'Marta, you never returned my *Espasa* Dictionary!' the *coronél* said. 'And you, Elenita, I hear you managed to get married anyway. What does your husband do?'

'A geologist, Father.'

'Interesting subject . . . .' The thought of geology had rather taken the edge off his voice. 'Where is he from?'

'He's English.'

'Oxford or Cambridge?'

'Oxford,' replied Elena, not to make too fine a point.

'You'll be all right then.'

Marta and Elena left after a difficult visit, neither having dared to suggest that he come to Majorca. On their way out they talked to Antonio's doctor. No, there was no cause for concern, the *coronél* was reacting well to treatment. Yes, he was a difficult patient, he had requisitioned the ambulance by outranking everyone else, and sent it with an orderly to the next town to buy a special bird-mix for his budgies. No, it was not normal to have budgies flying and messing all over a military hospital room. However, a *coronél* was a *coronél* . . . . Antonio died the following summer, but not from his cancer. With no one but his housekeeper to terrorize, he tired of living and starved himself to death.

After Antonio's death, his widow Maria-Luisa returned from America and settled in Palma. She proved an excellent mother-in-law. She was convinced that all men were tyrants like her late husband and stood curiously in awe of me. She never visited us in Deyá, and rarely called Elena if she thought I might pick up the phone. We went to see her whenever we were in Palma, but Elena saw no reason to correct her mother's impression of me.

8

In 1966 when Father stayed at St Thomas's Hospital for his gall bladder operation, he was visited by his eighteen-year-old god-daughter Juli Simon. A professional ballet dancer, she was slim and pretty with black hair and a strong nose faintly reminiscent of Laura's. Her father, Dr George Simon, was an eminent radiologist; her mother, Joanna, a musician. They had become friends of the family during the War. Juli came every day to the hospital and, finally, told Father that she loved him. Father laughed it off, but when he returned to Deyá they corresponded and he began wondering whether the White Goddess was not sending him a new Muse.

The following year, Father still seemed as obsessed as ever with Cindy. The day I took Juan down to Palma to Dr Darder and the hospital, Father came to Ca'n Quet with a telegram for Cindy, asking Elena to phone it through to the Post Office. He appeared quite unconcerned about Juan, although he knew I had taken him to the doctor; all he could talk to Elena about was Cindy. Elena was so incensed that, when he left, she dropped the telegram in the wastepaper basket.

However, Father was already cooling towards Cindy: when he discovered that she had been living with another man whom he regarded as 'evil', Father angrily wrote to Selwyn concerning the Torre, his new guesthouse:

> The house I was going to prepare for Aemilia is now not hers, not mine, but its own: for friends . . . . The Sillitoes are the first occupants and brought feather pillows and Chinese lamp shades. [RG to SJ, March 1967]

There was also a serious problem with Father's letters to Cindy. During the five or so years of being Father's Muse, she received a large number of letters from him. As in the case of all letters, although they physically belong to the recipient, the copyright belongs to the sender. Cindy could sell them, but could not publish them without Father's permission. However, in one of the calmer periods in their stormy relationship Father had written to Selwyn:

Half my writing is letters to Aemilia: one day they'll be printed. I've given Aemilia the copyright and she'll use it honourably. [RG to SJ, April 1966]

He had evidently been thinking in terms of publication after his death. It was an act of great – and unmerited – faith in his Muse. Not unexpectedly, during their next quarrel, she had threatened to sell his letters for publication. Over the next two years the threats to publish persisted until finally, through a strategy master-minded by Selwyn, Father managed to defuse the situation with the promise of greater riches:

I think you had better be guided by Selwyn . . and have the letters sold by him to a University or library who will pay twice as much when I freely add your letters to me which make sense of them. Eventual publication will have to be arranged, not less than 10 years after my death . . . with the agreement of Lucia and Tomás: for everyone's sake. If you die before the ten years are out they should have the copyright . . . .[RG to AL, February 1968]

In the event, Selwyn persuaded Cindy to sell the letters and the copyright to a Canadian university for the princely sum of $10,000.

In the summer of 1968 Cindy returned to Deyá. Father put her in the rented cottage by the Mirador, not in the Torre, the house that he had originally bought for her. Cindy still visited Canellún and hung around him as if everything was the same. However, when Juli arrived in Deyá for a visit, Cindy suddenly realized that her Musedom was in jeopardy:

Aemilia was fine for a while but suddenly flipped; be-cause Juli had come here for a good-bye on her way to join the Royal Ballet at Oslo and disturbed her mind while she was here and Aemilia was impelled to tell me cruel and most circumstantial lies about her (after her departure) which I believed. However *that's* settled now. [RG to SJ, July 1968]

It was at this time that the Deyá Town Council honoured Father by making him an 'adoptive son' of Deyá. The ceremony was planned to take place in August, and Father hoped that nothing would spoil it, especially through Cindy. As usual, Cindy mixed with the pot-smoking crowd, and Father worried that she might get caught. In his next letter to Selwyn he says:

> I had to send Aemilia away: things got a bit dangerous for her; but I made peace with her first. [RG to SJ, July 1968]

The day of the ceremony arrived. A large table and grand chairs for the dignitaries were placed in front of the entrance to the Town Hall. Folding chairs, normally used for the village celebration of the feast of Sant Joan, were brought from the storeroom, dusted off and set up in the Porxo square for the audience. By six-thirty in the evening, half an hour before the event was due to begin, all seats were taken by villagers. Those who arrived early reserved the chairs next to their own for family and neighbours. The *estrangers* stood at the rear of the square with summer visitors, including most of the Ca'n Quet guests. By the time the ceremony began, the Porxo was packed.

Father had invited the dignitaries for a drink at the Torre before the event. He and the Civil Governor now walked towards the Porxo – with Juli's pretty sister Helena between them. Others, including Nobel-Laureate-to-be Camilo José Cela, and Gaspar Sabater, my old schoolmaster and now a well-established Palma journalist, followed them. As they took their place at the table, they were welcomed by Joan Vives the Mayor and the Town Councillors. Father wore one of his light blue seersucker suits, a white shirt, and a red kerchief fastened with a gold clip; his black *sombrero* he carried in his hand. When he sat, he perched it on his knee.

Don Gaspar made the presentation speech. He spoke about Father's years before the War but, in deference to Mother, did not name Laura. He managed to draw parallels between Father's life and those of Chopin and the *Arxiduc*. The Mayor then thanked Father for his help in getting electric light for Deyá and for attracting so many *turistas*. Father got up and thanked them all. He said that, over the years, he had turned down many great honours, his Somme campaign medals being honour enough for him. However, he said, the title of 'adoptive son of Deyá' was more than an honour, it was a duty, a duty he was happy to undertake to the end of his days. He meant it.

Shortly after the ceremony Cindy showed up again. One day Father received an invitation from Peter Ustinov and his wife to dine on their yacht, which was anchored in the port of Soller. Father liked Peter Ustinov, whom he had known for many years, and he asked Elena and me to come too, so that I could drive him and Cindy down to Soller.

'Only if Mother comes,' I said.

Father, surprisingly, acquiesced, Cindy was left behind, and we had a pleasant evening together. This, for me, marked the end of Cindy's Musedom. Not long afterwards Cindy left and, to everyone's relief, Juli was raised to full Muse status.

9

Ca'n Quet continued to be a success with our guests. Some were returning two or three times during our seven-month season. We even had the odd permanent guest. But I was barely breaking even. As a hotel we were too small and too down-market, given our government-imposed prices, to be profitable. Should I try to enlarge it? As always I sought Selwyn's opinion.

'What about building a new hotel on the other side of the valley?' he asked.

'Of course, there's always the land below Canellún,' I said. 'But I don't know whether Father would go along with the idea.'

Father was, in fact, agreeable. Unwittingly, I had chosen the same spot on which, before the Civil War, he and Laura had planned an hotel with which to help finance the university. It was Mother who, I sensed, was not happy with Selwyn's idea. Nevertheless, I had an architect draw up a plan of the projected hotel and obtained an estimate from Pep Salas the builder. In the autumn of 1967, Elena and I drove to London – leaving Philip with his grandparents – to see if we could raise money to finance the project: I had a couple of contacts in the City. Unfortunately, the sums did not work out to the satisfaction of those I approached and we returned to Deyá empty-handed. That winter I found myself back in Libya to make enough money to tide us over until we opened again in the next spring.

During the 1968 season, Ca'n Quet had more bookings than we could cope with. We rented rooms in the village for the overflow but I still had to turn customers away. We were also having difficulties with the Ministry of Tourism inspectors. Our kitchen was old and unhygienic; nor could we provide the hot water they required. That winter, I got Monsieur and Madame Coll's permission to undertake the improvements at my own expense in exchange for their extending our lease a further five years. Father lent me part of the funds I needed, and the rest I paid off over the following season in exchange notes. I did not go to Libya: I realized I could save more money by overseeing the workmen than I could earn by mud-logging.

Our improvements were a great success. When we reopened for Easter 1969, we had two rooms with private baths; four new rooms in the attic; a propane hot-water system; a remodelled kitchen; and a facelift to our drive. Our two rooms with baths were always in demand; the new propane-fuelled stove in the refurbished kitchen could serve more casual trade meals. The Ministry of Tourism inspectors were much easier to satisfy. Even the sums looked healthy. Had I stuck with Ca'n Quet and consolidated on what I had, it might have been a viable business. It was then that I was approached by Dowling College, in New York, to house their Mediterranean Institute.

According to the prospectus they sent me, the Mediterranean Institute was to be a two-semester, fully academic programme. A trial group, consisting of thirty students and their professors, was to spend the winter in Deyá – from September 1969 to May 1970. Students would obtain credits in Creative Writing, Art, History, Poetry, Music, Spanish Language and Literature and French. The staff would consist of two professors and their wives and a young couple to counsel the students. There would be famous guest writers, such as John Cheever, Colin Wilson and Anthony Burgess, in residence for brief periods. Father was to give the occasional talk and a poetry reading. It was an exciting idea and the terms I negotiated to house them seemed to be good. Nevertheless, I did not want to spoil our Ca'n Quet trade, so we took on a second pension.

What was now Pensión Ca'n Gelat had once been the *Fàbrica*, where I had been given my first ever supper in Deyá; where we had our pig killed; where I had seen Old Gelat's corpse laid out. The top floor of the building had been extended over what had been the Salón, and now there were seventeen guest-rooms. Young Gelat owned it, and lived beneath in an apartment he had made out of the Salón. The tenants who had been running the pension had just left. I had my qualms about doing business with Gelat, for it was from him that Father had had to buy back his land. I remembered Father's curse. But if I wanted to keep Ca'n Quet as it was, there was little choice, and so I leased Ca'n Gelat for two seasons – 1969 and 1970 – with an option to continue.

During the five months before the students' arrival I tried to run Ca'n Gelat as we had Ca'n Quet. The building and surroundings lacked Ca'n Quet's charm, but it was in the village itself, Erna Low still provided excellent clients and our cook took care of both kitchens with a good assistant in each. Elena answered the breakfast-time questions at Ca'n Quet; I did the same at Ca'n Gelat. We engaged Pep Salas's pretty daughter as a receptionist to stand in for me but, even so, I found myself driving all day between the two establishments dealing with problems.

The Mediterranean Institute started off well. Its students were American, an even mix of young men and women. None had ever been abroad; few had even been away from home; nor had they ever been confronted by a foreign language. At first they were quite happy with the food and with the accommodation. The Teix towering above Deyá was greeted with the amazed 'Wow, man!', as were the village stone houses, or the little Seat-600 cars. It was September and they could go to the beach; there were still remnants of the summer crowd in the cafés. The students rose early and went to their classes. I felt that perhaps the Institute could be a success.

However, as autumn passed and winter approached, the novelty wore off: the students got bored. There was no television, no cinema, not even a pool table in the village. They became tired of our cooking, the various forms of pot-au-feu and minced meat we served them. They complained they did not like Spanish paella on Sundays. They demanded steak and French fries at every meal, which I could not afford on my food budget. They also disliked the plain whitewashed walls of their rooms which they began to paint themselves. Furniture got broken. The professors and the counsellors explained their bad behaviour as culture-shock, but did nothing to remedy it. Then the young couple who acted as the students' counsellors moved out and joined a hippie commune. Without anyone left at Ca'n Gelat to impose a routine, the students took to sleeping until lunchtime. My staff could not enter the rooms to clean them, and quit in disgust. The students then decided that the pension had 'bad vibes' and quite a few moved to houses in the village, taking with them our bed-linen and towels, and even our Butano-heaters. Those who remained stole keys of rooms they knew to be empty, and installed their passing friends.

By the time we opened Ca'n Quet again in April 1970, Elena and I were sick of students, staff, local residents, the lot. I tried to keep a friendly face when I was with our guests but it was not easy. I had been working harder than I ever had done on the oil rigs and there was still no money coming in. The staffing of both Ca'n Quet and Ca'n Gelat and the students' demands had eaten into my profits. Yet, our problems with pensions and students paled in significance when compared to the crisis that awaited us.

10

Elena had never had my good health. As a child she had caught every disease, from mumps and measles to whooping cough and chickenpox. She was always so thin her mother put her on fattening diets. Before we were married she still weighed only forty-six kilos: Miguel, her boss, nicknamed her 'Skinny One'. She had her appendix out; she suffered severely from kidney stones and allergic sneezing-fits. In 1967, two years after the Caesarean birth of Philip, she became pregnant again: a second analysis in England had revealed she was not Rh-negative after all and there was no reason not to have another baby. Unhappily, she miscarried after three months. We badly wanted a second child and in February 1970 she once more became pregnant. However, she had worked throughout the winter looking after the students, and her defences were low. In May she caught pneumonia.

I rushed Elena to the Palma hospital but, because of the baby, her gynaecologist would not let her doctors use the strong antibiotics she needed. Elena got worse. Maria Elena, her aunt, came

246

over to stay with her in hospital. By this time the students had returned to America but I was beside myself trying to run the two pensions on my own and look after Philip.

The phone rang at Ca'n Quet and one of the twins came on the line: 'One minute please while I connect you.' It was Elena.

'You'd better come, I've got pneumonia in both lungs now,' she said weakly.

I rushed down to the hospital. Elena was breathing shallowly, very pale, with beads of sweat on her brow.

'If I don't make it, Guillermo, look after Philip,' she said as I took her hand. I hardly understood the meaning of what she was saying. She was being calm, smiling, and as ever encouraging me: but there were traces of tears on her cheeks. She knew that she was dying. At the eleventh hour her doctors panicked: they stuffed her with antibiotics and, mercifully, she responded. A week later I drove her home, and carried her in my arms up the steep staircase to our bedroom in the Posada. Though four months pregnant, she weighed little more than a child.

I carried on running between Ca'n Gelat and Ca'n Quet, and coped with most of the problems. In the middle of August, Alfonso the Chef, who looked after both Ca'n Quet and Ca'n Gelat, quit and, although both his assistants stayed on and could provide the guests' meals, I had to take over cooking at the barbecue.

Slowly Elena recovered her strength, and moved down to our room at Ca'n Quet. As before she sat at the bar and kept the guests laughing with her stories of the *coronél*. But her worry showed through. From her medical interests she knew the reason her gynaecologist had tried to avoid giving her antibiotics: risks of foetus malformation were high. Having been prescribed a daily injection she, typically, decided to give it to herself in the buttocks. It was unpleasant, but safer than either the village doctor or the nuns who still did not have disposable needles.

The events of the previous five years had changed me. Perhaps Father was right that we Graveses are late developers. Determined to make my home in Deyá with Elena, I had run a business but had not managed to make it work. My youth and inexperience – I was still only thirty – were important factors; but so was Deyá itself. I had been too involved emotionally to see the limitations of the business. Now, finally, I had come to realize that, however full Ca'n Quet might be – I was giving up C'an Gelat anyway – and however much of a success among our guests, I could never make it pay with our level of staffing. After five years' work, the bank account remained in the red. But I could not reduce my staff: Elena was still weak and, even if the baby she was carrying was all right, she would certainly not be able to help me with Ca'n Quet the following season. What in the end made me take the decision to give up Ca'n Quet was the fact that Philip needed new shoes, and I could not afford them.

CHAPTER XIV

1

We closed both Ca'n Quet and Ca'n Gelat towards the middle of October 1970 – the end of the normal season – and I returned the keys to the Colls and to Gelat. On the twenty-third of October, early in the morning, Elena went into labour. This time it was not the easy ride into Palma we had had when Philip was about to be born – listening to the radio in the Karmann-Ghia. The road from Deyá to Valldemosa had just been rebuilt and resurfaced and our tyres lifted tarmac and gravel in a constant spat on the bottom of the Seat-600. The noise made it impossible to talk. We were both wondering what the baby would be like, whether we could hope for it to be normal after Elena's heavy dose of antibiotics. We went to the Palma clinic where Elena had survived her bout of pneumonia, and were given a cheerful room overlooking the garden. As soon as the midwife arrived, Elena was taken to the delivery room. Outside, in the corridor, I paced nervously up and down. I could hear Elena's screams: the birth at least was natural; then a different sound: the yell of a newborn baby. In due course Elena was wheeled out on a stretcher, and I followed her into the room. She was under a light anaesthetic. Soon afterwards the nurse came into the room with a little bundle. She unwrapped it and there was Sofia: a perfectly normal, beautiful baby girl.

All the oil companies to which I had written had turned me down – five years as an hotelier had not helped my curriculum vitae – so I took another job mud-logging in the Algerian Sahara. Although our separation was hard on Elena – I came home for only two weeks after being away for six – we both realized that with a job like this we could at least live where we chose. We remained at the Posada, and were under no pressure from Father to leave. A telephone was installed so we could talk to each other if and when I was near one at the other end. Although our two weeks together were short, we found we really savoured them.

For Philip, now a strapping six-year-old, my arrivals and departures became a way of life. He had the Graves looks. The villagers would shake their heads and say, 'There's no doubt: he's definitely from Canellún.' But Philip also had Elena's eye for detail, and his grandfather Antonio's gift for engineering. He was fascinated by the aeroplanes in which he saw me come and go, and he could already distinguish a DC-9 from a Caravelle. Philip was completely bilingual. One day in a doctor's waiting room an English lady was showing him wildlife pictures in a magazine.

'*Esto es un hipopótamo*,' she said, assuming he was Spanish, and pointing at a horned beast.

Philip looked at her, deadpan. 'It's not,' he replied in English. 'It's a rhinoceros.'

When I showed him a bookcase with his grandfather's books, he was impressed.

'Really? The *abuelo* made each one?'

'Yes, he wrote them,' I replied.

'So he did not really *make* make them?' he asked with an air of disappointment.

Philip loved helping his *abuela* in the Canellún garden. A friend of Mother's asked him to show her around.

'This is the lawn,' explained Philip, 'and this is the date tree; this is the sandpit, this is the sinking pool and sometimes there is a frog here.' It was the small concrete pond formed by the irrigation sump, which had so fascinated me as a child.

'The sinking pool?' asked the friend.

The Canellún cats were not neutered and Mother had prepared a kit to control the population. It consisted of a large sock, a stone and a bottle of vodka. She kept one or two kittens per litter, the others she drowned at birth; the vodka was to recover her strength after the deed.

'Yes,' replied Philip, 'this is where the *abuela* sinks the kittens.'

Sofia suffered no ill effects from her precarious gestation, other than a minor hearing problem, which was operated on when she was three years old. In many ways her personality was like Beryl's. She was a very private child who disliked being fondled. She was congenitally tidy. Philip went to bed with his teddy bear, two lorries and a Marmite sandwich; he woke up the next morning as if a typhoon had swept through his room. Sofia went to bed taking only her Copito, a white toy lamb, which she placed on the bedside table. When she got up you could hardly tell her bed had been slept in.

When Philip was two years old, we sent him to the village kindergarten run by the nuns. He came back happily and showed Elena a perfectly formed set of toothmarks on his arm. Fortunately the skin had not been broken.

'Who did that, Philip?'

'My friend Lorenzo. And Pepito made caca in his trousers.' Little seemed to have changed from the days when Lucia and Juan went there. When Philip was four, Elena and several other *estranger* mothers of small children clubbed together and engaged Francisca Heine, a qualified teacher who had married an American painter, to teach them reading, writing and 'new math'. School was held in a house in the Clot and Philip went back and forth by himself.

While we were at Ca'n Quet, these were satisfactory stopgap solutions. By September 1971, though, Philip was almost six and was due to begin the national curriculum at the boys' school where I had been taught by Don Gaspar. We had little faith in the new master and felt Philip needed a better education. We moved to Palma.

2

Karl places the beginning of the decline in Father's mental faculties at the prostatectomy he had in September 1959 at St Thomas's Hospital. The entries in Father's diary show that his treatment was badly handled. He was operated on on the seventh of September, but kept having haemorrhages afterwards. He had a further two operations to stem the bleeding and by the twenty-fourth of September he notes that he has '. . . expended 45 pints of borrowed blood'. Only on the second of October did the St Thomas's blood specialist return from holiday, to find that Father had a then rarely diagnosed condition called fibrinolysis, which accounted for the bleeding. This was sorted out, and after 34 days in hospital Father went to recuperate at my cousin Sally's in London. From there he wrote to Karl complaining:

I forget if I told you – I forget everything . . . . [RG to KG, October 1959]

Although I have never seen an official report on the 1959 operation, I do have a copy of a report from St Thomas's Hospital, written at the time of his gall bladder surgery in 1966. At the time, Father was seventy-one. In it the houseman finds him 'Pleasant, robust type, seems younger than actual age. Loquacious, scattering ideas.' However, in his neurological examination, the houseman encounters a disturbance called the 'equivocal plantar response', which sometimes indicates brain damage. The St Thomas's houseman also notes that Father had contracted the '1918 influenza', which brought neurological sequelae to many.

The cause of the decline in Father's faculties is not clear. The process seems to have been too slow and too late in life to be attributed to Alzheimer's disease. Did he, however, during one of the many haemorrhages in September 1959, go into physiological shock and suffer brain damage as a consequence? Could the sequelae of '1918 influenza' – of which he nearly died – have had some bearing on the process? And what was the effect of the high dose of 'sacred mushroom', taken shortly after the 1959 operation, which produced an extended priapism? Whatever the cause, the final result was senile dementia.

Father's mental decline began insidiously. None of us realized what was happening, although in retrospect, I can chart the early signs. In 1961 in a BBC TV interview with Malcolm Muggeridge, he forgot a quotation, a previously unheard-of occurrence, and was quite upset. When Muggeridge then asked Father how he knew about a certain event he had described in *I, Claudius*, he answered angrily: 'Because I was there'. A couple of years earlier, he would have explained his use of analepsis in his historical novels. In 1962 when I first went to the Sahara, Mother and Father were in London for his Oxford Poetry lectures. They had rented a flat in Montague Square, off Baker Street, close to where he and Laura had lived in 1938. Mother wrote: 'Father knows this district well, so is less lost than usual.' At the same time Father wrote complaining about the central heating, 'which becomes too close for thinking and shrivels up shoes and brains'. In 1964 when I was in Greece, I received two letters from him, within two days of each other, both announcing he was coming for his TV show. It seemed as if, in the second, he had forgotten he had written to me already.

Then there were other signs. He frequently mislaid his reading glasses and 'where are my bloody glasses?' was a phrase we all knew well. Later, he took to pocketing any glasses or pens he came across and I often had to recover my sunglasses from his desk. One day Lucia was walking up from the Cala and she saw a set of false teeth on a rock by the side of the path. She told Mother of the 'disgusting sight'. Father, meanwhile, desperate at the loss of his dentures had gone up to the Puig to ask the priest when in the pulpit at evensong to offer a recompense for anyone finding them. When Father got back to Canellún, he had Mother drive up to the church to cancel the announcement, while he rushed down the path to the beach to look for his teeth in the lentisc bush where Lucia had kicked them.

Until Karl left, he helped keep Father's prose to his previous standard and the last major work, *The Hebrew Myths*, written jointly with Raphael Patai and published in 1963, has become a textbook on the subject. After Karl's departure, Father's only book – other than several slim volumes of poetry, and some collections of essays and talks – was his *Omar Khayaam*, a new translation in collaboration with Omar Ali-Shah and published in 1968. Omar, Idries Shah's brother, translated a 'hitherto unknown contemporary manuscript' which, he claimed, belonged to his family and predated the one from which Fitzgerald had worked. Father worked from Ali-Shah's typescript and turned it into verse. *Omar Khayaam* received poor reviews, and the 'manuscript' was almost universally considered to be suspect. Ali-Shah promised to produce his manuscript when the time was ripe. Father wrote to Selwyn:

> The Khayaam business is getting a bit sticky and the Arberry clique are libelling Omar Ali-Shah and me in reviews; but patience, the time bomb will explode in Allah's own time. [RG to SJ, February 1968]

However, Ali-Shah's manuscript was never produced, and sadly Father shouldered the blame, if any, for a literary fraud. The only satisfaction Father had was when it was discovered that Professor Arberry, one of their most vociferous critics, had himself been fooled into buying a forged Omar Khayaam manuscript for a Cambridge library.

Father had habitually struck up acquaintance with strangers on the beach or walking to the village. Now, with less work and more time on his hands, he brought these protégés back to Canellún and introduced them to the family.

'Beryl,' he would say, 'this is Bill Smith. He is the world's expert on chick-sexing.'

Every one of his friends was becoming a 'world expert' if not 'the boss of . . .'. Father boasted that I was 'running' the oil fields in the Sahara. Whereas until now Father had always based his work on facts acquired from the classics or other reputable sources, he now picked up 'facts' from his new 'friends'. Such was his fame and presence that he got away with the most sweeping statements:

> . . . there are some sacred places made so by the radiation created by magnetic ores. [Deyá] is a natural kind of amphitheatre enclosed by mountains containing iron ore, which makes a magnetic field. Most holy places in the world . . . are of this sort. [Interview, *Playboy*, 1970]

or:

> [homosexuality among men is . . .] partly due to heredity, partly to environment, but largely because men now drink too much milk . . . . It's a fairly wide-spread medical view. [Interview with Edwin Newman, 1970]

As a geologist I can vouch that there is no more than a trace of iron minerals in the limestone mountains surrounding Deyá, nor is there any 'magnetic ore'. As for homosexuals and milk . . . .

The turbulent Cindy Musedom was largely due to Father's mental condition. No longer able to concentrate on writing prose, he poured his still ample energy into poetry. When Margot ceased to be his Muse, he found it imperative to find a new vessel for the White Goddess. Perhaps Father subconsciously picked the correct Muse for the moment:

> Aemilia was so violent a Muse that I am really much in her debt . . . for what she awakened in me. [RG to SJ, February 1968]

Father's 'Aemilia' was entirely of his own creation: what he saw in Cindy bore little relation to the real person. Nevertheless, she satisfied, once more, the apparent need for humiliation which he had experienced with Laura, and which drove him to write such wonderful poems to his Muse. Thanks to his Aemile, he managed to preserve his poetic faculties, when others were beginning to fail.

I have wondered, sometimes, whether I would have acted differently had I known that his behaviour towards Elena and me during our first years of married life was, in part, due to incipient senile dementia. However, this was never a clear-cut condition. Even when he was no longer fully in control of his faculties, he was still producing some good poetry; and he remained a much-respected and powerful public figure. Indeed, many of his highly intelligent friends, such as Selwyn Jepson, appeared not to suspect anything was amiss. Father's excellent physical condition also made his mental deterioration difficult to recognize. He could still rush down to the beach, climb around the cliff to his rock platform, belly-flop in, swim to the middle of the bay, and be back at his desk within the hour. It is only with hindsight that I can accept that his behaviour was part of a terrible and irreversible process.

3

For our first year in Palma we borrowed the Guillermo Massot flat from Mother and Father, and then we rented a more suitable one nearby.

The lay school we had chosen for Philip turned out to be full.

'Tell them that he's Robert Graves' grandchild, and they'll take him,' counselled my friends.

'In that case, I wouldn't want him to go,' said Elena.

From the beginning we had been determined that Father's fame should not affect our children's lives. He should be no more than a grandfather to them. In the end, it was the Jesuits who took Philip, even though Elena told them that he had not been baptized. As for Sofia, when she was old enough, she went to a kindergarten; and then to school at the Sacred Heart. Catholic schools still offered the best education in Palma. But we were not entirely happy with them.

In 1976 when Philip was ten and Sofia was five, we decided to move to Madrid. Our home language was Spanish, so Philip's English had progressed little now that he was no longer exposed to the English-speaking guests at Ca'n Quet; Sofia spoke no English whatever. In Madrid, therefore, we sent both children to a British school. They followed the English curriculum and learned to live in the big city, to use the buses and the *Metro*, enjoy the cinema, be critical of television.

Although we could have done with the extra money, Elena decided against taking a job. She was convinced the children needed at least one parent to welcome them back from school, and she never once missed being home when they arrived. She baked them bread, sewed on their buttons, listened to their problems; she took them to the deer park, to the vulture sanctuary, to pick mushrooms; she cared for their table manners, for their tidiness, for their language; she praised them and she punished them. Whether I was at home or away, Elena's was the final word.

After two years I left mud-logging and the Sahara and was transferred to the North Sea as a rig geologist. With the limited communications on a rig, I was very much my own boss, and I found the job satisfying. I spent four weeks on the rig and had two weeks off. In 1975 I became self-employed but I continued working the same routine. My new nomadic life took me to oil rigs in the North Sea, the Sahara, West Africa and the Middle East. On average I spent at least five months a year with Elena and the children, and I was never away from home for more than a month.

In 1981 we took a small flat in London. Philip wanted to take his 'A' levels in England, and it made sense for all of us to move. For, although both he and Sofia now went to boarding schools, Elena wanted to be at hand for weekend visits and half terms. Whether we lived in Palma, Madrid or London, we returned to the Posada during all school holidays. The children enjoyed Deyá but did not pine for it as I had once done. When they no longer needed us, Elena and I eventually moved back into the Posada. Both got university degrees, Philip in Mining, Sofia in Mathematics and Education. Their kinship to Robert Graves made little odds in their careers, as in mine, and they kept it quiet.

4

By 1970, the year we left Ca'n Quet, Mother was having to look after Father more and more. She was worried about his absent-mindedness, as she called it; however, when she took him to see a Harley Street specialist, who diagnosed senile dementia, she rejected his findings. With Cindy's departure, Father had calmed down. Juli was now his Muse. When Juli did not write, Mother would get someone to remind her to. Her letters kept him happy.

Father continued writing poems until 1975 but he had trouble with prose. Indeed, by then he no longer wrote letters, claiming that his eyes bothered him. Mother would write letters for him. In 1974 he was working on the half-page foreword for his short book of poems *At the Gate*. Mother sent it to Selwyn Jepson:

> Robert spent a long time writing this one and it turned out to be almost word for word the same as the fore-word to *Timeless Meeting*! [BG to SJ, March 1974]

On his eightieth birthday, in 1975, I left my oil rig for our joint birthday party. As I walked up the Canellún drive, Father barred my way.

'Who are you?' he asked aggressively.

'Don't be silly, Robert,' cried Mother, coming up behind him, 'it's William'

One moment he would not know even who Mother was; the next he was talking quite normally.

Father began getting up in the middle of the night and walking to the village. Lost, he would knock on the first door he recognized. Francisco Mosso opened his door:

'Don Roberto, you're out late tonight. Wait for me to get dressed and I'll take you home.' The villagers looked after him.

The film on which Father had always staked his hopes was finally made. When David Putnam's production of *I, Claudius* was shown on Spanish television, the Deyá villagers finally understood how famous a writer Father was. Unfortunately, Father's own attention span was now too short for him to enjoy it. Although the television series made him little money directly – he had long before sold the film rights – thanks to the increased sales of his books, Mother could now afford a male nurse to look after him.

Perhaps the most horrible stage of the now accelerating process was when Father's war neuroses and shell shock returned. It was tragic to see the terror in his eyes as he tried to run away, supported by his nurse and a walking stick, from the ghosts of the Somme. His lucid periods grew shorter and shorter. Nevertheless, there was still a constant stream of friends and strangers wanting to visit him. Many were very helpful to Mother, sometimes a long way beyond the call of duty. Some, however, just knelt beside Father in the wheelchair, talking to him in a voice used for young children: 'So, how are we this afternoon, Robert?' and smiled at the camera which recorded their meeting with the 'Great Man'. Those made me cringe.

Mother continued to looked after Father unflinchingly. Up at all times of day and night, she sometimes drove his nurses to distraction. Even when Mother fell seriously ill herself, she would not relinquish any of her responsibilities. Every morning she hoped he would wake up with a clear mind once more. Indeed, long after Father showed the last glimmer of recognition, in the quiet of the evening when no one else was around she would read him Shakespeare's plays, just in case he heard and enjoyed them.

5

I was relieved to be permanently back in the Posada. Mother had transferred the title deed to me. Can Torrent was now in Lucia's name, and the Torre belonged to Tomás. Juan had the beautiful house Margot had given him. I had never really been happy away from Deyá, although the village we returned to was not the one I grew up in.

Outwardly, Deyá looked much as it always had: new houses were built in stone, thanks to Father's efforts in the early Sixties. Whereas Canellún was once one of only a handful of houses on the Soller side of the valley, it had now become one among many: the new ones were being built mostly by wealthy Germans. There were now two luxury hotels and Ca'n Quet had become an up-market restaurant with its own swimming pool. The Deyá-to-Valldemosa road had been widened and one could no longer walk to Canellún without being passed by a steady stream of cars and buses. Even Laura and Father's road to the Cala had been black-topped by the Deyá Town Hall. The metamorphosis was complete. Deyá was an up-market holiday resort.

Of course many villagers remained, but most worked in the hotels or in the building trade. No longer did the fishwives bring the morning catch to the village; no longer did one hear the rattle of the carob beans being knocked down; no longer was the café filled with smoke and the cries of the *Truc* players on a Sunday morning.

Only in the memories of the older *Deyanencs* does my childhood Deyá still exist. Francisco Mosso, who loaded the bomb from the grotto into the lorry during the Civil War, is my neighbour and looks after the Posada key when we are away. He is above all a hunter and, in spite of his gammy leg and his almost eighty years, can out-walk most youngsters on the hills. The *Patrón* still mends his nets seated on the old wooden crate. They both tell me stories of Laura and Robert, and of the Civil War, the smuggling, the hunting and the olive picking on the terraces. My Deyá also lives in the memories of my school-friends such as Toni, who runs the *Patrón*'s terrace restaurant on the Cala with his brother Joan; or Xesc, the village carpenter and Justice of the Peace. But memories are like old photographs: they are real only to those who were there.

6

'Guillermo, I think you'd better come back quickly, your father isn't going to last many more days.' I hung up the phone. If Elena thought that the end was near, then it certainly was. I was in Tunisia. I finished my end-of-well geology report, and flew to Palma the next day. I arrived late at night, so it was on the following morning that Elena and I walked to Canellún. It was the seventh of December 1985.

Father was in the pressroom, which Mother had converted into a bedroom for him. He was stretched out on a striped canvas chaise longue in his dressing gown. I knelt to hold his limp hand: there had been no recognition on his part now for some five years; nevertheless, I found it comforting to be with him. He had wasted away to the bones. His breathing was shallow, and his face very pale; he showed no sign of suffering. Just then he sighed. Elena and I looked at each other. Mother had gone to the kitchen to prepare him some jelly. Elena reached for his pulse and shook her head. It was over. I was strangely thankful he had waited for me to be with him, as if to underline there were no hard feelings. I went to find Mother.

'I think Father is ill,' I said. 'Perhaps we should put him back to bed and call the doctor.'

Elena and I did so. Mother sat by the bed, held his hand, and then kissed his forehead. She knew that he was dead.

I arranged Father's funeral that same evening. Other than Lucia and Ramón, who were in Barcelona and came over at once, all of us were in Deyá. Having sorted out most of the details with Mother, the Mayor and the priest beforehand, everyone knew what to do now the time had come. Xesc the Carpenter brought a coffin from the Soller depot. Francisco Mosso dressed Father's corpse. Half an hour before the funeral was due to begin, the village men came up to Canellún and collected the coffin to carry it to the church. Toni March, Xesc the Carpenter, Pere of Son Beltrán and his brother took first turn as pallbearers. Others took over every so often, and carried candles to light the way. As the men of the family, Juan, Tomás, Ramón and I led the cortege. The moon was down, and the stars shone brilliantly in the crisp December night. As usual in the winter sky, Orion stood out above all the other constellations. On the Puig, the church bells tolled the death of the *senyor de Canellún*. No one spoke: just the shuffle of feet. I hadn't walked in a Deyá cortege since Old Gelat's death forty years before, but nothing had changed. As we climbed the road up to the church, the pallbearers began to grunt and whisper: their load seemed to get heavier.

I had planned a short service in keeping with Deyá traditions: it was the simplest way for the villagers to pay their last respects to their 'adopted son'. Unfortunately, the news of Father's death had broken on the wire services at about one in the afternoon and many of Father's friends and admirers had driven from Palma: the church was packed when we reached it. Journalists and camera crews were hovering but I refused to allow them inside. This was a service for the villagers, not for the media.

The pallbearers set Father's coffin in front of the altar. My brothers and I followed, down the aisle, past villagers, friends, and people whom I only vaguely recognized, and sat in the front pew on the left. Mother, my half-sister Catherine who was over from Australia, Lucia and Elena, had driven up to the church and were already seated in the pew to our right. The priest, Don Pedro's successor, said the first interdenominational mass ever celebrated in Deyá. After the Blessing, our family stood in line – I at the head, being the senior male present, though Sam would have come before me had he been there – while the congregation filed past. All the villagers, the *Patrón*, Francisco, Toni, Xesc, the Carrillo twins, Antonia of the Puig, Pepe the Widow, in offering their condolences, uttered the old formula: 'I am with you in your grief.' Many knelt, touched the coffin, and crossed themselves as they went out.

Next morning we buried Father in the cemetery, a stone's throw from the Posada. Only Lucia, Ramón, Elena and I and a couple of friends were present as the coffin was lowered into the grave. It had been dug into the hard soil of the Puig, beneath a tall cypress tree: a fitting place for him. Once buried, Salud Carrillo's husband, Toni, who worked for Pep Salas, made a simple cement plaque and, while it was still wet, inscribed on it:

Robert Graves

Poet

24-7-1895 to 7-12-1985

RIP

7

Making the arrangements for the funeral had seemed a natural thing for me to do. As the eldest son of Canellún it was expected of me by the villagers. However, my ties with Canellún had been broken when I married Elena. Mother had been looking after Father's literary affairs and I assumed she would continue doing so. But I began to worry about frozen bank accounts, and how she would manage.

After the burial we all returned to Canellún for breakfast. Coffee was made and we sat around the kitchen table. The Aga was lit and the *ensaïmadas* were warm. Mother fed the cats.

'Is there a Will, Mother?' I asked.

'I think so . . . .' she replied, and went upstairs to look. Presently she came back to the kitchen carrying an envelope. She sat down and read the contents. Lucia, Catherine, Elena and I waited expectantly.

'I'd forgotten,' she smiled enigmatically. 'He named you his executor.'